MEAT ON THE BONES

MEAT ON THE BONES

FIVE LIVES AND AN ENIGMA
FROM A NEW ENGLAND FAMILY HISTORY

BARRY J. MACDONALD

Printed by Create Space, An Amazon.com Company.

Available from Amazon.com, and on Kindle and other devices

*"every life leaves behind an echo that is audible
to those who take the trouble to listen."*

Amitav Ghosh
The Glass Palace

For Leslie, Bryan, Lynn, David, Anika, Emerson, Willow, Ruby, and Sadie.

This book tells one small portion of your story.

CONTENTS

PREFACE

A genealogy can simply be thought of as a group of ancestral names with associated dates and places of birth, marriage, and death along with the evidence of the linkages between those names and subsequent generations. Family history, however, is much more than that. Behind each name was an individual of flesh and blood. Behind each name was substance: a personality, an attitude, and actions shaped by the historical circumstances and societal norms of the times. Each individual in a family plays a role, whether major or minor, in the history of their moment on earth. Some of these people may be famous, but the world is primarily composed of others who are less well known or, more often, not known at all. Nevertheless they all have stories to tell.

This book is primarily a study of five lives from my family history. The five are: my mother; a veteran of the First World War; a 19th-century newspaper publisher/politician on Nantucket Island; a land speculator in the 17th-century Massachusetts Bay Colony; and an Englishman who landed at New Plymouth with the Pilgrims in 1620. Their collective lives span two continents and roughly 400 years, from the late 16th-century to the beginning of the new millennium. Yet, geographically, these five people spent a significant portion of their lives no more than 100 miles apart in what is now Massachusetts.

The genealogical bones—the names, key dates, and connections between generations—are the foundation on which each of these portraits has been constructed. Searching for the bones themselves is often a complex and frustrating task. At times my search seemed fruitless: many avenues pursued, numerous clues examined, many a hypothesis proven false. Then, after years of searching, a key fact would fall into my hands that opened generations to my understanding. I've woven a bit of that process of seeking for the bones into each portrait. At the end of the book is the detailed genealogy that demonstrates the family linkages between me and each of the highlighted individuals.

As I worked on the bones, I often found material that revealed much about the actual personality and deeds of some of my ancestors. Putting this meat on the bones is the heart of this book. In order to be more than just a name, an individual must have put down on paper, or some other medium, something about themselves—or friends, public authorities, or enemies must have done it for them. Such records are not always easy to find, but are more common than one might expect. Identified in each chapter is how and where I found these key materials.

No one lives his or her life in a vacuum. For those like my mother, who lived in our contemporary world, there is minimal need for additional historical context. For others, who participated in events in the early part of the 20th-century or prior to that time, I have found it necessary to add material from a wide range of political, social, economic, and geographic sources that helps explain the world in which each of these individuals lived.

In the concluding chapter, "The Ironic Enigma," I have chosen to discuss my search for the family that bears my own surname, *MacDonald*, and to make plain the consequences of not gathering family history data from the living when one has the chance. This is a cautionary tale. My grandfather, who could have probably answered many of the key questions about the MacDonalds, about whom I have long sought answers, actually lived in our home for the last four years of his life while I was a child. Unfortunately, much of my grandfather's history was lost when he passed away—the questions unasked, or the answers never given.

The process of finding the individuals and their stories discussed in this book has been full of seemingly endless reels of microfilm and, in recent years, an equally endless list of websites. The search has also included a good number of historic newspapers, manuscripts, and those still valuable commodities—printed, hard copy books. The portraits I have constructed from these materials touch on many of the fundamentals of our common human experience: altruism, perseverance, patriotism, materialism, and the search for adventure, to name a few. Getting to know these and other ancestors has held my attention for many years. I hope the handful of portraits in this book holds your attention for at least a few hours.

ACKNOWLEDGEMENTS

Meat on the Bones owes its existence to the assistance and guidance of a great many people, including a number of members of my immediate and extended family. My mother June MacDonald's interest in her own ancestors was a constant source of both encouragement and information throughout the development of this book until her death in 2009. Her Covert cousin, Barbara Bates, was the first in the family to develop a genealogy on my mother's side of the family. Her generosity and willingness to share her efforts are the foundation on which my subsequent work on my mother's side of the family is based. My mother's aunt, Grace (Covert) (Fox) (Brown) Bird, collected everything related to her Covert family that she could lay her hands on, including news articles (many of which I am convinced she had a hand in writing), photographs, Bible records, and military records. These materials are a treasure trove of information on the maternal side of my family that has proven invaluable in writing this book.

From an institutional perspective, the key resource for developing the genealogical foundation—the "bones" if you will—on which the lives in this book rest, is the New England Historic Genealogical Society. The Society's amazing array of experts, genealogical library, and on-line databases is invaluable to anyone with as many New England ancestors as I have. Special thanks to NEHGS's Managing Editor of Periodicals, Lynn Betlock, who guided me in publishing two articles, based on material in this book, in NEHGS's quarterly magazine, *American Ancestors*.

The book's first chapter, focused on my mother, June (Pennell) MacDonald, depends a great deal on the unpublished narrative I requested she write of her early life prior to her marriage to my father, Irving MacDonald. Without it, this chapter would have none of the descriptive richness involving personalities and places that only she could provide. Also of importance are the 1933 and 1935 diaries of my maternal grandmother, Helen (Covert) (Pennell) (Jepson) Barry, which contain important references to events in the life of her family that add poignancy and pathos to the story. I must also thank Ms. Susan Boucher, Director of Placement, Planning, and Training at the Monson Developmental Center, for her personal assistance in guiding my mother and me on our 2005 tour of what was once the Monson State Hospital for Epileptics. Ms. Boucher also opened the way to obtaining the amazing set of documents of my mother's stay at that hospital from 1935 to 1943.

The second chapter on Percy Covert, the Doughboy, owes its existence to the aforementioned Grace Bird, Percy's sister. As family chronicler, she kept every letter that Percy sent to her from his time in France with the 26th (Yankee) Division during World War I. I expanded on this key material by the use of many first-hand accounts of other members of the 26th Division and other units of the Allied Expeditionary Force who wrote about their experiences in the "war to end all wars." James Fahey of the Braintree [Massachusetts] Historical Society also kindly lent his great expertise and archival materials on the Yankee Division.

The depiction of the life of Samuel Haynes Jenks owes much to the Nantucket newspapers that Jenks and others edited, preserved at the Nantucket Atheneum, and other newspapers of the time, preserved by America's Historical Newspapers, an archive maintained by Newsbank and the American Antiquarian Society. Other materials about the Jenks family, its associates, and activities were reviewed at the Research Library of the Nantucket Historical Association. The author also expresses appreciation to Nathanial Philbrick whose *Away Off Shore, Nantucket Island and Its People, 1603 - 1890* contains an invaluable series of historical sketches of the movers, shakers, and events that shaped the history of Nantucket. Many thanks also to Barbara Ann White whose *A Line in the Sand, The Battle to Integrate Nantucket Public Schools* is the in-depth source for understanding the remarkable school integration battle which took place on Nantucket in the 1840s.

The story of the life of Richard Thayer began for me with William S. Pattee's description of the "land troubles" involving Thayer in early Braintree, found in Pattee's 1879 book, *A History of Old Braintree and Quincy.* His description of the events surrounding these particular "troubles" is still the most comprehensive account I have found. I supplemented Pattee's material with additional records of events, land transactions, and court cases that are maintained by the Massachusetts Archives in Boston. I also benefitted greatly from the genealogical and historical records compiled on the Thayers of Braintree and their descendants by such writers as Patricia Thayer Muno and Waldo C. Sprague. My thanks again to Jim Fahey of the Braintree Historical Society for introducing me to its collection of materials concerning the history of early Braintree. Thanks also to the Braintree Town Clerk's Office for showing me the original and providing me with a copy of the 1665 Indian Deed which is an essential part of Richard Thayer's story. I have also profited from the review and commentary on some of my material for this chapter by Robert

Charles Anderson of the Great Migration Study Project, and a leading expert in the field of 17th-century New England genealogy.

Writers such as Caleb Johnson, Kieran Doherty, and Hobson Woodward have extensively documented the life of Stephen Hopkins. I acknowledge in particular the use of material from Caleb Johnson's *Here Shall I Die Ashore—Stephen Hopkins: Bermuda Castaway, Jamestown Survivor, and Mayflower Pilgrim*, including his re-print of the first-hand account by William Strachey concerning the wreck of the *Sea Venture* on Bermuda. For the early history of Plymouth, I made extensive use of William Bradford's irreplaceable account, now known as *Of Plymouth Plantation*, as well as material by Bradford and Edward Winslow found in *Mourt's Relation*.

The basis of what little genealogy I have on my M(a)cDonald ancestors on Prince Edward Island began with material held by the Prince Edward Island Provincial Archives and the Prince Edward Island Heritage Society. My initial guide to these and other sources was Beryl Barrett, a PEI genealogist introduced to me by the Heritage Society. On the maternal side of that family, the unpublished genealogies prepared by Arlene (Carr) Sorensen and Arlene Hood provided the bulk of what I know about my Carr ancestors. My thanks to Arlene Sorensen for meeting with our family to discuss the Carr line during one of our sojourns on PEI in the 1990s.

I must also extend great appreciation for the editorial services of Elizabeth Jane Sherman. May the final product come close to meeting Janie's exacting standards. And special thanks to Gary Daines who designed the cover, developed the interior layout, and created the index. It would not be much of a book without all of these key features.

Finally, I must thank my wife Vicki, who is always first in my life, for all her help and, above all, for her great patience in putting up with the time I have invested in this and other genealogical projects, and of course, for all the work yet to come.

All those noted above played vital roles in the creation of this book. Of course, any errors of form or content are mine. Any comments may be forwarded to *bajmacdonald@hotmail.com.*

CHAPTER 1

THE WILL TO ENDURE:
JUNE MIRIAM PENNELL MACDONALD

Family historians can spend a great deal of time digging out a few facts concerning an ancestor who lived many generations ago in, say, colonial America. For anyone with a colonial American heritage like mine, the pull to study these early pioneers is often irresistible.

As for those in the present, like parents, we already know them. Or do we? By the time we arrive on the scene, parents have likely lived a quarter or a third of their lives, sometimes more. Do we really know what they did in that formative period?

My mother, June Miriam (Pennell) MacDonald, is a case in point. When I was a child, she often made the remark that her life would be good grist for a novel. At some point in my adult life, I recognized that I really didn't know much about that grist that made up her early life. I began to ask her questions about her childhood and early adulthood, and then suggested that as presents for birthdays or Christmas, she give me a piece of her story. This she did over a number of years, often writing in longhand on eight and a half by eleven-inch sheets of pink paper. From her well-written personal account, many a long personal conversation, and some other remarkable source materials, I have come to understand how little I knew of her early life. For me, what I have learned is an inspiring story.

June Miriam Pennell was born in June, of course, 4 June 1919 to be precise, at home at 75 Ellsworth Street in Brockton, Massachusetts (hereafter, Mass). She was the second child of Leon Pennell and Helen Cornelia Covert. On the cover of her baby book, published by Borden's Condensed Milk, a haloed child is surrounded by two rather menacing-looking storks, while on the frontispiece, a smiling nurse parts a curtain to announce, "It's a _____," with the handwritten addition of "girl." The booklet notes that the attending physician was E.W. Clark, the nurse was Orella Chareth, and that June had a brother, Willard (actually Leon Willard). The Chareths and Pennells were neighbors, as an event almost exactly a year later made clear.

Who were these Pennells? When I first began researching this story, the Pennells were virtually unknown to me for reasons that will become apparent; but, some work at the library of the National Society of the Daughters of the American Revolution in Washington, D.C. quickly revealed that the Pennell name had a long history in New England dating back to the arrival in Gloucester, Mass, of two brothers, Thomas and Clement Pennell, in the early 18th-century. Their predecessors were from the Isle of Jersey in England's Channel Islands where the surname morphs to Pinel; and, all the first names take on a decidedly French character reflecting the complex French and English heritage of Jersey. As far as I can trace it, the family line runs back to a Jean Pinel, Rector of Grouville, Jersey, in the early 1600s. Later, members of the Pinel or Pennell clan moved into southern Maine and New Hampshire. Some of them began building ships near Brunswick, Maine, around 1760. A community grew up around this business that even took on the family name, Pennellville.

The link between the Pennells of Gloucester and southern Maine and my grandfather, Leon Pennell, became clearer when I found a typewritten manuscript in the LDS Family History Library at Salt Lake City entitled, *The Pennell Family in Portland, Maine*, written by Clara Pennell Phinney in 1916.

On page 134 of this manuscript is the name of John Pennell, Jr., born at Kittery, Maine, in 1839, in a line that runs from John Pennell, Sr., to a Joseph Pennell, and from Joseph to Clement, one of the original brothers from Gloucester. According to Clara Phinney's record, John Pennell, Jr., married Annie Clark, daughter of Captain John Clark of England. They had three children: an adopted boy, George, who died at the age of one; another adoptee named George Woodbury (or Woodberry in other records), who survived to adulthood; and their own child, John, who also died at age one. Phinney fails to mention one other child, Freddie, born at Chelsea, Mass, in 1871. I have yet to pin down the actual provenance of George Woodbury Pennell, born, supposedly, around 20 November 1869. No other document found to date supports Clara Phinney's assertion that he was adopted. I have not yet found a birth record for George, regardless of the fact that some documents indicate he was born at Chelsea, Mass. Despite this mystery, it is clear that he was the father of Leon Pennell.

One of the truly intriguing characters in this story is Annie Clark Pennell, wife of John, Jr. A U.S. Census record shows that by 1880, John, Annie, and their son, George, were living at 325 Saratoga Street in Boston. In this record, Annie was

June M. Pennell on graduation from nursing school, 1946.
Collection of the author.

listed as born at sea and her occupation was listed as a "clairvoyant." Evidently, this was no passing fancy for Annie since, when she married for a second time to a Gideon Oliver at New Bedford in 1895, the vital record lists her occupation as "medium." My guess is that her interest in the popular spiritualist movement of the day eventually took John and Annie to one of its centers in New England— Onset, Mass. Revered by the local Indians in days past as a spiritual center, Onset became a key watering hole for spiritualists during the Victorian age. Annie would certainly have been right at home in this environment. Intriguingly, the vital records of Annie's marriage to Gideon Oliver in 1895 show her as a widow, but her first husband, John, lived until 1910 when he died at Wareham, Mass. I have not found a record of a divorce.

Regardless of how they got there, the extended Pennell family was well en- trenched in Wareham, of which Onset is a part, by the 1890s. In 1892, John and Annie's son, George, married an English immigrant named Harriet (known as Hattie) Beswick at Wareham. Three of their children: Robert Earl, George, and Leon (my grandfather), are listed in the Wareham town records as born at either Onset or Wareham. Leon was born at Wareham itself on 10 February 1897.

Sometime in the late 1890s, George and Hattie's family made the move to Brockton, Mass. By 1900, the U.S. Census of Brockton shows them all there at 179 Elliot Street. Leon attended Brockton schools, including Brockton High School, where, the family story goes, he met Helen Covert. That the family was in Brockton in 1908 is confirmed by a letter from Leon to a member of his moth- er's family in England. This letter came into my hands in a rather remarkable manner. Since I knew little about Leon, I did what most anyone is likely to do these days when looking for information; I plugged his name into the Google search engine on the Internet. That led me to a query on a genealogical site from a Helen Shields, living in Wales, who stated that she had a letter in her possession from a Leon Pennell, an 11-year old boy from the U.S. who was writing to cous- ins in England. Helen's family no longer recognized the name of the writer. She requested responses.

After we finally made contact, Helen Shields sent me an electronic copy of Leon's letter. The letter, dated 6 January 1908, is typical of an 11-year old boy: "I have no doubt that you will be glad to hear from me. I have never written to you before. . . . I thought I would scribble off a few lines as I had nothing else to do. Grandma has often told me to write time and time again." The letter was written from 1211 Main Street in Campello, the southern section of Brockton. The residence has now disappeared, replaced by commercial development on Main Street. Leon noted in his letter that he was attending the Huntington School. This school is one that I attended myself for a year as an elementary school student when we lived in an apartment not more than two blocks from 1211 Main Street. Clearly, the letter was written by my grandfather and is one of the few tangible pieces of his life now in my hands. Recognizing that I was closer to the writer than anyone in the family now remaining in England, Ms. Shields sent me the original. One can only speculate as to why an English family would keep a letter for nearly 100 years from an 11-year old boy to a distant cousin. As one of the few people in the world who would have a reason to answer Helen Shields' query, I am certainly glad that they kept it.

On the other side of June Miriam's parentage, we find the family of Leroy Covert and his wife, Edith Gertrude Wood, and their one son and six daughters: Percy, Ethel, Grace, the aforementioned Helen, Ruth, Harriet, and Edith. While Leroy and Edith Covert died long before I was born, I knew personally, or had at least met, all their children. Many of them were very close to each other and to my immediate family.

The name Covert is easily traceable to a Teunis Jans Covert, or Coevers, who emigrated from Holland to New Amsterdam in the 1650s. He married Barbara Lucas van Kessel in Holland, and when they arrived in New Amsterdam, there were already four children in this family. Five more would be born in New Amsterdam. Remarkably, all of these children lived to adulthood. Their descendants are, of course, legion. As the following Covert generations disbursed from New Amsterdam, many moved first to New Jersey, and later, some became pioneers along the fringes of the country in the Finger Lakes region of New York. To this day, there remains a small village of Covert in Seneca County, New York, between Seneca and Cayuga lakes (Fisher, et al.).[1]

Leroy's grandfather, John E. Covert, eventually settled in Michigan thanks to a set of events that are described in Chapter 2 of this book. That fact, and the growth of Detroit as a major employment magnet in the industrial age, accounts for the birth in Michigan of some of the family members previously

---

[1] References to sources are inserted parenthetically throughout this text. For a detailed description of each source, see the Sources section of the book, organized by chapter.

mentioned—Percy, Ethel, and Grace. It also accounts for the frequent movement between the east coast and Detroit of Covert family members, including my grandmother and my mother.

Leroy Covert's father, Martin Covert, a son of John E., was a Civil War veteran. Martin's wife, Affa (or Effie) Antoinette Davis was born in Michigan near Detroit. Her mother was a Caywood. There are many Caywoods who were originally from the Finger Lakes region in New York. My assumption is that the Covert and Caywood families were well acquainted before the 1867 marriage of Martin and Affa Antoinette, which took place in Ovid, New York, in the Finger Lakes region.

Eventually, the Covert and Pennell actors in this story all converged on the town of Brockton, Mass, and later, the adjoining town of West Bridgewater. Why? I have no hard evidence. Most likely, the answer was the same one that brought hundreds of thousands of people: Irish, Italians, Canadians, Armenians, Latvians, and a plethora of other nationalities, to towns like Brockton in the late 19th- and early 20th-centuries—jobs. Brockton was a factory town with a single product, shoes. By 1920, more than 80% of the town's employment was tied to the production of footwear. During World War I, it was said in town that U.S. soldiers marched to war in boots made in Brockton. Names like Keith, Knapp, and Walkover were synonymous with shoe products made in the city.

When I was growing up in Brockton in the 1950s, the Howard and Foster shoe factory stood right across the street from where we lived for several years. By then though, the shoes had long been on their way out, first to the non-union southern U.S., and, finally, to low-wage countries like Indonesia or China. Brockton has never really recovered from the loss; but back in the days of the flapper, jazz, and the rise of the automobile, Brockton was a boomtown. Streetcars plied Main Street where at least three movie theaters offered the latest in entertainment. Edison himself came to inaugurate one of the first public electric lighting systems in the country, and a brand new state-of-the-art high school was built there. At one point in the 1920s, with the electorate heavily composed of recently arrived European workers with a radical tilt to their politics, Brockton elected a socialist mayor, a fact somehow missing from my history classes in the post-World War II Cold War environment. So, there is little doubt in my mind that the Coverts and the Pennells moved to Brockton for work, and that work was almost assuredly associated, at least initially, with shoes. (On Brockton, see Carroll.)

Because of those moves, Leon Pennell and Helen Covert got to know each other in high school at Brockton. Given their birth dates, Leon was most likely ahead of Helen by a year in school. But, by the spring of 1916, Helen had graduated, and by 28 November 1916, Leon and Helen were married in Bellows Falls, Vermont. Their marriage record can be found in Rockingham, Vermont.

Why Vermont for the marriage? And why did the great family historian, my mother's Aunt Grace, not collect a story from the local press about this marriage, as she had done for herself, her brother, Percy, and her older sister, Ethel? One clue may lie in the birth date of Leon and Helen's first child, Leon Willard. Leon Willard's baby book, this one produced by Cook and Tyndall, a local retailer of "Everything for Baby and Mother," states that Leon was born at 9:05 AM on 6 May 1917 at 16 Wheeler Avenue, the home of his grandparents, Leroy and Edith. Edith Covert served as the maternity nurse. When I asked my mother about the dates involved in this marriage and birth, she said that, indeed, the two of them had eloped because of the impending birth of a child. Her mother advised June that this was not a good way to start a marriage. In fact, from the evidence available, this marriage was not always on the firmest ground, and would be tested in ways that would shake the strongest of marriages.

These circumstances still do not fully explain the location of the marriage in Vermont. The family story was, and a few documents state, that Leon worked as a telegrapher associated with the railroads, another great engine of economic growth in the early 20th-century. My mother said that he worked as a night operator for Western Union. Whether he worked for Western Union itself or directly for one of the many New England railroads of the day, it is clear that he was already based at one of the railroad stations along the Connecticut River Valley that forms the border between New Hampshire and Vermont. All of the towns named in documents that make mention of Leon Pennell, in the days from his marriage forward, fit that mold: White River Junction, Bellows Falls, and Rockingham in Vermont, as well as Wells River and Woodsville in New Hampshire. So, the most logical answer to the marriage location question is that Helen and Leon eloped to Vermont because Leon was already working there.

There is little firm information on the life of Leon and Helen immediately following their marriage. It appears that Helen, and probably baby Leon Willard, lived for a time with Leon in Wells River, New Hampshire, near the Vermont border. But, it also seems that Helen shuttled frequently back and forth between either New Hampshire or Vermont and her extended family's homes at Brockton and vicinity. An undated news article from the indefatigable Grace's collection states that on one such trip Helen contracted typhoid and was hospitalized for some time at Brockton. By 1919, Leon and Helen had returned to Brockton and established a home at 75 Ellsworth Street as indicated by June's birth record. What brought them back to Brockton, I do not know.

Almost exactly one year from the date of June's birth, this home was the scene of the first major tragedy to strike this family. Under a headline that reads, "Little Body Swept 1000 Feet," the *Brockton Times* of Tuesday, 8 June 1920 reported: "Leon W. Pennell, 3, Son of Mr. and Mrs. Leon Pennell, 75 Ellsworth Street, Drowns in Coldstream Brook Monday Evening — Was Playing Happily When Last Seen — Men Pull Tot from Water Long Way From Accident." The paper further reported that little Leon was playing in front of the house with friends, Rosamond and Roy Chareth, and then ran around to the rear of the house. Evidently, he circled around to the brook and stumbled in, unseen by anyone. When his body was recovered, police officers hurried to the scene with the "lungmotor," but they discovered that resuscitation was useless. On Wednesday afternoon, Leon Willard's funeral was held at the home. Grace's archive contains a handwritten copy of a poem read at the funeral, "He is Passed Away," by James Whitcomb Riley. The poem begins, "I cannot say and, I will not say, that he is dead. He is just away." Leon Willard was buried in Union Cemetery at Brockton. No stone marks the grave.

Sometime after the death of his son, Leon returned to his work on the border between New Hampshire and Vermont. In her story of those days, my mother states that she and Helen joined him, but at some point, Helen and June left. This is clear from a very small clipping from Grace's collection, undated, and without reference to the name of the paper in which it was published. It reads: "My wife having left my bed and board, I am no longer responsible for bills except those of my own personal contraction. Leon Pennell. Woodsville, New Hampshire." This separation occurred sometime in the early 1920s. Was it the result of further strain caused by the death of little Leon Willard on what may have been an already fragile relationship? My mother, very young at the time, never even realized that there had been a break-up until, as an adult, she saw this news clipping in her Aunt Grace's collection.

My mother, however, did know about and related to me the basics of the next tragedy to strike the family. Sometime, also in the early 1920s, Leon was involved in a work-related accident. This may have occurred at White River Junction in Vermont, but the specific details are unknown. My mother's understanding was that Leon was somehow hit in the gut by a piece of railroad equipment. Leon was seriously injured. Eventually, he was moved to Long Island Hospital, a facility for the indigent and chronically ill on Long Island in Boston Harbor. This move may have happened when, again according to my mother's recollection, someone in the family attempted to sue Leon's company for negligence, and the company then withdrew its support for his care.

While Leon attempted to recover from his injuries at Long Island Hospital, Helen at some point decided to take June and head for Detroit where her sister, Grace, had taken up residence. Then, an old family friend heading for California, Doris Hambly, arrived on the scene and persuaded Helen to take June and join her. They got as far as Kansas City where the car gave up the ghost and they collectively ran out of money. Helen was forced to take a job as a cashier at an amusement park, and June got "shipped back," as she put it, to her Aunt Grace in Detroit.

Then, in late 1923 or 1924, June moved again, this time to the Leroy and Edith Covert home, now at West Bridgewater, Mass, just south of Brockton. From my mother's account:

> The house is still there—a big white square house about three houses from the center of town. There was a small apple orchard in the back of the barn and there it was fun to perch in the branches and be Rapunzil the girl who let down her golden hair so her lover could climb up it and rescue her. And small matter that my hair was neither golden nor long. There was also a thick hedge between the property and the adjoining field and this was where all the princes were stuck trying to rescue 'The Sleeping Beauty.' Wonderful what imagination can do for a little girl.

> The house itself was a big, high-ceilinged barny place. No electricity, a pump in the kitchen sink and a small house connected to the woodshed for necessities—complete with a Sears Roebuck catalogue! Fine in the summer but a bit uncomfortable in the winter.

> As to the inhabitants, there was Great Grandma Wood [Nancy Ann (Tower) Wood], Great Grandma Covert [Affa Antoinette (Davis) Covert], Grandpa

Covert [Leroy Covert], Grandma Covert [Edith Gertrude (Wood) Covert], and Aunt Harriet, Aunt Edie [Leroy and Edith's last two children], and I.

Grandpa Covert was the typical male of that day. Went to work each morning, six days a week. Came home and read the paper in his rocking chair and had little to say to us kids. He started having epileptic seizures when he was a young man but they were few and far between. He loved to play cards and Saturday night was card night. He also liked to go fishing. He had an old Model T Ford and he and Uncle Percy would take off most Sunday mornings. His word was law and we all did as he said.

My Grandma Covert appeared to me as an overworked, harassed woman. Probably no different than many women of her day, but she had a big household to manage and few conveniences. My recollection of her is one of always cooking and flying around that big house cleaning. I have pictures of her laughing and enjoying herself, but with all she had to do she had little time to pay attention to a little girl. Also she was beginning to suffer from the cancer that would eventually take her life. She would cook all day Saturday—pies, doughnuts and beans. Sunday night the house would be full . . . and by Monday all the food would be gone.

I shall always remember with fondness those Sunday nights. [The extended family and friends would arrive]. Eventually we would all gather around the piano and sing—all the old songs and hymns. Aunt Gladys [Percy's wife] was a gifted pianist and sometimes Grandpa would get out his fiddle and play for us. In later years, people would wonder how I knew so many songs. It was all due to those Sunday nights at my Grandma's house.

In spite of being low man on the totem pole, life at Grandma's was good and always busy with so many people around. They must have been very poor but that didn't bother me. Then a big change came into my life. My mother [Helen] was coming home! Now I hardly remembered my mother but I was filled with natural curiosity. And come home she did, across the country with two men—not to be done in those days—but she did, knickers, bobbed hair and all. A 'Thoroughly Modern Millie' of the twenties! But she was good fun and I accepted her.

Virtually the only recollection June had of her father was, at age five, going to see him with Helen at the Long Island hospital. It was near Christmas, 1924. My mother recalls that Leon frankly told his estranged wife that the only way he was likely to leave the island was in a box. He tried to make a present of another box, one containing Christmas candy, to June, who was highly disappointed when

Helen allowed her daughter to take only one piece of the candy. That is the extent of my mother's recollection of this final meeting.

On 5 March 1925, at 9:05 AM, the same time as the birth of his first child, Leon's prediction came true as he succumbed at Long Island Hospital to pyelo-nephritis, a kidney disease sometimes brought on by trauma to the kidney. June's handsome father, for so he looks in the few pictures I have of him, was dead less than a month after his 28th birthday. He was buried in the Union Cemetery at Brockton in the same grave lot as his son.

My mother told me that following the death of Leon, the Pennell family made an offer to adopt her. This did not wash with Helen who was determined to keep her girl. The estrangement between Helen and Leon, and probably with the rest of the Pennell family, was clearly deep, since less than two months after Leon's death, on 3 May 1925, Helen married for a second time. Not surprisingly, there were no Pennells attending, as recorded in the little album that marks this wedding, but there are no members of the groom's family either—only the extended Covert clan and their friends. For little June, still shy of her sixth birthday, it was a fateful day in an already tumultuous life. My mother picks up the story:

> His name was Harold Jepson, although everyone called him Jeppie. Short, prematurely bald with a slightly indented chin, he was certainly not much to look at. . . . I heard rumors that he was 'sweet on my mother' and someday he would be my step-father. Now that had a bad connotation and being a great lover of fairy stories, I conjured up all sorts of bad images of step-mothers and fathers. Also, it meant I would have to leave my happy life at my Grandma's. I was not happy about it.

> In those days, children were seen and not heard, so I was not consulted and my mother became Mrs. Harold Jepson. Sorry to say I didn't start off very well in this new venture. When Harold picked me up to kiss me after the wedding, I wriggled away and said, 'You put me down, I'll never call you daddy.'

> But of course I did, and all seemed to go well. We went to live in a house on South Main Street in West Bridgewater. Somewhere during that period, we went to live in Indianapolis for a short time. . . . I imagine Harold went there to find work as even then work was becoming scarce. It was to be the story of my life with Harold. We were always moving. He could talk himself into a job and just as fast talk himself out of it. He was a great talker and, as with most insecure people, a great bragger.

Back from Indianapolis, June started school again in West Bridgewater. She spoke of the old school, now only a memory except for the library which is presently a commercial building.

> Next to the school was a small store that sold candy and various things to tempt youngsters. It also sold hotdogs and on bad days my mother would call the school and tell them to keep June through the noon hour and send her to Mrs. Bisby's for lunch. Oh bliss; oh joy! How I prayed for poor weather! Even then I liked to eat out!

Another move within West Bridgewater and another series of jobs, or attempts at jobs, for Harold, then:

> One morning Harold woke me up and told me to get Grandma, and go to school with Edie (her Aunt Edith). This frightened me as I had never known my mother to be sick, but Grandma didn't seemed to be alarmed and shooed me off to school saying there would be a nice surprise for me when I got back.

> And what a surprise! A big fat baby boy. — Why didn't I know? In those days, things like that weren't talked about. Also the fashions of the day were loose, shapeless garments, and all women wore big aprons. Maybe I just wasn't observant. Anyhow it was a total surprise to me. He was christened Lawrence Leroy, but to me he was my Lollipop.

Another move ensued, this time to a duplex near the center of town that would later become a professional building. It has since been torn down to make way for a small shopping center. During this period, my mother wrote of going to the Brockton Fair, a major annual event. She visited her first, very exotic Chinese restaurant and saw Chinese people for the first time. She then attended her first movie, *Rough House Rosie*, starring Clara Bow. June also spoke of her double promotion from the first grade to the third grade, and of coming home with the news and asking, "Mama, Mama–can I march in with the third grade?" And so she did. Again, my mother picks up the story, but not on such a positive note:

> My happy life in Bridgewater was drawing to a close. My Grandmother died that Christmas Eve and the family was broken up. My Great Grandma Wood went to live with friends. Grandpa Covert moved to Brockton to room in a hotel. Harriet [June's Aunt] was married to her Mickey [Malcolm Weston]—a marriage that was to last sixty years. And Edie [the youngest of the Covert children] was sent to live with Aunt Grace in Detroit. So the close-knit family was scattered.

The circumstances surrounding the death of Edith Covert at the end of 1927 were major news in the *Brockton Times*. Under a headline that reads, "Leaves Death Bed to Rescue Husband," the article goes on to relate the collapse of Leroy Covert who fainted and fell across the blazing logs of an open fireplace about a week before Christmas.

> Forgetting her own suffering and regardless of the fact that any sudden exertion might end her own life, Mrs. Covert dragged herself from the bed and across the room and succeeded in pulling her husband away from the flames and extinguishing the fire in his clothing. . . . The drain on Mrs. Covert's feeble strength proved too great and the end came shortly before midnight Sunday.

Despite the drama in the newspaper's telling, my mother's understanding is that her Aunt Edith, at home at the time, had a lot to do with getting her father out of the fire. Leroy had suffered an epileptic seizure. Edith Covert was terminally ill with stomach cancer that claimed her life late on Christmas day.

My mother continues: "We moved two more times—both in Brockton. Then in 1929, jobs being scarce, we moved—again—to Detroit." So, in an era when many people stayed put for life, June, at the age of ten, had lived in several towns in Massachusetts and Vermont, once in Indianapolis, and twice in Detroit. She had lost a father whom she hardly knew, a brother shortly after her own birth, and was now living with a stepfather who never seemed to be able to keep a job, but found the time to be highly verbally abusive to both his wife and stepdaughter. This time in Detroit though, she was old enough to remember the experience:

> Our first apartment was a basement flat right on the main street—Woodward Ave. consisting of two rooms. One was a large living room with one end curtained off to make a bedroom with a small part of that curtained off in which there was a small bed for my brother and me. The back room was a combination kitchen and dining room. I don't remember a bathroom but there must have been at least a toilet. With the traffic, the streetcars and people going by constantly, it was noisy and dirty.

> It was Christmas time and my mother made the best of it. She convinced Lolly [June's brother] and I that a big tree would be out of place in our tiny apartment so we were content with a small table tree. She thought it would be fun to make our very own decorations so we pasted paper chains and strung popcorn. I never realized until much later that it was all we could afford. My mother made it all seem like fun. We hung our stockings on the bedpost and

somehow 'Santa' found us in that basement room and left us an orange, a box of raisins and in the toe, a shiny penny!

Fortunately, we didn't live there very long. Harold got a good job at the Cadillac Motor Company and we went from rags to riches, or so it seemed to me!

We moved to a brand new apartment house. For some reason, I still remember the address—2116 Hubbard. Three sunny rooms and a real bathroom with a shower and all the hot water you wanted! No more taking a bath in the middle of the kitchen floor or, if it was winter, in front of the stove! There was a roll-away bed—the first one I had seen—that folded all up and went into the closet. My parents slept on that while Lolly and I shared the bed in the bedroom. A nice warm bedroom too. No need to build a fire, so I got rid of the hateful job of filling the woodbox.

Harold and my mother eventually separated. My brother was boarded out, my mother went to work and I became a latchkey kid, only they didn't call us that then. It didn't bother me a bit. I could get up, have what I wanted for breakfast and pick out what I wanted to wear to school that day. No one to scream at me or tell me how clumsy I was. Sometimes I would fix my breakfast, then jump back into bed and pretend my maid served it to me! The old imagination was still working.

We moved again and that was to be the pattern of my life. My mother and Harold would make up and then separate, and we would move. I hated being the new girl— 'everyone say hello to June, our new girl'—while I stood there, embarrassed to tears.

I finally learned my way around the city and could go from one end to the other on the trolleys. One thing I remember clearly is 'The Golden Tower of the Fisher Building.' . . . One of the things I liked to do was go and watch them broadcast. Radio was new then and still a wonder. Gradually I grew to like the city and the life, but it was time to move on again. As usual, Harold had lost his job. He decided to go back home and so we left Detroit and went back East, this time to Plymouth, Massachusetts.

'My joy knew no bounds when my family moved to Plymouth.' Thus I began a composition in the seventh grade and even now I still love to go to Plymouth. We settled in a flat not far from town. Harold had a good job managing a dairy plant and we should have been happy. But Harold still went into his jealous rages and he and my mother fought terribly. He still made my life miserable with his verbal abuse. I could do nothing to please him. He never physically abused me. Sometimes I wished he would hit me and shut up! Verbal abuse leaves no visible marks and he was always kind to me when anyone was around so no one was aware of what he was doing to me except of course my mother. She was so afraid of him that she dared not interfere. It was inevitable that something would happen.

Something did happen. Like her grandfather, Leroy, June began to have seizures. It was epilepsy, something I did not know my mother had until I was an adult. In her mind, there simply was no need to discuss it after it had been brought under control. Why raise a subject that had brought so much hurt and pain, on top of all the other turmoil in her life? In her words:

> Little was known about it and there was very little could be done for it. It is a horrible disease if only for the fact that it isolates you from daily living. No one wants you around to play with and you are barred from all the regular activities, I could not play basketball or field hockey or any gym. I could not sing in the church junior choir or be in any of the school activities. But the biggest disappointment of all was the graduation cantata. It was the bicentennial of George Washington's birth [1932] and the eighth grade was going to put on a big cantata for its graduation exercise. Each teacher was given a scene and she could choose her singers. Every day I read the list of the ones who were chosen for a part, but I waited in vain. I can understand their reasons, but it still hurt and the hurt remained for years.

> There was one consolation. My mother bought me a beautiful white dress and took me to a beauty shop to have my hair waved. So I graduated. At least my affliction did not affect my brain and I graduated third in my class.

> We were on the move again! Harold and his big mouth! He knew more than the owners of the dairy did and told the wrong people, so he was fired. A short trip to Brockton, then back to West Bridgewater to Harold's mother's house. It was not the happy town I had known before. Harold was out of work, food was scarce and it was a bad time for everyone.

But, in the midst of the Depression, the bad times in West Bridgewater were about to get worse. I have in my possession diaries that my grandmother, Helen, kept for two years—1933 and 1935. Excerpts from her diary of 1933 now pick up the story:

> *Tuesday—14 February:* Harold . . . going to Springfield tomorrow. Gee if Harold can only get work. How we need the money no one knows.

> *Wednesday—15 February:* Rainy day. Went to an all day meeting of the Mission Circle. Harold went to Springfield. My precious Boy forgot to come

home from school and now he is gone. Poor poor darling. How can I go on now. He and little Kenneth Taylor were drowned.

Friday—17 February: Pleasant day. Just waiting that's all. Life is so strange. It seems as tho' I cannot go on. Things are too hard to bear. Harold has got the work in Springfield. Hope he'll make good and I'm sure he will.

Saturday—18 February: Pleasant weather. We buried our little darling today. Oh God how can life be so cruel. May he be safe with you and my loved ones there till we can all be together again. I think my heart is made of stone.

The deaths of my mother's brother, Lawrence, and his schoolmate, Kenneth Taylor, were front-page news in the *Brockton Times* of 16 February 1933. The article appeared just below the main headline of the day, the attempted assassination of President Franklin Roosevelt in Miami. Apparently, the first graders could not resist sliding on the ice on the frozen Town River on their way home from school and, sadly, both plunged though. The Taylor boy was found near the hole in the ice; Lawrence's body floated into a net that had been set by the police below the site of the accident. A double funeral was held for both children. Helen's 1933 diary continues:

27 February: June went to the show and was ill. Poor girl – what can I do.

05 March: June was ill.

03 April: June went to the Dr's. I don't think he helps her.

17 April: June was ill and fell downstairs.

03 May: Nice day. Home all day and evening and it's my eighth anniversary. Wonder what the next 8 will bring. Some peace and happiness I hope for I get so blue at times. Life is so queer. Guess it's all a game.

13 May: Had a terrible row with Harold. He is very cruel to me. How can he do it.

03 June: How can Harold be so cruel. The terrible things he says. He hurt me so I don't care to go on. Tried to die but failed.

04 June: My head is so sore I can't lay on it.

05 June: I still feel very sick. Don't believe my taste will ever return.

08 June: June didn't go to school; she fell ill in the morning. School will soon be done, then she can rest poor girl. She has had a struggle this year. Hope she gets well this summer.

09 June: Grandma [Harold's mother who had come to stay with the family] drives me wild. Will she ever shut up.

27 June: No money today—wonder what we'll do.

09 August: Walked to the cemetery with flowers for my little angel. Wish I was with him.

12 August: I went up and got $2 from Pa. I hate to take what little he has, but I must do something. How much longer can it last.

21 September: Harold can't find work.

During the month of September, Helen recorded that June started school in West Bridgewater, but June eventually moved to Plymouth to stay with the Avery family. The Averys owned the dairy from which Harold was fired earlier. While they clearly had no more use for Harold, the Averys had developed a close relationship with June. My mother remembered them with great fondness. Again, from my Grandmother's diary of 1933:

04 October: June had a bad spell and got burnt.

14 October: Another nice day. Harold and his mother went to Bridgewater and sold the house. Now we'll all have to get out. I won't go and live with her so guess I'll go by myself somewhere. God will take care of me.

18 October: Nice fall day. Have got my things all packed up now and will make a break soon. I think it is the only thing to do for I certainly am miserable.

19 October: Pleasant but sort of cool. Well I finally made the break and got out. I couldn't stand the life with Harold and his mother any longer. I am at Ethel's [Helen's sister] for the present. Hope I can get work. Went to Plymouth at night [probably to visit June].

My mother reported in her story that she never saw Harold again, although he and Helen were not formally divorced until 1937, some four years later. For the second time, my mother's family, never very stable to begin with, had come apart at the seams. The toll on Helen had become so great that she had tried to take her own life. When I asked my mother about this episode, she said that Helen had swallowed iodine. The constants in the family's story had become: unemployment, moving, verbal abuse, the death of family members, and June's illness which grew progressively worse, possibly exacerbated by the conditions under which she lived.

By the time Helen picked up her diary entries at the beginning of 1935, she was in the hospital after what appears to be an automobile accident that occurred in December 1934. Despite the accident, things seem to be looking up for her as she refers to "her dear." The "dear" in this case was Herbert H. Barry, constantly referred to in the diary and known to everyone as Bert. In days past, Bert was a noted sportsman for Brockton High School and captain of the football team at Syracuse University in 1910. Now in 1935, he owned what in Massachusetts was euphemistically called a "package store," more generally known as a liquor store. This would prove to be a potent combination for Helen: a new man to lean on, this time with the resources to actually support her, and a new means to cope with all the sorrows of the past—alcohol.

And, what about June? There are many references to June in the 1935 diary, but they are usually associated with the word "Palmer." When I was a child, I would occasionally hear my mother refer to Palmer in conversations with my father. Gradually, I came to realize it was a place, a town in central Massachusetts that was somehow associated with my mother's epilepsy. Much later I would learn that the rural town of Palmer (and more specifically the neighboring town of Monson) had been the location for an evolving series of state institutions. In the mid-1800s, the traditional town poorhouse in Monson had been transformed into a state-run almshouse, primarily to cope with huge numbers of Irish and other immigrants who did not always succeed in their new life in America. During the post-Civil War period, the almshouse gave way to a training school that housed orphans and children from broken families, which was a predecessor to the foster care system that replaced it in Massachusetts in 1897. (See *History of Monson State Hospital.*)

By 1898, the Monson facilities had been converted into the Massachusetts Hospital for Epileptics with just over 200 patients. In its early life, nurses went there to train in a specialized program focused on the care of epileptics. Because of the Depression, however, the nurses training program was closed for lack of funds, and the institution was faced with other problems. In one of a series of articles on what came to be known as Monson State Hospital, a Superintendent of the institution, Dr. Ronald Rosen, wrote in 1978: "Many hundreds of persons who would not ordinarily have been admitted to State institutions were admitted from 1929 to 1935. . . . Many came from families who, if times were better, could have kept their relatives at home." The hospital, primarily for epileptics in its early life, also began to absorb more and more patients with other forms of brain-related illnesses as time went on. At one point, Monson housed over 1,600 patients. As of 2005, when my mother and I visited, it housed about 160 patients with various forms of severe mental illness.

One day, when my mother's epilepsy became more of an open topic of conversation in my adulthood, I asked her about Palmer. She said she had gone to Palmer because the State hospital was there. Blithely assuming that she had probably been in this place for a couple of months, I asked her how long she had actually been there. She replied, "seven years."

I remember standing in our kitchen where this conversation took place, speechless, because of the length of time, as well as the time of life involved—my mother's teenage years and part of her young adulthood as well. I felt like one of those old Looney Toons cartoon characters who had just experienced a great shock of some kind, with their lower jaw on the floor. In fact, the hospital records show my mother was at Palmer, as she always referred to it, from the age of 15, until she was more than 23 years old. So, my mother had it wrong; she was actually at the hospital for eight years. Noticing my shocked expression, she said something that I will never forget, "Oh no, don't worry; I was happy there." Such a phrase was a hallmark of June's grit, determination, and ability to rise above the past. On the other hand, if you think of her past from the vantage point of 1935, it is not surprising that she could be happy being away from the shambles of her family life at that time.

So how did June get to this place? Some of that story lay buried away until 2005, when I asked my mother if she would like to return to Palmer, an attractive town set in the rolling hills of central Massachusetts. We made the trip. Monson State Hospital, now the Monson Developmental Center, is still run from the same Administration Building that was its headquarters in the 1930s, and was one of the few buildings my mother was able to immediately recognize. I inquired there if we could tour the campus and was directed to a member of the staff, Susan Boucher, who turned out to be the third generation of her family to work at the hospital. Since my mother's ability to walk was quite limited by this time, Ms. Boucher came out to the car and proceeded to conduct us on a driving tour of the place. She was a font of information as we toured the campus. She had to know the history since many of the buildings clearly had been abandoned for some time and were beginning to crumble and disappear into the weeds that surrounded them. Later, my mother would say that she hardly recognized anything since the trees had grown up so much around the campus in those 70 years since she was first admitted there.

After the tour, we chatted further with Ms. Boucher. She said that we could obtain the records from my mother's stay at the hospital, but that my mother would have to make the application. We explained that these days my mother could not write much and only with great difficulty; at which point, Ms. Boucher instantly organized in her office the production of a typed letter of request which I carried back to my mother in the car for her signature.

About two weeks later, an envelope arrived from the hospital containing copies of what probably is every piece of information about my mother's eight-year stay at Palmer that now exist. There were several photos, medical records, a list of visitors and the dates of their visits, letters involving my mother's eventual departure from the hospital, and the correspondence between my grandmother and the hospital that covers June's admission to the institution. Of particular interest is a letter from my grandmother dated 13 August 1934. Neither I, nor my mother, had ever seen it, of course. Below is a transcription of the handwritten original:

To the Head Social Worker

Monson Hospital, Palmer, Mass.

A few months ago I filed admission papers to your hospital for my daughter June Pennell. I realize there is a long waiting list but do you ever make an exception?

Here is the situation briefly. June's father is of course dead. Her stepfather was very abusive to her and myself also. Under medical orders for my own health and June's terrible condition I was forced to do something so broke up the home.

An old lady friend of mine and very fond of June [undoubtedly Mrs. Avery of Plymouth] gave her a home, but thru sickness in her family can no longer keep her. I received word this afternoon, hence this letter.

Work is scarce and I am working out as a housekeeper (all I could get to do). A good place where I get my board and room but only a small amount of cash (namely: $4). Unfortunately I cannot have June here and I do not make enough to pay her board anywhere.

The girl needs physical care. Her nervous condition grows worse and her mentality I find is failing her. It's hard to admit that. I wish she were under your care for she needs it.

I have no home for the girl and no money. The situation is desperate, I feel. Won't you please advice [sic] me if there is any way you could help me or do you know anything or any way I could get help.

Can't you make an exception for her.

> Respectfully yours,
>
> Mrs. H. Jepson

Please reply soon.

On June 28th, the hospital had replied to Helen's earlier application, stating that the hospital was overcrowded with a long waiting list. Nevertheless, the abject tone of Helen's letter of August 13th, supported by other letters from the Head Social Worker at the State Hospital in Foxboro who had helped out in June's case, turned the tide. On August 15th, the Superintendent of Monson State Hospital replied to Helen, in part, as follows: "Our wards are crowded but in view of the situation which you describe, we will make some arrangements to accommodate her [June] and you may send her to the hospital at your convenience."

Little time was lost. On August 21st, June was at Palmer and admitted to the hospital. On their records, even though she left the hospital as a regular patient by mid-1942, June would not be formally discharged until 26 November 1950, several years after her marriage and a number of months after my birth.

Most of the records from the hospital are, not surprisingly, clinical in nature, such as medical examinations and mental health tests. The medical records cover a fall as a result of a seizure in 1939 that resulted in a hematoma and a fractured skull with subsequent aphasia or difficulty in speaking which, uncannily, mirrors another such event in June's life that happened over 60 years later. Other than this incident and the recurrent epileptic seizures, treated primarily with the drug, Luminal, to lessen the severity, June's health remained quite fine throughout her time at the hospital. The hospital records also show that this was not an institution where they locked patients in and threw away the key. Since there was no question regarding mental stability, the epileptic patients at Palmer were free to make visits home when conditions allowed. The records show that June left the hospital two or three times a year for several weeks at a time during her permanent stay there. After mid-1942, these leaves became the rule rather than the exception, with June only showing up at the hospital for periodic check-ups.

There were also visitors to Palmer, most frequently, June's mother, Helen. For the first several years, there were many such visits. They began to trail off at the end of 1937 once Helen's address changed to 124 Spring Street at Brockton. The address is that of the Barry family. Bert hung onto the property, adjacent to his liquor store, throughout his life. It is a very familiar address to me since our family lived there for a number of years when we first moved to Brockton in 1953. The house would become the victim of a protracted probate case following Bert's death. Vacant for a number of years, it was eventually burned to the ground by vandals. The adjacent liquor store would finally be torn down too. In more recent times, there was a doughnut shop on the lot.

Another visitor in 1939 was a former patient at Palmer who became my mother's lifelong friend, Dorothy (Dotty) Rushforth. In 1941, Dotty visited again, but this time as Mrs. F. [Fred] Esty. All through my childhood, we would visit the Estys. They would play an important part in my mother's life until the end of her days. The last entry on the visitor's list is Helen's visit on 24 August 1942—probably to take June home for good.

So, during those eight years, what was there to be happy about at this medical institution in the middle of the Massachusetts countryside? This never was June's favorite topic for casual conversation. But over time, she told me a bit about her long stay there. For one thing, there were dances every Friday night. Once a year, the chief pharmacist and his wife would put on a major musical production; my mother's vocal talents, so cruelly shrugged off in that eighth grade cantata, "Ode to George Washington," at Plymouth, would be put to good use in starring roles. There was no stigma attached to having epilepsy at this place.

The patients were employed at Palmer, a key part of the institution's philosophy on treating epileptics. My mother pressed many a piece of clothing in the laundry, not necessarily a job designed to produce great happiness, but it was something productive to do. And while the men and women lived in separate buildings, there was plenty of time on the job, at meals, and at the dances to get to know one another. My mother related that her first real boyfriend was from her days at Palmer. There was an attempt to establish a high school, but evidently, the hospital's available resources were not up to the task—a major disappointment. My mother also made clear that while there were happy times, this was still an institution that operated on a strict schedule, using bells to signal the major events of the day, and without the freedoms any budding young adult would expect to experience in the U.S.

The early 1940s offered her a great opportunity though. Medical advances were being made in the drugs that were used to treat, and sometimes control, epilepsy. At one point, June was selected for an experimental trial of a new drug known as Dilantin, still in wide use today. In her case, the drug worked. Dilantin was capable of bringing her seizures under control except in periods of heavy stress or excitement. It opened a doorway to freedom from the constraints of hospital living, and my mother was more than willing to step through it. She was 23 years old, and ready to lead a normal life. The question was whether the world was ready to let her do it:

> Home at last! To be able to do what others take for granted! To choose what time you want to get up, what you want for breakfast, to go where you want to go unescorted. These little things make a big difference in your life and anyone who has lived by bells and regulations knows what I mean. To be able to control your own life to a certain extent means a great deal.

> For a few months it was wonderful, visiting relatives I hadn't seen in a long time, going downtown when I wished and even joining the local church. I was twenty-one [actually, she was twenty-three by this time], in good health and anxious to be out in the working world. I could understand my mother's anxiety and her wish, backed up by her new friend, Bert, to keep me at home and quiet, but after all I had worked daily at the hospital and knew it was good for me to keep active.

So, June went on a job hunt. Her first job was in the nearby town of Stoughton in a shoe factory, boxing shoes. She recalls the thrill of the first paycheck, followed by the realization that the job itself was boring and that she was an outsider among the mostly immigrant workforce that tended to speak in languages other than English. The shoe factory was followed by a stint at the lunchroom in Kresge's Department Store in downtown Brockton; however, the noise and confusion of that environment, along with the deboning of chickens in the store's basement for the next day's chicken salad, were too much.

After giving up on Kresge's, June saw an ad in the local paper for work as a housekeeper at Brockton's Goddard Hospital. Since she was certainly familiar with hospitals, she decided to give that a try: "I began my work there and finally found my niche in life. I did routine housework and because it was wartime and they were short of nurses I was allowed to do simple nursing chores. There was a group of nurses about my age and I became friendly with them." June's experience at the Goddard Hospital convinced her that she could do nursing work. The war was on and there was a great need. She persuaded her mother that she should give this a try, and she was off.

I had long heard of June's training at the Harley Hospital, an institution no longer in operation, in the Dorchester section of Boston. The Palmer records also contain several letters that make mention of a Marlboro Hospital. Why had I never heard of this place? The answer was simply because it was an episode my mother preferred to forget. Epilepsy at that time carried a great stigma. It is clear from the Palmer record that the prevailing sentiment among the medical professionals, as well as society in general, was that those with epilepsy, controlled or not, should be sheltered from the world, particularly the world of everyday work. So, June took the only course she thought was available; she did not tell the Marlboro Hospital about Palmer or the epilepsy. She was admitted to their training program, but in June of 1943, she had a seizure on the job, and the truth became apparent. When we discussed this rather sensitive subject, my mother told me that since she was doing well, she decided to wean herself off the medication that controlled the epilepsy. That approach obviously did not work at that time.

Given the circumstances, June lost the Marlboro training opportunity. The report of the Household Nursing Association and Training School for Attendant Nurses of Boston dated September 1943, stated: "Hospital Physician advised attendant to give up nursing in any form and go into other work."

June did not see it that way and continued to appeal for reinstatement. In February of 1944, in a letter full of doubts, the Household Nursing Association wrote to the Monson Hospital asking for their advice on readmitting June to their program. In the same month, the Superintendent of Monson replied in these highly encouraging terms:

Dear Madam:

Referring to your letter concerning June Pennell addressed to Dr. Forrerr, the information you have concerning this patient is substantially correct. Miss Pennell gets along very well on medication but you realize of course, there is always the possibility that she may have an occasional seizure. This patient is still on our records and in case of necessity, could be returned to this hospital at any time.

Very Respectfully, _____Superintendent –BONDS FOR VICTORY–

After making it difficult for June to obtain entrance to the hospital at Palmer, it seems that the institution was now highly reluctant to let go of one of its long-time patients! Nevertheless, in July 1944, the determined June once again appealed to one of the doctors at Palmer for a recommendation that would allow her to get the formal training she needed to become a nurse. She noted that she had been working in a nursing home on both day and night duty under conditions that were substantially the same as in a regular nursing position. June concluded: "Will you please send me such a letter that I may start looking for a school which I may enter. I failed once through my own foolishness and I am anxious to prove that I have profited by my failure and can really do it." The physician responded as follows:

Dear June:

I am glad that you are getting along so well, but I really would advise you to consider some other line of work rather than nursing.

If you wish to give Doctor Hodkins as a reference or any member of the Hospital staff, the best we could do would be to give an actual report of your condition as we knew it.

Sincerely yours, _____ –BONDS FOR VICTORY–

Clearly, the medical bureaucrats at Palmer were not going to go out on a limb for June. She had to return to Helen and Bert's home on Spring Street at Brockton. But there, circumstances had also changed. In August of 1944, Helen and Bert had finally married. They had waited for years since Bert's staunchly Catholic mother was opposed to her son marrying a divorced woman. But, they finally took the plunge. My mother was now definitely, as she recounted it, "the fifth wheel."

Once again, the newspaper ads brought word of another training program, this time for Licensed Practical Nurses, at the Harley Hospital in Boston. Clearly going nowhere without a clearance from a doctor, and knowing that she must be up front about her epilepsy this time, June found a doctor in Boston who was able to give her a clean bill of health. As she put it, "At this point they were so short of nurses they would take any warm body, and I was accepted." My guess is that the Harley Hospital staff also may have noted how determined this young woman was to succeed. And succeed she did. In her own words:

Five of us gathered to pass inspection under the eagle eyes of our inspector, Miss Cecilia Whitman. With a checked dress, a very starched apron and hat,

black stockings with seams very straight up the back, black oxford shoes and
hair pulled back off the collar, we waited while Miss Whitman looked us up
and down and gave her approval. It was a small hospital and only five had been
accepted to train under the government program.

In those days there was no such thing as a five day week or an eight hour
day. We worked from 7 AM until 7 PM with four hours for classes and lunch.
We had one afternoon off and a Sunday a month with a late pass. There was
no ward maid, so after we had bathed our patients and [provided] C&B [chair
and blanket] to those who were able, we had to tidy up—dust mop the floor
and clean the utility room. The patients stayed in bed a lot longer than they do
today so that meant cleaning and sterilizing bed pans and basins. As we learned
how, we passed medicines and gave treatments. They were very short of nurses
due to the war and we were taught and allowed to do many things we were not
supposed to do. And then there was night duty from 7 PM to 7 AM. One time
I worked nine weeks in the nursery and I vowed I would never do that again.
Well, I stuck to my word as far as night duty was concerned, but the nursery
became my life's work.

It was not all drudgery and hard work. It was wartime and Boston was
teeming with soldiers, sailors, and all types of service men. There was always
a brother or a sweetheart home on leave or stationed around Boston who was
looking for a girl for a buddy. It was funny, we'd come off duty, tired out and
longing for a shower and a nice bed. Then the phone would ring and somehow,
somewhere we would get our second wind and off we'd go, dining, dancing,
roller skating, movies, whatever the night had to offer.

The hospital was built on a hill surrounded by a stone wall. We found if we
walked close to the wall, we would not be detected if we happened to be late!
Also the night supervisors were careless, particularly in the cold weather. They
were supposed to come up to the Nurses Home, which was several doors up
from the hospital, and see that we were all there. They would, instead, call and
whoever answered the phone would assure her that we were all in! Oh yes,
of course, we got caught now and then but they were so short of nurses, they
needed all the help they could get, so we got off with a reprimand and the loss
of our caps for a while.

A year and a half later, out of the initial five, there were only two young women
left in the class, June being one. They completed the program and then took the
State Boards, which both passed, and were awarded the dark blue ribbons to wear
on their caps that signified they were board-approved LPNs. My mother noted,
"I had reached my goal and I was very happy!" Years later, when I was a boy, my

mother's cap went missing at the hospital where she worked. At the time, I didn't understand why she was so upset about it. Now I know what that cap symbolized to her.

June decided to stay on at the Harley Hospital, working for room and board and $87 a month. But there was another reason June decided to stay put. June had met a fellow named Irving MacDonald on a double-date arranged by one of her schoolmates, and immediately dubbed him "Mac" in order to get around calling him Irving. Her verdict after the first date, "This guy is not going to be much fun." Right at that time, the hospital put June on the 3-11 PM shift, not exactly conducive to social activities, but, June and Mac managed a church play on the following Sunday and developed a routine that wasn't exactly ideal, but kept them together:

> When I was on 3-11, Mac would take the trolley from Codman's Square to Upham's Corner, pick up some doughnuts and make his way to the hospital. The nurses would put him in an empty room until I got through. Then we would go to the Nurses home where I would make coffee. The other girls would smell the coffee and come tripping down. 'Gotta see Mac,' was their excuse. No privacy! So I saw him on Tuesday, Thursdays and most week-ends.

> That was our routine for two years. I was getting tired of the hospital—no chance for advancement. So I decided to leave and try a bigger hospital, maybe go to New York where I knew there was a big maternity hospital. However, when I told Mac my plans, he said, 'Don't go away. I have plans too.' I said, 'Do your plans include me?' He said, 'Of course,' and that was my proposal.

> One Saturday near Christmas, I was making plans with another girl for the following Saturday when Mac, overhearing us, said, 'You can't go there. We have to go in town. 'Why?' I asked. 'Well, you want a ring don't you?' My romantic Mac!

So, the wedding plans went forward. June decided on a big church wedding, "with all the trimmings," having had no school graduation party and no celebration when she finished nurses' training. Their plans were met with no great enthusiasm from either family. June was three years older than Mac, a fact that didn't sit well with his mother. Mac's younger brother didn't want to act as best man. Bert, June's stepfather, simply refused to come, and June's mother was not planning to attend either until her sisters finally persuaded her. Helen was heard to remark, "He's a nice boy, but he'll never set the world on fire."

Despite all the family grumblings on both sides, June and Mac did, indeed, get married on 31 May 1948. Mac's older brother, George, finally stood up for him, and since June was short on family members that wedding day, Mac's Uncle Clarence gave away the bride. As my mother reported, "At least Mac and I were happy." And so they remained for 37 years, and undoubtedly, would have for many more, if later events hadn't conspired against them.

June and Mac lived for five years in the Dorchester section of Boston in a flat in a tenement on Whitfield Street right across from where the senior MacDonalds (Theresa and Alfred) lived. Mac held a series of jobs during those days: carpet layer, worker in the Baker's Chocolate factory, and worker in the Eagle Oil Company, an establishment that made oil-based materials. In 1950, I was born at the Harley Hospital where my mother had trained. The birth, however, triggered my mother's epilepsy, and the heavy seizures so upset my father that the idea of a larger family came to an end; thus, only one child came of this marriage.

In 1953, a request came from Helen and Bert. They had decided to live on a regular basis at Bert's property on the river in Wareham, Mass, and commute from there to his store at Brockton twice a week. That would leave the long-time Barry home on Spring Street at Brockton empty, so would June and Mac consider moving to Brockton to live in the place rent-free? This offer was a bit of a two-edged sword. My mother and Bert had never been close, and the idea of being beholden to him for the roof over our family's heads was not appealing. On the other hand, my father was not fond of his job with the Eagle Oil Company, and some of my mother's relatives who worked as custodians for the schools at Brockton said they would help Mac get a job in the system. I also think putting a little distance between the in-laws and herself, particularly the rather domineering personality of her mother-in-law, had its appeal to June. So, despite the misgivings, we made the move, back to a town in which my mother had vowed she would never live again.

I have very clear memories of the house on Spring Street where we lived for five years: sitting with my father on the downstairs porch watching the theatrics of a summer thunder storm; watching the ice man haul blocks of ice with an enormous set of tongs into my grandfather's store which had no electric refrigeration; listening in the summer time for the once-yearly clop of hoof beats and the sound of metal-rimmed wagon wheels on the street as the midway rides were brought from the train station to the Brockton Fair grounds, passing right by our house.

During this period, June, having fought so hard to get her nurses education, finally persuaded my father that she should go back to work. She would work on the 3-11 shift so that she could care for me during the day. From that point forward, she worked at the Brockton Hospital in the nursery for close to 30 years.

After a year's interim stay in an apartment near Main Street, we moved into our own home on 69 Carl Avenue, at Brockton. This would be the family home until the early nineties. My mother was much in favor, while my Depression-scarred father was terrified to make the purchase. What if they couldn't make the payments? What if they lost the mortgage? What if they lost their jobs? My mother's argument was that as long as people continued to have children, they would need nurses to care for them and schools to attend, so there was little chance that either of them would lose their jobs. She was proven right.

At the time, Carl Avenue was only partially paved, so in essence the street was an over-large cul-de-sac. At one time, it had been a Swedish enclave in a city defined by the ethnic neighborhoods of shoe factory workers. In the 1950s, the Swedes were still a plurality in this neighborhood: Johnsons, Andersons, Pearsons, Magnussons among others, all members of the Lutheran church that was not far away; but others, like the MacDonalds, were moving into the area.

From this home, June not only cared for her immediate family and continued her nursing work, but she also cared for the needs of the previous generation as they approached old age. In 1962, Bert died, leaving Helen isolated at their home in Wareham. As mentioned previously, Bert's line of work, the liquor store, was not kind to Helen. She had lost much in her life, two boys and two previous husbands to death, separation and divorce. She had lost her remaining child for many years to epilepsy. For those reasons, or perhaps others more complex, the alcohol in Bert's store became a haven, a source of solace, or perhaps simply an addiction. By the time I came to know her, she was a shell of what she had been in earlier days.

What to do? June contacted Doris Volk, the former Doris Hambly who had partnered with my grandmother in the previously-mentioned adventure that ended in ruin in Kansas City. As it turned out, Doris was in need of a situation, so she moved to Wareham to provide a home life for my grandmother. Every Friday, my mother drove the 35 miles from Brockton to Wareham to take care of business, lay in a supply of groceries, and attend to the maintenance of the house. This went on for many years until Doris could no longer handle the effort.

During the same time period, another relative came to live with us, my grand-father, James Alfred MacDonald. My parents converted a "sun-room" at the back of our house into a bedroom for Alfred, as he was always known. My mother and father supported him and cared for him until his death by cancer in 1964.

Similarly, my mother's Aunt Grace, with whom she had lived from time to time as a child in Detroit and elsewhere, came under my mother's wing in her later years. Grace had no children of her own and June's relationship with her was close to that of a daughter. While she never came to live with us, it was my mother who provided for Grace and assisted her in her later years until her death in 1983.

Along with everything else, June also went back to high school. The abortive attempt at a high school at Palmer had left her without a degree. So by attending night school, she was finally able to get her diploma in 1966, two years before I received mine. My mother told me many times that her biggest regret was that she did not continue on with college classes which would have allowed her to become a Registered Nurse and, as such, would have enabled her to teach nursing students.

As for me, I never wanted for anything of any significance as a child. But, when it was time to go to college, despite a scholarship from the school, there still was a shortage of cash to cover all costs to attend Syracuse University. The solution was for June to switch from part-time to full-time work, thereby covering all the remaining bills and enabling me to complete college, debt-free in 1972. That degree would be the catalyst that would eventually lead me to a career as a Foreign Service Officer with the U.S. Agency for International Development (USAID). USAID would take our family, ultimately of four children, overseas for a total of fifteen years.

Our first overseas assignment was to Mauritania in West Africa, beginning in 1981. This was still a time when communications were not what they are today. Computers were new and, of course, there was no Internet. International telephone service to this part of the world was still very difficult. So, it would take a letter from my father, a very rare, almost unique event, to get the news that my mother had developed a non-cancerous but highly dangerous brain tumor that would require surgery. While the surgery was successful, all of the tumor could not be removed. This fact resulted in the gradual loss of some motor skills along with periodic vertigo that would eventually end June's long and hard-won nursing career, which, unfortunately, ended without any kind of a pension for her long service in the nursing field. The tumor also somehow triggered my mother's epilepsy, requiring her, once again, to use medication to control it.

In 1984, I was transferred to Kenya. The following year, early one morning in August, I got a rare call from my mother. My father, who had found employment years ago with the school system, was determined to get his school ready for the new school year. In the process, he attempted to carry a heavy machine up a staircase by himself, but he had heart trouble and the staircase climb was too much. Not even his wife of 37 years saw him alive again. All I could do was go home and speak at the funeral, spend a bit of time with my mother, then return to Kenya. I would call periodically to find out how she was making out, to which her so-typical response was that everything was fine. It took me years to realize that this was certainly not always the case and how greatly the death of my father had affected her.

The following Christmas found June in Nairobi, along with my in-laws, for the holidays. During this trip, June revealed that the brain tumor had regrown and that there was need for more surgery, which would be set for 1986 when we would be back in the U.S. on leave. That surgery took away another swath of her mobility. By the early 1990s, June recognized the need to give up the home on Carl Avenue, so she moved to a two-bedroom apartment in the adjoining town of Bridgewater. Later, she would move to an assisted living complex, back again at Brockton. Despite her increasing health problems, she hung onto, and substantially improved, the summer property in Wareham that she had inherited on the death of her mother.

The 1990s, though, would bring June something totally unexpected in her life. In this period, Dotty Esty, her old friend from the days at Palmer, passed away. At some later point, Dotty's husband, Fred, visited the Wareham house to help my mother out with some maintenance. They struck up a lasting close acquaintance, and the support and comfort Fred provided my mother will never be forgotten, nor the ties between the two families, now 80 years long.

And never forgotten will be this remarkable woman of the iron will, steadfast determination, and great heart—June Miriam (Pennell) MacDonald. This woman, who triumphed over a broken childhood, a stigmatizing disease, and all the naysayers who said she couldn't when, indeed, she knew she could. This woman, who cared for so many, even those who should have cared more for her when they had the chance, but didn't or couldn't. This woman, who, in later life, continued to face personal loss and physical adversity with the same indomitable spirit with which she faced epilepsy and the death of family members in earlier days. This woman, who in the face of challenges that would have crushed others, was able to report, "I was happy there."

If I still felt I was missing something in June's story, I was fortunate to have the opportunity to ask the ultimate source until 3 April 2009 when my mother died at Boston. Ironically, it was the epilepsy, her old nemesis brought under control long ago, that killed her. I had noticed earlier in the year before her death that she might have reached a point where she was beginning to lose track of taking the medication that kept the epilepsy at bay. I was about to arrange for the staff of her assisted living unit at Brockton to help keep track of it for her. But it was too late. On a Wednesday, June had been out on her usual weekly shopping trip for groceries. Everything seemed to go fine. A bit later though, the assisted living staff heard a crash, entered June's apartment, and found she had had a seizure, hitting her head as she fell. June was moved to a Boston hospital by helicopter where several days later, she passed on.

Amazed to have made it to eighty years of age, and then to have lived to see the new Millennium, June soldiered on until just two months' shy of her ninetieth birthday. She was, of course, slowed by disease and age in her last years, and in the end, the loneliness of those years began to show as she appeared to grow somewhat tired of day-to-day living. But, that is not how I will remember her. The portrait I will always carry of her is the one I have chosen to include in this book, the strong, vibrant young woman wearing her cherished nurse's cap, who was the heart of my childhood, and my lifelong example of endurance and fortitude.

CHAPTER 2

THE DOUGHBOY:
PERCY LEON COVERT

The costs of war are well known: physical destruction, massive human suffering, huge financial losses, and sometimes, political and social upheaval on a global scale. Despite these costs, some wars ultimately produce great benefits. The Second World War clearly saved us from lunatic fascists who wished to dominate the world.

From a family history viewpoint, many wars also produce an ironic, but significant, collateral benefit. The bureaucracies that support them produce mountains of data cataloguing who was involved, where they served, what they did, and also, to whom they were related. This material is a major source for those seeking basic genealogical facts, as well as the details of their family's involvement in these catastrophic events that, unfortunately, define so much of human history.

Another major source of material comes from the participants themselves. They often record their memories of the drama, as well as the humdrum of war, in letters, diaries, pictures, or books that are saved and passed down in families as a means of remembering the unique service that wars engender. What follows in this chapter depends heavily on a series of such letters written by a soldier in France to his sister in America during the First World War.

A Military Heritage

I came very close to taking part in the war that occupied my generation, the Vietnam War. But, by 1972, when I was eligible to participate, the war was beginning to wind down, and the military decided that it did not require my services. So in my immediate family, I have to step back to World War II to find those who were involved in a conflict. It is not hard since nearly everyone of that generation was involved in some fashion. The start of my mother's nursing career, previously described, owes much to the war. My mother-in-law and her sister were welders on blimps being constructed at Moffet Field in California. My father was with the Army Air Force, spending his service years in India and Burma. But, other than my father's photos, I have nothing in writing about his service. For that sort of perspective, I have to take another step back to World War I.

Once again, I am indebted to my Great Aunt Grace. Her brother, Percy, was the only male of his generation in the Covert family. When the U.S. finally got involved in the war in 1917, Percy took part. He was a prolific writer all through his stint in France, even turning out an occasional letter on a typewriter. Most of those letters have been disbursed to parts unknown and lost over time. But, of course, Grace kept hers, as well as every article involving Percy's service that she managed to get printed in the local newspaper. Given the closeness between Grace and my mother, all this material is now in my possession. To have this personal record of service in the "war to end all wars" is a tribute to Grace's tenacity in holding onto her family's history. It provides an eyewitness account of a great conflict that has now disappeared from living memory into the history books.

Leroy and Edith Covert and their family of seven children have already been introduced in Chapter 1. As noted, the first Coverts in this ancestral line lived in the colony of New Amsterdam, moved to northern New Jersey, and then to the Finger Lakes region in the state of New York (Fisher, et al.). Percy and his two oldest sisters, however, were born at or near Detroit. What took his family to Michigan? Ultimately, the cause was another war.

In looking into the history of the Coverts, I came across an often-used source for family history information, a family association. The Covert Association, maintained by Diane Broderick of Tampa, Florida, introduced me to Robert (Bob) Covert of Port Charlotte, Florida, now deceased. Bob provided me with a great deal of information on several generations of Coverts, including John E. Covert, Percy's great-grandfather. Supported by copies of John E.'s service record from the National Archives, Bob Covert showed that John E. had served in the War of 1812, and that he had been given two land grants for his service. He apparently sold the original 40 acres he was given in 1851, but, evidently, John E. settled on the 120 acres he received in 1855 since he is next heard from in 1871, applying for a pension for his war service from the town of Mundy, Genesee County, Michigan. Mundy is near Flint and not far from Detroit. So, the family story that the Coverts of Leroy's and the next generation went to Michigan to get work in the auto industry is likely only part of the answer. Members of the extended family had already been there for at least two generations.

Edith (Wood) Covert's family background, on the other hand, is nothing but Massachusetts for generations. What was she doing in Michigan in the late 1800s where she married Leroy Covert? Once again, it is Aunt Grace who provides the story, as told to her niece, Barbara Bates. According to Grace, Edith's mother, Nancy Ann, was running a boarding house in Braintree, Mass, near a tanning mill, when a half-sister, who had "gone West," sent for her to come out to Detroit. Nancy Ann had saved some money and had the choice of going to Michigan or investing in telephone stock. At that time, telephones were new and she wasn't sure about their longevity, so she chose to go to Michigan. Nancy Ann took her 11-year old daughter, Edith, with her. The year would be 1882. Later, at the age of 18, in early 1890, Edith met Leroy Covert at a dance at Fort Wayne where he was stationed with the regular army. Less than two months later, Leroy and Edith were married before Leroy was redeployed to Texas. The dates in this story match known birth and marriage records. Alexander Graham Bell established his first joint stock company in 1877 in order to promote his new telephone. So there is quite a bit of plausibility to this story. It certainly would be useful to have the destroyed U.S. Census of 1890 to confirm who was living in Detroit at that time.

By the next U.S. census in 1900, both the Wood and Covert families were back in Massachusetts, living in the town of Holbrook. The elder Coverts, eventually joined by Nancy Ann Wood, stayed in Massachusetts until their deaths during the period between the two world wars.

According to his letters, written during the first of those wars, Percy joined the National Guard in Massachusetts around 1909 when he was 18 years old. Why would he join the Guard? Possibly, he was following the tradition of military service in his family, including not only John E., but both of his grandfathers in the great conflict of their day, the American Civil War. The enlistment and service records of Martin V. Covert are found in the National Archives. He was assigned to Battery A of the 3rd Regiment of New York Light Artillery and served the bulk of his time in New Bern, North Carolina. There was a battle at New Bern in 1862, leading to its occupation by Union forces for the duration of the war. In December of 1864, the muster roll indicates Martin was "Absent on Detached Service (Expedition)." What sort of an "expedition" is not clear. May 1865 finds him sick in the Foster General Hospital at New Bern, with what illness is not clear, and it was from that hospital that he was discharged on 02 June 1865. In later years, Martin acquired a pension for his service in the war and spent the last years of his life in the Soldier's Home at Bath, New York, where he died in 1915. Martin Covert is buried in the National Cemetery at Bath.

Similar records exist for William Henry Wood, Percy's grandfather on his mother Edith's side. William Henry enlisted at Randolph on 07 April 1862 for three years and was assigned to Company E, 35th Massachusetts Volunteer Infantry. He got as far as Alexandria, Virginia, where a heart ailment of "five years duration" took him out of the war. He was discharged from the military on 28 December 1862 at the New Convalescent Camp, near Alexandria, Virginia. The muster rolls make clear that he spent most of the period of his enlistment in the hospital. By 1900, he received a small pension for his service. William Henry died in 1903. Despite his shortened term of service, his gravestone at the Central Cemetery in Randolph, Massachusetts, carries only the following inscription: Wm. H. Wood, Co. E., 35 Mass. Inf.

So, Percy came from a family with a strong military tradition which, if traced further, shows that William Henry Wood's grandfather, Barnabas, was also a veteran of the War of 1812, and that William Henry's wife, Nancy Ann Tower, was directly descended from participants in the American Revolutionary War and the French and Indian wars that preceded the Revolution. I believe that Percy knew at least part of this history. But, one piece of the military tradition he knew for sure was that of his own father.

Again, thanks to Aunt Grace, I have in my possession several documents that relate to Leroy Covert's military service. These documents are worn and heavily soiled, bearing all the evidence that they were once carried on the person of the owner as prized possessions. One of these is a "To all whom it may concern" document on Leroy's discharge from the Army of the United States as a Private in Company A of the 23rd Regiment of Infantry which he had joined in 1889. The discharge was given on what appears to be 23 December 1890, at Ft. Sam Houston, Texas. There is a reason given on the document, but it is now illegible. One likely reason, however, is his newly married wife who was still in Michigan. The reference as to character is listed as "excellent."

There is also an 1899 Honorable Discharge from the Michigan State Troops, a Michigan-only defense force. The final document is an Honorable Discharge from the 10th Company of the Coast Artillery Regiment of the Massachusetts National Guard given on 29 April 1917, by reason of "Instructions, M.B. 220.81 Mass. April 9 1917." These instructions relate to the reorganization of the Guard unit as part of the 26th (Yankee) Division of the American Expeditionary Force (AEF) following the United States' entry into World War I. Family lore, support- ed by information in Percy's letters from France, indicates that Leroy wanted to be part of the fight and was severely disappointed when he was discharged from the service despite being 46 years old with a wife and three children still at home. But, if Leroy was too old, his son was not.

With such a soldierly heritage and a father who clearly was proud of his military service and wished for more, it is not particularly surprising that Percy would move with his Guard unit (the same unit from which his father was discharged) into the Yankee Division of the AEF and, thus, into the war. By 1917, however, Percy's decision to fight in this war was not a simple matter.

On the 28th of June 1910, at the age of 18, Percy had married Gladys Morton Dean, also age 18, at Brockton, Massachusetts. By the next day, the word was out. Despite an attempt at secrecy, it was in the local paper, the *Brockton Times*. The article reads in part:

> For a joke the young folks had planned to keep the wedding a secret from their friends for a short time, and when a reporter appeared at the house this noon and informed the bride that the secret was out, Mrs. Covert, who is 18 and pretty, was surprised beyond words. She smilingly confessed the truth and admitted that she hardly expected she could keep it secret for long. Mrs. Covert first met her husband a little over a year ago, when she was entertained at his home, and it was Miss Grace Covert, the sister of the groom, who first introduced them, and who gave away the secret of their marriage this morning.

Hardly likely that Grace would keep a secret like that when it could be turned into such a fine news article! The bride and groom, however, may have had reason for a bit of privacy regarding their marriage since Percy and Gladys were already expecting their first child, Alta, who was born on 26 January 1911. Whatever the circumstances, Alta was the first child of the new Covert generation, and shortly after her birth, there appeared in the *Brockton Times* a five-generation photo of members of the family to commemorate the occasion: Alta, of course, with her father, Percy; his mother, Edith (Wood) Covert; Edith's mother, Nancy Ann (Tower) Wood; and Nancy Ann's mother, Susan (Snow) (Tower) Leach, who was born in 1822 in northern New Hampshire. It is a fabulous picture to have in the family album, and the accompanying news article as well.

By 1912, there was another child in Percy and Gladys' household, Alliston Dean Covert. Two years later, on the first of June 1914, two more children were born. Perhaps these twins were premature as one child died immediately. The other twin hung on for two weeks, dying on the 14th of June. These children were not given names in either the birth or death records of Brockton, Mass, or in the Covert family Bible. There would be no further additions to Percy and Gladys' family.

The War and U.S. Involvement

Across the sea in Europe, two other deaths in June of 1914 would, ultimately, alter the lives of millions of people worldwide, including Percy Covert. On 28 June 1914, a Serbian nationalist named Gavrilo Princip shot the Austro-Hungarian Archduke Ferdinand, heir to the throne, and his wife, Sophie, in the streets of Sarajevo. They died the same day. The Austrian response to this event would touch off a cascade of actions that would lead to a worldwide conflict. While the Sarajevo murders were a trigger, the overall rationale for the war rests in a matrix of past territorial losses, a complex series of alliances, militaristic traditions, growing industrial power, the restiveness of vassal states of various empires, and those empires' attempts to repress them, among many other reasons. The industrial power which fueled the war assured that any early hubris on any combatant's part of quick victory would be crushed by the power of mechanized arms, clouded by the use of chemical weapons, and sucked down by a sea of mud and blood in trenches and barbed wire entanglements that would stretch across France in the west, Russia in the east, and a variety of other fronts in Italy, Turkey, Africa, and the Middle East. When America entered the war in 1917, millions of soldiers and civilians were already dead in a quagmire that offered little hope of resolution any time soon.

At the start of the war, the Americans held a neutral position toward what they regarded as a European conflict that they had had no role in perpetrating; however, attacks by German submarines against neutral parties, including the infamous sinking of the liner *Lusitania* in May of 1915, had a role in reshaping American attitudes toward the war. In early 1917, the Germans ended a year-long hiatus on submarine attacks against neutral shipping and American boats were once again in their crosshairs—a provocation, among other concerns, to which the Americans responded. Those other concerns included the close American relationship with England, and a growing sense that France, which had supported

America in its war of independence, and a fellow republic, could not be left without American support in its hour of need. That sentiment would be most famously stated when, once in France, American troops marched in Paris to the tomb of Lafayette and an American colonel cried, "Lafayette we are here!"

Percy Covert clearly had a good set of family reasons to steer away from this war. Many married men with families were exempted. But, it is clear that Percy saw himself, like his father, as a military man. Just prior to the institution of mandatory draft, Percy made his registration on 5 May 1917, along with millions of other young men. Percy's draft registration noted his wife and two children and his employment as a motorman for the Bay State Street Railway (a local trolley company) located at Brockton. That registration put in motion a string of events that would take him to France for the balance of the war. He welcomed the call.

A 1918 Brockton City Directory shows Percy as head of household at 359 Pleasant Street. Clearly, he was not in residence that year, but this is the same address of his in-laws, Edgar and Louisa Dean. So, it appears that Percy's family went to live with the Deans while he was away in France.

The United States was hardly ready to conduct a war in 1917. The regular Army was small. It had recently been involved in fighting along its southern border and in Mexico, hardly great experience for the trench warfare that had raged for three years in Europe. As noted, the U.S. instituted a draft to assure it had sufficient manpower for the effort. But there was another source of men ready at hand, the National Guard. The 26th Division was stitched together from National Guard units from throughout New England, including Percy's 10th Company of the Coast Artillery Regiment from Massachusetts. These part-time military men were made full-time soldiers in dramatic fashion:

> The second line of defense, the National Guard, under mobilization orders since the declaration of the war, was called into active service at twelve noon, July 25, 1917, and mobilized in their respective armories all over the Union.

> On that unforgettable day, at exactly noon, fire bells, whistles, and sirens were shrieking out their message in multiples of five, for the alarm call to arms was 5-5-5. Startled people ran into the streets in wonder, leaving their noon day meals untouched. Such excitement prevailed with everybody talking of war, that one would have got the impression that the enemy was only miles away. (Albertine p 10)

Not only were trained soldiers in short supply, so were barracks needed to house them, weapons, and the ships needed to transport men and materiel to Europe:

> The flood of troops strained the supply of available equipment. A shortage of rifles saw some recruits drilling with wooden sticks. Hand grenades, machine guns, artillery pieces were all in short supply. Indeed, artillery was so scarce that the French would supply virtually all of the guns used by the American Expeditionary Force in France. (Hallas p 24)

Despite these obstacles, the American war effort pulled itself together. The 26th Division was the second AEF division to reach France, making the trip in September of 1917. Since U.S. ships were too few, many elements of the new 26th Division went "across the pond" on English ships, many of them converted passenger liners.

Percy's unit, the 101st Field Artillery Regiment, sailed on September 9th on the *RMS Adriatic*. The *Adriatic* was one of the "Big Four" passenger liners of the British White Star Line. Built in 1909, it was the first ship equipped with an indoor pool and a Turkish bath. She had been captained on her maiden voyage across the Atlantic by the White Star's Commodore, Edward Smith, sometimes known as the "millionaires' captain." He had originally made a name for himself ferrying British troops to South Africa during the Boer War. It was on the maiden voyage of the *Adriatic* that Captain Smith made his famous comment that modern industrial techniques had made major shipping catastrophes a thing of the past. In the *Adriatic*'s case, Smith's words were prophetic. The ship came through the war without incident and would sail until 1935. Smith's words, however, proved less sound during the maiden voyage of the last vessel under his command—the *Titanic*. The *Adriatic* took Percy's 101st Field Artillery to England where less upper-crust transport was arranged to take them across the English Channel. By 25 September 1917, the unit was in France.

In France with the 26th (Yankee) Division

Unlike many others involved in the war effort, Percy was highly literate, and as his letters to Grace make clear, he wrote to a large range of correspondents. Some, like Grace, kept at it for the duration. Others, Percy complained late in the war, eventually gave it up. As his 26th Division was one of the first to arrive in France, Percy was involved in nearly all the "drives" against the enemy in which the AEF, commanded by Major General John J. "Black Jack" Pershing, participated, from early 1918 until the Armistice on November 11th of that year. He wrote about

Percy L. Covert, the Doughboy, about 1917/18.
Collection of the author.

it all. Due to the secrecy imposed on troop movements, however, most of these letters were written from, "Somewhere in France." While it has not always been possible to specifically locate Percy himself at any given moment, I am indebted to the series of sources listed in this book for helping me identify where the 26th Division as a whole, and Percy's artillery regiment in particular, were at any given time during their service in France.

Percy's first letter to Grace is dated 5 October 1917. Many of these letters note Percy's specific unit within the 26th Division: Headquarters Company, 101st Field Artillery Division (of the 51st Field Artillery Brigade). The "Somewhere in France" in this case is the Coetquidan Camp (referred to in another letter as "Cocky Dan") where the American artillery brigades were sent to train. Located near the town of Neufchateau in the northeast of France, Coetquidan Camp had been a French artillery training site since the time of Napoleon. From its landing place at Le Havre, the 26th Division moved to the camp by train, in rail cars famously known as "40 hommes, 8 chevaux" (40 men, 8 horses). The men often stood in these cars for hours since there was not enough room to lie down, and, at any rate, they quickly learned that laying down on the vermin infested straw that often came with the cars was not to their advantage. Much of their baggage from the trip across the Atlantic arrived at Coetquidan two months later, at least the part of it that was neither lost nor stolen.

The rapid mobilization of the AEF meant that many of its units, without sufficient arms or the ships needed to take them to Europe, spent months in the States in training. Those elements of the AEF that did make it to France early in their service, like the 26th Division, would spend months in training there, often under the tutelage of the French who would show them how to fight this particular war. Percy wrote in the October 5th letter: "We are drilling like sixty every day and I like it first rate only I miss the boys of the old 10th. . . . Before long I expect to see action at the front." He was right about the heavy training; he was wrong by months about moving to the front. Neither the other allied nations nor, in particular, Black Jack Pershing, were anxious to insert U.S. troops into this vicious war without proper training.

As this letter continues, Percy regretted the absence of his father in the war effort: "Poor old dad. I wish he was along. I know just how bad he feels getting his discharge and you folks can never realize for you never was a soldier and it sure would be hard for me." It is clear that Percy took his soldiering very seriously.

All these letters are signed with his full name and rank, in this case, Sgt. Percy L. Covert. Another name appears on the letters, usually with the inscription, "OK," that of the censor.

The rationale for the censorship was simple. In the business of trench warfare, a spy might somehow obtain some reference in a letter to a troop location that would assist the enemy in targeting its attacks. Among those skeptical of this policy was the *Boston Globe* reporter Frank Sibley, who was "embedded" in the 26th Division for the duration of its time in France. As stated in Sibley's book, *With the Yankee Division in France*, much of the fighting was conducted in the Alsace-Lorraine area, which had been traded back and forth numerous times between the Germans and the French, and where there were many sympathizers with the German cause. Sibley noted that if you wished to know where the Division was headed next or when the Division would be involved in an attack, a discussion with the local townspeople would usually produce very credible information. Clearly, if the townspeople knew, so did the Germans.

In Percy's next letter, dated 26 November 1917, small pieces have been cut out—most likely evidence of the censors at work. Even the meticulous professional Sgt. Covert appears to have included a bit too much in this letter. In the note, he told Grace what he'd been chosen to do during this war:

> I am a telephone operator now myself [Grace was also a telephone operator by profession] only I carry my switchboards with me and set up my central most any place. I have a 20 drop board of the old style. You know, ring the bell and the drop falls. . . . I am the telephone sgt. in the regimental detail and have to set up communications for the whole regiment.

And in this note, he opened a theme that would occupy a part of most of his letters, one that was common throughout the army: "I don't know of anything that I want outside of tobacco and candy and you can't send too much of that for I smoke a lot and sweets are very scarce." Elsewhere, Percy noted that the food was not bad and that they were generally well supplied with the basics; however, having more than the basics certainly helped. He carried on an incessant dialogue throughout his letters to Grace about sweets, especially chocolate, and the all-important tobacco, since what could be obtained locally, particularly in the early going, was deemed of very poor quality.

Then came a shock to the soldier who, it appears, hoped that this war would help him make the Army a full-time career. In a letter dated 5 December 1917, Percy described his demotion from sergeant to corporal:

> I almost hate to write home this time for I got the worst slap in the face last night that I ever received since I first joined the Army in 1909. The captain called me up to his office last night and told me to write out a request that I be reduced to a corporal as he had a better man for the job. . . My chance of getting my com. [commission] passed when I was transferred from the coast. If I had stayed there I had a good chance but it is all off now.

Conveying this news to his father must have been devastating. Despite the loss in rank, Percy carried on. In the same letter, he lectured his sister, the news-hound, on keeping his letters out of the local paper: "I don't like to scold Grace, but please don't give any more of my letters to the papers. I didn't come over here to get a lot of bull put in the paper about me and you give any more I'll stop writing." It is clear from this and many similar remarks that Percy was afraid that Grace would manage to get something printed from one of his letters that would be regarded as sensitive, and then he might find himself reduced to a private for the duration.

The balance of December 1917 and January 1918 passed off with little of sub-stance to say since the regiment remained in training mode at Coetquidan. Of course, there was Christmas and that meant gifts from home, referred to in a letter dated 26 December 1917:

> Your very welcome package was an Xmas present indeed. It reached me yes-terday afternoon along with your letter of Dec 3. I have just finished off one of the cans of sardines and part of the Uneeda [the original Nabisco cracker] and they sure went great. . . . The candy and sweets are nearly gone for we share our bundles as they come to us. You wanted some suggestions of what you could send. Well smokes are always in order. Sweet chocolate, dates, figs, nabiscos, salted peanuts and candy are amiable and go very good. . . . In fact any kind of smokes and eatables go good. While we get plenty of good substantial grub these little extras from home sure polish off a feed. . . . I don't know how much I have gained but this outdoor life sure agrees with me and my belt hardly fits me now.

In another note, Percy commiserated with Grace on her break-up with her first husband, Roy Fox. Throughout these letters, there are frequent references to the comings and goings of Percy's mother and father, and his sisters and their spouses, those old enough to have them. There are fewer references to his wife, Gladys, whom he calls "Muff" in these letters and no references at all to his children.

The "outdoor life" of which Percy spoke so positively was about to change though, as finally the early arrivals among the American units, including the 26th Division, were judged ready to be tested in limited action. From a letter dated 20 February 1918: "Answering yours of Dec 23, the day after I got it we left the camp for the front."

As noted earlier, there were many fronts in World War I since the combatants were European empires with colonial and other interests around the world. But the Western Front in France was the focal point for much of the most intense action. Not long after the declaration of war in August 1914, the Germans had mobilized a massive force that took the path of least resistance through neutral Belgium on their way to Paris and what they thought would be the end of a short war. That thinking was mirrored by every other power involved:

> Five Empires were at war by midnight on 4 August 1914: the Austro-Hungarian Empire against Serbia; the German Empire against France, Britain and Russia; the Russian Empire against Germany and Austria-Hungary; and the British and French Empires against Germany. If the war was to be over by Christmas, as many believed, or at the latest by Easter 1915, tens of thousands might be killed or wounded before the guns fell silent. Every army believed that it could crush its opponents within a few months. German troops were as confident that they would soon be marching in triumph along the Champs-Elysees in Paris as French troops were that they would parade along the Unter den Linden in Berlin. (Gilbert p 34)

The Germans made quick work of any Belgian resistance to its shattered neutrality and poured into northern France. Eventually they were slowed and then stopped short of their goal by the French, a much smaller contingent of British troops, and the Belgians who could stay neutral no longer. By 1915, many of the original professionals who had fought the war had been killed or disabled and all sides were fighting with new volunteers, and later, conscripts. The conflict had evolved into the trench warfare for which it is now famous. Through most of 1916 and 1917, there was plenty of action, drives that were designed by both sides to break out of the stalemate and move on toward victory. But, the result from any of these individual battles was usually carnage, with many thousands dead, and the front shifting no more than a few thousand yards, if that. The names of some of these often lengthy and horrible engagements, Verdun and the Somme, resonate down to this day.

Over the course of 1917, that same sort of stalemate did not apply to the Eastern Front. Less than a month before the American declaration of war against Germany on 6 April 1917, Tsar Nicholas II of Russia had abdicated. Shortly after the U.S. came into the war, the German and Austrian High Command had sanctioned the departure from Switzerland to Russia of an individual who would do much to change the short-term outcome on the Eastern Front and the longer-term history of the 20th-century, Vladimir Ilich Ulyanov—Lenin. Following the abdication of the Tsar, a provisional government had been created which eventually came to be led by the socialist, Alexander Kerensky, who promised to keep Russia fighting. But it was not to be. By November 1917, the Bolsheviks had seized the government and begun the process of taking Russia out of the war. While much of the fighting on the Eastern Front had been undertaken by the Austro-Hungarians, there were also large numbers of Germans involved. The end of the war in the east meant that the Germans could relocate a significant number of soldiers and weapons to the Western Front. The idea was simple, overwhelm the Allies in France and end the war before the growing number of Americans became a significant factor in the equation.

In the beginning of 1918, when the Americans first began to enter the front lines, the Western Front stretched from its northern tip in Flanders on the Franco-Belgian border, then moved nearly due south through Artois and Picardy until it began to curve in a southeasterly direction at Soissons, only some 75 miles northeast of Paris. From Soissons, the line generally moved to the southeast toward Verdun, where it turned further south into the Vosges Mountains along the Franco-German border. The front ended in the Swiss Alps.

In the general area of Soissons was the Chemin des Dames Sector located on one of the innumerable ridges or other high ground that often anchored the front. The 26th Division moved into this sector in early 1918, some 100 miles northwest of their training camp at Coetquidan. These men operated under the overall direction of the French officers responsible for the sector. While the individual units of the division maintained their organizational integrity, all of these units were interspersed among the French units who had been fighting this war for nearly three years. The French were not about to entrust any part of the line entirely to the untested Americans.

This sector was known to be "quiet" at this time, but the Germans who faced them knew the Americans had arrived, and in a series of tit for tat raids they tested each other. In early February, the 101st Field Artillery lobbed its first shells at German positions, and during that month, the infantry of the 26th Division saw its first action. While most of these initial actions were not part of major thrusts, the Germans, who at times used very experienced storm troopers in these actions, learned that the Americans, though green, could and would fight. The first Americans from the 26th Division died as a consequence. Percy had this to say about being at the front in his 20 February letter, although as a telephone man at brigade headquarters, it is important to recognize that he was usually quite a distance from the actual front lines:

> You were right about the place but—you must learn not to speak or write about where us boys are. . . . If you hear anything forget it and then you can feel that none of Uncle Sam's lads were killed or shot up through any aid you may have given to the enemy unintentionally. . . . I am chief operator, supervisor, trouble shooter, general manager, janitor and all the rest. . . . You ought to hear me talk French to the operators in the French centrals when I have to call through their lines. I'll bet they near bust laughing. . . . I am feeling swell and getting lots of excitement these days. We have air raids and bombing nearly every moonlight night. . . . There was two French planes fighting four Germans right over our heads last week and way down low too. It was a fine sight and a good scrap. The anti gun shells were bursting all around them leaving puffs of smoke hanging in the air and pieces of shrapnel dropping all around. It is very exciting to watch. . . . Well I guess I'll call it a letter for this time and bid you bon nuit.

A visit to the wing of the Smithsonian Air and Space Museum near Dulles Airport in the Washington, D.C. area brings you face to face with some of the aircraft being flown in this war, not long after the dawn of aviation itself. They look so flimsy and fragile. But they were not a trivial part of the conflict. While the Allied-German dogfights were a spectacular sight, the use of reconnaissance aircraft to pinpoint enemy positions for artillery bombardment was much more deadly. By 1918, well over 1,000 Allied aircraft and some 500 German aircraft took part in battles related to the St. Mihiel offensive.

Air power, as well as tanks, improved machine guns, marine torpedoes, mountains of barbed wire, and ever larger artillery shells, including those filled with poison gas, available to all parties involved in the conflict, assured death to millions, soldiers and civilians alike. Percy described the landscape of the battlefield in the Chemin des Dames sector in a type-written letter dated 2 March 1918:

> I have plenty of chance to see the country, but it is pretty badly shot up so it isn't very beautiful. It must have been grand in its day for all the buildings are built out of limestone and very prettily constructed. I took a walk over the hill yesterday and the ground was all shell holes everywhere and some of them were 6 or 7 feet deep and 10 or 12 feet across. You could hide a horse in them in a cinch. . . . You can't imagine what it is like. Big trees shot off, buildings blown all to pieces, big holes everywhere and general destruction any place you go.
>
> You ought to see the old trenches and barbed wire entanglements around here. . . . I can't describe the wonderful works I have seen. You must actually see them to realize the magnitude of this war outside the actual fighting.

Despite such passages, it is clear that Percy was not dwelling much on the horrors of this war in these letters to his sister. Percy's communications to his father were evidently more graphic. He made reference to one of his letters to his father in another of his missives to Grace and suggested that she read it since he knew his mother had read it and "stood it," as he put it. While I do not have Percy's evidently more graphic letter to his father, Corp. Horatio Rogers, who may well have worked with Percy, given his occupation in Percy's 101st Field Artillery Regiment, makes the horror of this war clear:

> One afternoon I was out alone repairing telephone wire in the waste of shell holes behind and to the left of our position when I heard faint groaning, I found two doughboys in a shell hole. They had been sleeping there when a shell exploded just inside the shell hole, blowing off their legs. They had done the best they could with first aid packets and tourniquets but they were moribund when I found them. There was nothing I could do. The same night I found a dead stranger in the trench leading to our kitchen hole. The back of his head was crushed in, I suppose by a large shell fragment. All this was beginning to get on my nerves. (Hallas p 276, quoting Rogers, *Diary of an Artillery Scout p 230*)

For the infantry on the front lines, "going over the top" of the trenches following an artillery barrage meant: facing withering fire from machine guns and other automatic weapons; the use of hand grenades and bayonets; and finally, hand to hand fighting with weapons such as trench knives. Major wars like this one tend to produce significant technological advances in weaponry. But, the most significant weapon of this war was still manpower, millions of men, used to gain a few yards that were frequently lost again the next day or the next month. The principal result for the men on the front lines was slaughter on a massive scale.

Keeping alive at the front, even when not in battle, was not a simple matter either. There were the endless trench systems, the "wonderful works" as Percy referred to them, with dugouts built behind or into the trenches in which to sleep. All of these works were filled with their share of the ever-present mud, rats, and lice, known to every Doughboy as "cooties." From Percy's 20 February letter: "I am living in a dugout now in the side of a hill like a rat and have lots of rats for company. They run all around the place at night. I don't mind them as long as they don't take a lunch off me."

In one account by Col. Frederick M. Wise, he described watching a rat on a trench embankment as he walked toward it. The rat calmly waited for the soldier to approach, then jumped on his nearest shoulder, ran across to the other shoulder, and then hopped onto the opposite trench embankment. The colonel's comment was that the rats were now so used to the human population that they were using them as stepping stones to get around in the trenches (Hallas p 65, quoting Wise, *A Marine Tells It to You* pp 183-4).

The vermin, cold, rain, and simple physical exhaustion from the never-ending toil of digging trenches, stringing the endless miles of barbed wire that separated the combatants, and moving the tons of munitions and other supplies needed to prosecute the war, took their toll. Many men died without firing a shot. Others received wounds and died of infections that in later wars would be halted by antibiotics and other drugs that did not exist at the time.

Between 18 and 21 March, the 26th Division was relieved in the Chemin des Dames sector. The Division was supposed to head back for some additional training, refitting, and rest west of the Coetquidan Camp where it had originally trained. Those orders, however, were revoked and the Division moved instead into the La Reine or Boucq Sector in the general vicinity of Toul, northeast of Coetquidan. The reason for this redeployment was straightforward. The German high command had now begun a series of offensives that would eventually encompass nearly the entire front as they sought to break through to Paris and end the war. This rapid redeployment of his unit probably accounts for Percy's letter dated 9 April 1918, which was begun in ink and finished later in pencil:

Right in the middle of that word [the earlier part of the letter] I was ordered to pack my kit and move to another town about 8 miles away and here I am. I forgot what I was going to say. It is now 1:30 A.M. and all I have for company is snores from a couple of orderlies in the other end of the building and the boom of the guns. We were eight days over the road on horseback reaching the front we are on now and it was some drill. It rained nearly every day and was cold riding. I got the cooties in one billet we put up in and I can't seem to get rid of them.

Any history or memoir of this war never fails to discuss the nearly ever-present rain and the mud created by thousands of men, horses, and tons of equipment moving over the same stretches of wet road. In the artillery units, this often meant the need for nearly superhuman efforts to haul heavy guns and caissons up hills that had been churned into vertical bogs. The horses used to haul the guns sometimes failed in the effort and were shot on the spot. The 2011 film, *Warhorse*, depicts the horrors inflicted by this war on man and beast alike. Men were reduced to total exhaustion. All one could do was push on, survive and, of course, provide a running sarcastic commentary on the conditions:

Mud splashed on the bottom of the dismounted men's slickers and from these plastered itself in a hard clammy cake all over their spirals [leggings] from shoe to knee. Feet stuck in the mud and the clinging clay made them feel well nigh unliftable.

Army slickers are unhappily never known as raincoats. They have in fact the opposite effect from any self-respecting raincoat. They act as one-way valves, permitting all the water to enter in an alarmingly efficient manner and allowing never a drop to escape. The cold rain mockingly defied all known laws of gravitation, running up the sleeves as well as down the neck and into the ears. (*Battery A of the 101st Field Artillery* p79)

Percy gave Grace a description of the fighting in the La Reine/Boucq sector in a letter of 27 April. While not possible to identify specifically, the fighting most likely involved battles around such towns as Apremont or Seicheprey. These fights, while not major, were aimed directly at the Yankee Division, with the specific idea of weakening the morale of the Americans. As Percy's letter indicates, that strategy did not work:

We are in the big scrap going on now and it sure is a whopper but we are giving them XXX- -!!! all the time and have come out best so far. . . . It is indescribable over here on the fighting lines. It's a perfect hell. High explosive shells, and gas shells are falling around all the time. . . . The Germans are throwing all their strength into this drive it seems. I think it is their last fling and the Allies are holding them splendidly. They don't seem to care how many men they lose.

It was not the German's last fling. In fact, by the end of June, the Germans had overrun the Chemin-des-Dames area where the 26th Division had started out, pushed down to the Marne River, and crossed it near Chateau-Thierry. West of Chateau-Thierry, the German advance was halted at Vaux and the Belleau Wood where, in a battle made famous for its ferocity even in this war, the Marine Brigade of the AEF's Second Division stopped them. By the end of June, the great series of German spring offensives of 1918 was spent, but they were not done yet.

Sometime during the Regiment's stay in the La Reine/Boucq sector, Percy got a change of venue, as described in a letter of 17 May:

I am in an army school wrestling with electronic problems on series, parallel and multiple series and series multiple, motors, dynamos, wireless and dozens of other things you don't understand and some you do such as operators sets, cards, plugs, jacks, etc. I think I'll start a telephone company of my own when I get home and I'll need experienced operators so I'll give you a job. . . . We can buy most everything we need now in the Y.M. canteens, the Salvation Army canteens or the commissary sales stores. So if you want to send me anything make it a P.O. money order and I'll buy what I need. . . . I haven't seen any rats for quite a while now. Yes I've had cooties a plenty since I wrote that letter and they sure do stick when you once collect them. I am rid of them now but I suppose I'll get a new bunch when I go back to the front.

By 11 June, he was back from the school:

I am living up on the third floor of an old chateau now [possibly Chateau Ferme south of Bernecourt] and one end of the roof has been blown in by a shell. The village I'm in gets shelled quite a lot and nearly every evening you can hear the gas alarms blowing nearby. . . . Two of us went down to a little pond near here for a swim the other day and while we were in the Huns started to shell and we had to grab our clothes and run about 50 meters into a dugout to dress. I don't think it's fair to throw shells at a man when he's in his birthday suit taking a bath.

The German drive on the Marne, in the vicinity of Chateau-Thierry, had produced a salient, a geographic bulge in the lines that, if not nipped in the bud, could be exploited to make further progress. The 26th Division was rushed into the Chateau Thierry Sector to assist in the reduction of this salient and to resist any German attempts to drive through it. If the Germans were successful here, then not much more than 50 miles to the southwest stood the greatest prize of all—Paris. In a letter dated 11 July, Percy wrote:

> I have been on the move every day for the last ten days but I guess we have settled again now for a while. I am living in a barn at a big farm now. I guess the old Huns have got more respect for the American boys than they had. We've beat them up proper every where we've had a brush with them. I think it will be over pretty soon. . . . My board is very quiet tonight. I haven't had a call for an hour. I guess I'll close this up and test out my lines. I hope they are all good for I hate to send my line men out at night especially if Fritz is firing.

As in any combat situation, communication links between units, and among units and their commanders, were vital. In this war, most of that communication was carried by actual telephone wires. These wires on the front itself were an enemy target and were constantly being cut. Toward the rear, they were always under threat from shelling. The best time for repairing the lines was at night, often the time of the most intense shelling. Evidently Percy had several linemen working for him by this time, a vital and dangerous occupation.

In mid-July, the Germans launched a major attack to further extend the salient they had created with its tip at Chateau Thierry. Their attack was blunted and the Allied counterattack began on July 18th. They threw the Germans back from the Marne, with the 26th Division taking the villages of Torcy, Givry, and Belleau itself. Months would pass and many more men were yet to die, but the Germans would not threaten Paris again. Percy wrote of this period on 12 August:

> Say Sis, if you think you have been busy you ought to have been with me for the last three weeks [probably speaking of late July]. We started a drive and got the Huns on the run and it was fight and follow day and night catching what sleep and eats wherever and whenever we could. But we sure did drive them and were relieved after we had pushed them back 18 kilometers.

In early August, the Division got its first real rest in months. This break gave all the men a chance to recuperate a bit and get cleaned up. Again, from Percy's letter of 12 August:

> We have been out of the lines for about a week now. Yesterday we all took a bath, drew new clothes and were thoroughly disinfected. Believe me it sure was good to get rid of those blamed shirt rats and get into some clean clothes. We have a couple of big tanks that stay in the rear and when we come out we tie our clothes and blankets in a bundle and put them into one of these tanks

and steam is pumped into them for a half hour. This is called delousing and it sure does cook the cooties. I am mailing dad two empty boche [derogatory term for German troops] one pounder cartridges and one of the popular French magazines. Tell him to have them polished and lacquered and they will make a couple of nice vases for the mantle when you all get together again and get a home established. [The family was on one of its periodic moves between Massachusetts and Michigan—this time to Detroit]. If you want to have them engraved they were captured at L'Esperance Farms July 1918. . . . We'll soon be back in the lines and it looks now as if we are nearing the end for the Allied troops are driving them all along the line.

By the beginning of September, Percy was right about being back in the lines, this time in the St. Mihiel salient. Here, the 26th Division was part of an Allied action that quickly pushed the Germans back out of the salient and back toward the Belgian border. The Allies were, indeed, driving the enemy, but the enemy was in no mood to surrender.

At the end of September, the Allies went on their last major offensive of the war, designed to push the Germans out of the Argonne Forest and beyond the Meuse River that would largely drive them from French territory. The 26th Division's task was to create a major diversion intended to distract the Germans from the major attack. At one point, elements of the Division were located in an area called the Haumont Ravine, tagged by some of the soldiers as the Valley of Death:

> The surroundings were certainly bleak: rusty barbed-wire and shell-torn earth for a foreground and for a background, blasted hills topped with gaunt fringes of shell-torn trees; wounded men and battered ambulances forever crawling along the tortured, mud-swamped road; broken wagons, smashed caissons, packs, blankets, towels, toilet articles, clothing, letters, dead horses—everything trampled into the mud; the whole outlook desolate and cheerless. The valley at this point was a veritable gas-pocket, for the poisonous fumes being heavier than air, rolled down from all sides and hung in the bottom eighteen hours out of twenty-four. (*Battery A of the 101st Field Artillery* p 18)

Percy painted a somewhat lighter picture for his sister in a letter of 20 September:

> This drive here was a corker and we are now on land that the Boches have held for years. . . . We captured beaucoup prisoners and supplies in this drive and believe me we fatted up our mess quite a bit with German potatoes, squash, salt fish and many other things from their gardens and storehouses.

He wrote further on 27 September:

> You make me laugh when you ask how many Germans I've killed. What do
> you think I do, call them up and then shoot in the transmitter and hit them in
> the ear? . . . I suppose I've helped kill a lot of them by connecting up the CO
> to the batteries.

The Germans had indeed been on this ground a long time and, consequently,
had been able to organize to live quite well. Many commentators noted the riches
in terms of food and fodder that fell into Allied hands as the Germans were
pushed out of this long-held territory.

As the Meuse-Argonne offensive progressed, the Germans stoutly resisted but
were driven steadily back. By this time, however, they also faced other major
problems affecting their war effort. The Allied commercial and economic block-
ade of the Central Powers, greatly aided by British naval power, had brought a
large part of the civilian population to the brink of starvation. Popular fervor
for the war was being replaced with threats of revolution. The German imperial
regime, as well as others among the Central Powers, was teetering on the brink of
collapse. Percy commented on the situation in a letter of 6 October:

> There are all kinds of Peace rumors going around here and we know for a fact
> that Bulgaria is out and Turkey all cut up and ready to follow suit. [and later in
> the same letter] Hurrah for good news!!! The communique just came in over the
> wireless and says Germany has requested a conference for a discussion of peace.
> That's great for a starter. I wonder if it will go through. Gee that will be great.
> No more whizz bangs or bombs and home soon. It seems too good to be true.
> Well Grace I can't write any more. Look for me home in about six months if
> that conference goes through. In the meantime send me some chocolate.

The chocolate would prove hard to come by, and peace was still a way off, but
the outcome now appeared inevitable. Percy's prediction of when he would be
able to leave France proved to be quite accurate. After four years of continuous
warfare, both sides were largely exhausted, but the insertion of nearly two million
Americans into the contest, after years of fighting, had turned the tide. By the
end of the war, most of the combatant countries had lost 20 to 25 of every 100
men involved in the fight. By contrast, the Americans had lost only two of every
100; and they were prepared to move more troops to the battlefield. With many
European governments on the verge of collapse, the end was near.

The end did not come without another enemy taking the field, a killer as effective as any bayonet, shell, or gas bomb, and one that did not care which side of the front it attacked. This was the infamous Spanish influenza. Late in October and in early November, Percy commented on the flu, not on the battlefront, but at home:

> *24 October:* They called the Fair off this year [the annual Fair in Brockton, Mass—a major social event] on account of the spread of Spanish Influenza so Muff wrote. Has it hit Detroit? Brockton had 8000 cases and over 100 deaths and we knew a lot of them. . . . It looks to me as if I am safer here than at home just now.

> *6 November:* Have you had a rage of the Fluey in Detroit? Brockton was surely hard hit and the spread of the plague is worldwide. The papers over here say every country has a rage of it. It bumped off a lot of my old friends in Brockton for fair. Hope none of you folks had it.

Back at the front, the Germans were being pushed back toward the city of Verdun that they knew they must hold at all costs. Behind Verdun lay key rail lines linking their industrial heartland to the front. If Verdun were lost, they would no longer be able to effectively supply their troops. Slowly the Germans were ground back, but they fought on. Finally, it was the collapse of the German political machinery needed to support the war effort that spelled the end as the country descended toward anarchy. As a consequence, an armistice was negotiated, to be effective on the 11th hour, on the 11th day, of the 11th month of 1918.

All commentators who were on the field of battle at the time noted the uncertainty surrounding this event. Would the armistice actually take place; would it hold? Commanders of both sides gave orders to maintain the firing, particularly the artillery, right up until the last minute before 11 AM. Batteries competed to see which would be the one to fire the last shot. Then, the time arrived. Percy didn't write about the event until 1 January 1919, from Varennes, Haute Marne (the names of towns appear in his letters after the armistice):

> Have got back from my furlough [to Aix les Bains]. . . . We had quite a time the day the armistice was signed. All the guns fired right up to 11 A.M. and then what a silence. We couldn't realize it was really all over and no more diving into holes like rats—and then the bunch let loose. We fired pistols, rifles and anything that would make a noise and at night set off all the signal rockets and flares we could find. . . . I'm surprised to hear that Muff was in the hospital. I haven't heard from her since November 15th.

After four years of the noise of never-ending bombardment, there was silence. Every writer who was there commented on the silence—"all quiet on the Western Front." The war was finally over. With hindsight, it now seems inevitable that the war would end this way, with an armistice, not a surrender. Both sides had lost millions of men. On November 9th, the Kaiser had abdicated and Germany was on the verge of revolution. The Allies, too, were in tatters. There had been more than one mutiny in their lines as well, particularly among the French. So it would end in an armistice. In 1919, at Versailles, the terms of peace for the Germans would be hard. But in November 1918, their troops left the field without unconditional surrender. From an originally secret AEF intelligence report of 23 November 1918:

> The party [I assume an Allied intelligence unit] caught up with the retreating [German] Army at Remach on the Moselle. The discipline and morale were perfect. From Remach to Treves by way of Wasserbillig there was an almost unbroken column. . . . There was not a straggler nor a symptom of disorder. . . . The troops seemed happy and full of spirits. . . . A triumphal arch was erected at the entrance to Treves, with the inscription, 'Welcome to our Unconquered Heroes.' (as quoted in Mead p 396)

One of those not satisfied with this outcome was General Pershing. His AEF troops had fought less than a year. By November 1918, he had roughly two million men in the field; he expected three million by 1919. Pershing calculated that such a force, along with the rest of what the Allies could muster, would be enough to force the unconditional surrender of the Central powers on the field of battle. But, it was not to be. I have seen several versions of the quote attributed to Pershing in his later years. Whatever his exact words, it marks a very prescient sentiment: "They never knew they were beaten in Berlin. It will all have to be done all over again" (Stallings p 374). Beginning 20 years later, it was, indeed, done all over again.

From November 1918 forward, what was required of the AEF was to undo what had taken the Americans over a year to build up, getting two million troops and support personnel out of France, at least those not chosen to participate in the occupation of Germany. This was a formidable task to which the writers of the book on Battery A of the 101st Infantry devote an entire chapter entitled, "Fighting the Armistice."

Percy's letters were briefer now as the 26th Division turned its back on the front and moved toward departure. A note card that he bought in Varennes in northeast France came to Grace from Guerpont, dated 24 November. It must have been custom crafted for the troops. On the front of the card is a charming drawing of a village scene with the inscription, in English: "Somewhere in La Belle France—A thousand leagues separate us but do not divide our Christmas Day." On the back, Percy wrote, "Not much chance to write now for we are moving a great deal."

A postcard sent on 6 December came from Aix les-Bains, Percy's furlough destination, with a picture of the thermal baths there. Percy sent a one-liner to Grace, now in Detroit, "Will write soon. Too busy now." He had time for longer letters on 1 and 27 January 1919, written from Varennes in northeast-east France.

By 15 February, on Knights of Columbus Overseas Service stationary, he wrote: "Now don't take any stock in what you read in the papers about the 26th Division being on its way home for we are stranded in Mayet (Sarthe) and don't know a thing about when we will move." Mayet was one of the major transit points for the AEF on the route home and lies some 20 miles southeast of Le Mans.

Two typed letters followed, both written from Mayet:

22 February: I wrote you from Varennes that I had received one box from England [mostly full of candy] and it was a humdinger. The girl who put it up sure knew what was good and what would stand the racket of the mails.

I kind of wish in a way that we had gone into Germany. I don't ever expect to get to Europe again and I would like to see all that I can while I'm here. I have been all over the northern part of France and over in the eastern part so that I could look into Italy and Switzerland . . . [there follows an idea of taking a leave down to Nice or Monte Carlo that never materialized]

I guess Muff isn't very busy with Florence [unidentified] or anybody else these days. I got the first letter from her since Nov. 15 last week and she has sure been a sick kid. She was taken to the hospital with a fever of 103 1/2 and the night she got there it went up to 104. I guess she darn near went west. She says she was unconscious for a week. She only weighs 90 pounds now with her overcoat on. She says she is feeling all right now and expects to pick up rapidly. She had old Doc. Clark and he fixed her up O.K.

14 March: I guess someone else has enjoyed your fudge and the two other boxes from England for they have not showed up yet. Wouldn't it be funny if they followed me home and I got them in Camp Devens or after I was mustered out and back in civilian life. I thank you just the same for trying to get them to me for that is more than any one else did. You have been very good and thoughtful to me while I have been over here and I sure realize it.

We will not hit Liverpool on our way home as we know definitely that we sail direct from Brest. I'd like very much to meet that girl [the English friend of Grace's who sent the sweets] for she sure knows what is good.

Well kid that is about all I can think of to write tonight. Don't write any more after you get this for I'LL BE ON MY WAY.

<u>Back Home</u>

After a total of some 550 days on French soil, including over four months of training, over 200 days at the front, and over four months of waiting to return home after the Armistice was declared, Percy's artillery unit finally made it out of the French port of Brest on 31 March 1919. The headquarters unit and other elements of the 101st Artillery sailed on the *USS Agamemnon,* formerly the *Kaiser Wilhelm II,* a German passenger liner which had had the good luck of being in New York City harbor when the U.S. declared war. They landed to a hearty welcome in Boston on April 7th. There were a Divisional review at Camp Devens on the 22nd and a Divisional parade in Boston on the 25th; then the whole lot was discharged from Camp Devens on April 29th. Some 25 years later, my father was discharged from his service in World War II on 8 December 1945 from the same place, relabeled Fort Devens.

There is one more letter in the collection, undated, written from Fort Heath, Winthrop, Mass, which described how Grace could visit Percy there if she wished. This letter must have followed his discharge from the 26th Division since he signed it: "Sgt. P.L. Covert, 10th Co. M.C.A.N.G. [Massachusetts Coast Artillery, National Guard], Fort Heath, Winthrop, Mass." Percy was back in the old Guard unit of which he and his father had both been a part, and he was once again a sergeant.

In his letters to Grace during the war, Percy often talked about visiting her and the Covert family in Detroit and perhaps relocating there. But in one letter, he noted that his wife, Gladys, wouldn't move there as long as her mother was alive at Brockton. He also mentioned his secure job in the Post Office at Brockton. This was a job that he must have acquired shortly before he left for the war and which he kept until he retired. In retirement, he lived at Wareham, Mass, in a house that, according to family tradition, he and his father built together. My grandparents, Percy's sister, Helen, and her husband, Bert, also had a place at Wareham. I spent a good deal of time with them when I was young, but despite the fact that he lived nearby, I only recall meeting Percy twice. On two different occasions on my birthday, he stopped by my grandparent's house and gave me books as gifts: *Black Beauty* and *Treasure Island*.

Percy died in December 1964. The Massachusetts Vital Records Index indicates that he died at Medfield, Mass. Percy was brought back to Wareham and buried in the Central Cemetery in a small area reserved for soldiers. His gravestone reads:

PERCY LEON COVERT

SGT HQ CO 101 FLD ARTY

WORLD WAR I

FEB 23 1898   DEC 20 1964

For many soldiers, their wartime experiences seem to overshadow much that follows in life. It is often the one event they choose to memorialize at death. This was the case for Percy Covert. Once a Doughboy, always a Doughboy.

CHAPTER 3

THE SANGUINARY NEWSMAN:
SAMUEL HAYNES JENKS

In the previous two chapters I have noted family members whose knowledge was the foundation of my understanding about the genealogy of the maternal side of my family. On my father's side, there was no one like them on whom to rely. How I managed to unearth what little I know about the M(a)cDonalds themselves is discussed in Chapter 6. What about the other side of the coin, my grandmother Theresa MacDonald's family? My father knew that she was a Fernald whose father Daniel was from New Hampshire. Theresa's mother was a Heaton, Minnie Heaton. The story was that Minnie's father was a hatter from Baltimore who made hats for Abraham Lincoln. Somewhere in the story, there was also a family named Jenks. That was it. So it was up to me to gather more facts and put some meat on whatever bones I might find.

Finding the Jenks Family

Theresa Fernald's birth record shows that she was born at Haverhill, Mass, and that her father was, indeed, named Daniel, born at Lee, a small town in southern New Hampshire. The birth certificate also names Theresa's mother as Maria P. Heaton, born at Baltimore. My grandparents' marriage certificate, from the State of New Hampshire, adds that Daniel (written as David on the transcription I received) was born at Lee around 1866, give or take a year, while Minnie (or Maria) was born at Baltimore around 1858. (See the Genealogy Section of this chapter for the full list of sources consulted on the Fernald, Heaton, and Jenks families.)

Eventually, I located a birth record for Daniel Fernald that confirmed the information in Theresa's birth record, and added that Daniel was born in October 1865 to Charles and Mary Fernald. Over time, it became clear that Daniel and Charles were members of a long line of Fernalds in southern New Hampshire that runs back to a Renald Fernald. He came to America probably in the 1630s. By 1645, he had settled at Strawberry Bank, now Portsmouth, New Hampshire. During the 1650s, Renald was Town Clerk for Strawberry Bank.

Minnie Fernald's death certificate from Boston shows that she died in 1919 of diabetes and nephritis. It also provides the name of her father, Richard H. Heaton, and indicates that he was born at New York City. For the first time, the Jenks family appears. In this record, Minnie's mother is shown as Eliza W. Jenks, born in Massachusetts. Another death record, this one for Eliza Heaton, states that she died at Boston in 1892. Eliza is listed as a widow and her parents appear: Samuel H. Jenks, born at Boston, and Eliza Williams. A death notice from the *Boston Evening Transcript* of 13 August 1892, reads: "Deaths: Heaton—At South Boston, 12th inst., Mrs. Eliza Williams Heaton, late of Baltimore, last surviving daughter of Samuel Haynes and Eliza Williams Jenks" (America's Historical Newspapers, hereafter AHN).

Thanks to the Internet and such valuable services as Ancestry.com, it is now possible to sit at home and look at every census that the U.S. government has conducted and released through 1940, for which records still exist. With such a tool, it did not take long to find the Richard and Eliza Heaton family at Baltimore in 1850, 1860, and 1870. These census records, confirmed by several trips to Baltimore to look at sources there, show that Richard was born in New York state (possibly at New York City) around 1823 or 1824, and that he and Eliza had a total of five children, including Minnie. Most of them were probably born at Baltimore. Baltimore records of the period appear to be incomplete, so the precise details remain elusive.

By the time of the 1880 census, however, the family situation had changed. Richard remained at Baltimore. The census shows Richard Heaton, hatter, age 57, living as a boarder with the family of Mahala Harris. Among the family members is a daughter, Kate Harris, age 50. But, the 1880 U.S Census shows that Eliza Heaton was now at Boston with two of her children, Minnie and George B. At some point, the only other surviving child of this family, Frank, also returned to Boston. Later census records indicate that, in fact, Eliza Heaton did not die a widow in 1892. In the 1900 U.S. Census for Baltimore, Richard Heaton, hatter, age 76, is still alive and listed as head of household. The only other member of the household is Katherine Harris, servant, age 71. Richard died at Baltimore in 1905.

Much about Richard and Eliza Heaton's family has come to light. But, despite a fair amount of effort, it has not proven easy to determine Richard's provenance. There are a number of Richard Heatons born in New York in the 1820s. Exactly which one is the Richard who married Eliza Jenks remains a puzzle. What about Eliza?

Living in the Washington, D.C. area allowed me ready access to two great genealogical resources, the National Archives and the library of the National Society of the Daughters of the American Revolution. Sorting through Jenks sources in the DAR library one day, I came across the *Genealogy of the Jenks Family of America*, written by William B. Browne and published in New Hampshire in 1952. In the last generation recorded in Browne's book, the sixth generation from the original immigrant, Joseph Jenks, is the family of Samuel Haynes Jenks. Among the children of this family is Eliza W. who was born at Boston on 16 August 1822, and who married Richard Heaton on 21 January 1847. A look at other sources at the DAR showed that Richard Heaton and Eliza Jenks married at Boston. The family group record in Browne's book shows that Eliza's father, Samuel, had a total of twelve children, born of four wives: Lydia Williams, Lydia Stevens, Eliza Williams (a sister of Lydia Williams), and Martha Coffin. The first three of Samuel H.'s wives died at a very young age. At least two probably died of the consequences of childbirth. The other, I was to learn, died of typhus.

The information available at the DAR also revealed that Samuel Haynes Jenks, while born at Boston on 20 September 1789, spent a good portion of his life on Nantucket and was owner and editor of a newspaper there, the *Inquirer*. Other materials, including Browne's book, showed that most of the Jenks line were mainlanders, living in towns such as Lynn, Saugus, Newton, and Boston in Massachusetts. So why did one of these mainlanders end up living on Nantucket? And why did Samuel H. Jenks, in a family noted for its interests in the foundry, blacksmithing, and other commercial businesses, end up as a journalist and a politician? Who were these Jenks and where did they come from?

I am indebted to several sources found at the NEHGS library at Boston for the history of the first Jenks of this line to appear in America. One such source is entitled, *Joseph Jenks, Colonial Toolmaker and Inventor*, by Stephen P. Carlson, revised in 1975. Joseph was a sword maker associated with a famous sword making operation established under the patronage of Charles I at Hounslow, Middlesex, England. How Joseph originally reached America is not clear, but by 1641, he was on the Agamenticus River in Maine running a blacksmith shop. In 1643 or 44, John Winthrop, Jr. and others visited Agamenticus as representatives of the Company of Undertakers of the Ironworks in New England. Bog iron had been discovered in Massachusetts, and the Massachusetts Bay colonists were eager to establish an iron industry that would free them from importing all their iron wares from England. By December 1647, Joseph Jenks had settled at Lynn, Massachusetts, with a patent in hand from the Massachusetts General Court. The patent, one of the first in the country, was for a water-powered mill to make scythes and other edged tools. He established his edged-tool forge at the aforesaid Company's facilities at Hammersmith, on the Saugus River. A highly skilled craftsman, and an early New England entrepreneur, Joseph died in 1683 leaving behind numerous descendants.

The genealogical line from Joseph, the immigrant, to Samuel Haynes Jenks runs as follows: Joseph Jenks, born in England, about 1603; John Jenks, born in Massachusetts, 1660; Capt. John Jenks, born at Lynn, Mass, 1697; Capt. Samuel Jenks, born at Lynn, Mass, 1731/32; and Capt. Samuel Jenks (Samuel Haynes Jenk's father), born in Massachusetts, 1766. It is not surprising that early successful citizens of such towns as Lynn would be involved as officers in the militias of their day, thus accounting for the many captains in this Jenks line. Some of them also maintained the family's traditional work in the iron industry. In 1789, a Captain Samuel Jenks (probably Samuel Haynes Jenks' father) owned "Samuel Jenks and Son, Blacksmiths and Bellows Makers" at Governors Wharf at Boston (Ancestry.com, *U.K. and U.S. Directories, 1680-1830;* see Genealogy section).

And, it was Samuel Haynes Jenks' father who also first forged the Jenks family's links to the island of Nantucket. Capt. Samuel Jenks first married Mary (Polly) Way of Philadelphia at Boston on 15 February 1789. It made the news at Boston's *The Independent Chronicle and the Universal Advertiser,* dated 19 February 1789: "Married—Mr. Samuel Jenks, jun. to Miss Polly Way, both of this town" (AHN). Polly Way's parents were Robert Way and Catherine Gandawill. There were Ways at Boston from the earliest days of the Massachusetts Bay Colony, and Ways on Nantucket by no later than the mid-1700s. I surmise it is the Way family that first introduced the Jenks family to Nantucket.

Capt. Samuel Jenks moved his family to the island in the first decade of the 1800s. Of Samuel's seven children by Mary Way, at least one of them was born on Nantucket. Four of these children married spouses on the island, several of them from long-standing Nantucket families, the Wyers and the Swains. After Mary Way's death, Capt. Samuel Jenks married Eunice (Wyer) Swain of Nantucket. The 1820 U.S. Census for Nantucket shows the families of Samuel Jenks, as well as Robert W. Jenks, one of Capt. Samuel's brothers, living on the island. Capt. Samuel and Robert, using the iron forging and blacksmithing skills so common in the Jenks family, constructed a clock for the South Congregational Church on the island in 1823 (Godfrey, pp 81-83). But, like most men on the island, Capt. Samuel would also invest in the main business of that time, whaling. Records held by the Nantucket Historical Association show that he held interests in several whaleships and made financial arrangements with individual participants in whaling voyages.

Given what we know of his father's history, it is highly likely that Samuel Haynes Jenks spent part of his childhood on Nantucket. And with that background, it is also not surprising that he would eventually marry into families with strong Nantucket connections, such as the Stevens and the Coffins. Even in Samuel Haynes' day, it was often said that practically the entire population could trace its history back to the original Coffin on the island, Tristram, one of the original English "proprietors" of the island.

Anyone who has read Melville's *Moby Dick* has heard of the Coffins and Starbucks of Nantucket. Written in 1851, one of Melville's first descriptions of the inhabitants of the island is as follows:

> Now Bildad, like Peleg [part owners of the Pequod], and indeed many other Nantucketers, was a Quaker, the island having been originally settled by that sect; and to this day its inhabitants in general retain in an uncommon measure the peculiarities of the Quaker, only variously and anonymously modified by things altogether alien and heterogeneous. For some of these same Quakers are the most sanguinary of all sailors and whale-hunters. They are fighting Quakers; they are Quakers with a vengeance. (Melville p 71)

Melville was, of course, setting the stage for the arrival in his story of that epitome of sanguinary vengeance, Captain Ahab. As Melville's classic novel makes clear, Nantucket in the early 1800s was made famous by the whaling industry. As Samuel Haynes Jenks would discover, the influence of Quaker society on the island sometimes set it at odds with more than whales.

The United States in the Days of Samuel H. Jenks

Over the course of Samuel H. Jenks' relatively long life, the country as a whole underwent tremendous growth, change, and challenges on its way from a nascent nation to the divisiveness and destruction of the Civil War period. The country's boundaries expanded dramatically through the practical gift of the Louisiana

Purchase, and other actions such as the war with Mexico in the 1840s. The growing European-American population, with its increasing demand for land, created
a rising level of conflict with the Native American populations that would lead
to their eventual displacement by Federal mandate, ever further westward. And,
the largely agrarian society that existed at the time of the early founding fathers
gradually gave way, particularly in the northern regions, to increasing industrialization aided by huge advances in transportation (canals, roads, and eventually
railroads), communications (the postal system, newspapers, and the telegraph),
and technology (first water powered, and then stream-driven). (See Howe.)

From the country's founding, there were strong arguments over the limits and
extent of Federal power. As time passed, debates raged concerning the extent
of control over the banking system, whether Federal monies should be used to
promote economic development by financing public works, and most divisively,
whether the institution of slavery should be expanded into the new territories
being brought into the Union. Not long after the country's founding, these arguments would lead to the development of the first political parties, institutions
that Washington and John Adams had viewed as unnecessary evils. By the time
Samuel Haynes Jenks became an adult, the party system in the political life of the
country was well entrenched. Through the medium of a largely party-controlled
press, the parties were the vehicle through which much of the debate over key
national issues raged.

Massachusetts

Massachusetts was one of the original founding states of the Union.
Massachusetts men like John and Sam Adams and John Hancock were key
figures in the Revolutionary period and, some of them remained prominent
in the debates that followed on how to shape the new country's government.
Massachusetts stuck to a strong Federalist approach longer than most states due
to the presence of influential politicians like those in the Adams family. In Samuel
H. Jenks' time, the Indian question did not factor as strongly in Massachusetts
as it did elsewhere since the Native American population in New England had
been largely decimated in the Colonial period by disease and armed conflict. As
for industrialization, whole towns such as Lowell would eventually be created as
a means of furthering the production of textiles in the state. The pitting of largely
agrarian interests versus increasing industrialization would be reflected in the
post-revolutionary Shay's Rebellion that began in the more rural, western half

of the state. Shay lost; industrial interests would be king in Massachusetts. (On Massachusetts History, see Brown and Tager.)

There were slaves in Massachusetts, some right up until the time of the Civil War. Also, there were Massachusetts shipping and commercial interests that worked in the slave trade. There were never, however, relatively large numbers of slaves in the state since its economy moved in the direction of industry rather than large-scale agricultural production. So, it is not surprising that some of the most strident and dedicated abolitionists, men like William Lloyd Garrison, were based in Massachusetts. The abolitionist movement found strong support among some elements of the population of Massachusetts, including many Quakers. Ultimately, slavery would fall. The issue of integration of the races, however, was quite another matter, not only in the south, but also in the northern states like Massachusetts. As we will see, it became a key issue on Nantucket during Samuel Haynes Jenks' time there.

Nantucket: Sheep, Whales and Quakers

One of the most startling facts I have learned in researching this particular story is that Nantucket was not, from the beginning of English colonization, part of either the Massachusetts Bay or Plymouth colonies. For quite a bit of its early colonial history, it was a power unto itself. In fact, its first colonial allegiance, and a tenuous one at that, was owed neither to Massachusetts nor to Plymouth, but to New York. Not until 1692, at its own request, did Nantucket become an integral part of Massachusetts. Why was Massachusetts Bay not formally involved in the early governance of Nantucket? First of all, the island sits some 25 miles from the nearest mainland. Even at its peak in the heyday of whaling, its permanent population was no more than 10,000, and there are few more than that living permanently on Nantucket today. Sometimes referred to as Nantucket Nation, it stands now as it did when the first Europeans set eyes on it, a small bit of land set apart by the broad Atlantic Ocean. (On Nantucket history, see Philbrick, and others, in the Source section.)

That characteristic has made much of its history unique. It would make it a bastion of Tory support during the Revolutionary War, in part to protect its large shipping interests since the British ruled the seas. It still considered itself so distinct at the time of the War of 1812 that some Nantucketers decided to sign their own peace treaty with the British, only to discover, as Jackson did following the Battle of New Orleans, that the war was already over. Despite this distinctiveness, the history of the island shows that the broader issues that affected Massachusetts and the U.S. in general, could not be ignored, even in far-off Nantucket.

In 1658, a small band of people from Massachusetts Bay, most from the town of Salisbury and environs, made its way out to Nantucket via Martha's Vineyard. There were Coffins, Starbucks, Macys, Folgers, and Swains in the group. Several of them seem to have been Baptists, not especially favored in that day by the Massachusetts Bay colonial establishment. Others had had run-ins with the government on non-religious grounds. It is clear that they very deliberately decided that Nantucket was a place to get away from Massachusetts Bay. They cut a sales contract with Thomas Mayheu, the Governor of nearby Martha's Vineyard, for 30 English pounds and two beaver hats, and signed treaties with the other occupants of Nantucket, the Native Americans who numbered perhaps as many as 3,000 on the island at that time. Despite the substantial Native American presence, the original English settlers each took shares in what became known as the "Proprietary" and, in essence, set up shop as their own independent territory.

One small problem confronted them immediately—how to make a living on this speck of land out in the Atlantic? For the first few decades of their tenuous existence there, the proprietor's answer was sheep. Sheep require land for grazing, thus, more treaties with the Indians to swallow more land. It did not take many years before the sheep were on their way to turning the island into a desert. By the end of the 1600s though, the English discovered something else they could do near the island, something the Indians had been doing for years—catch whales. At first, there were so many whales in the immediate vicinity (mostly right whales) that the whaling business was handled from on-shore using small boats. Later, the business would expand to the Atlantic, and finally would come the epic voyages of years' duration to the whaling grounds in the Pacific that are the stuff of story and film. Not long into the 1700s, Nantucket became the whaling capital of the world, and so it would remain into the 1830s.

About the time the English discovered whaling as a business on Nantucket, the Quakers made inroads on the island. Melville's statement that the island had been "originally settled by the sect" was not accurate. But, early in the 18th-century the Quakers were quite successful in converting to their faith some key members of some of the principal families on the island, the Starbucks being one. Gradually, Quaker membership increased to the point where they became not only a religious force, but also the commercial and financial center of gravity on the island.

Samuel H. Jenks — Early Days

While Samuel H. Jenks eventually returned to his occasional boyhood haunt of Nantucket to make a name for himself, he was no Nantucketer by origin and no Quaker. He was born at Boston in 1789, the year the U.S. Constitution was ratified and Washington was elected President. By his own account, he was educated at Boston's public schools. Samuel H. began his career in commerce at Boston and maintained business interests there all his life. He was by religious profession an Episcopalian and later in life, he became a Mason. So, to Nantucketers, Samuel H. was an off-islander, or a "coof" as they were known, a fact that was often raised in his subsequent battles with his many born-and-bred Nantucket antagonists.

The Nantucket which Samuel H. decided to make his permanent home sometime around 1819 was then, thanks to whaling, the third largest port in all of New England. It was an island where Quaker mores and influence were strong, but by no means exclusively so. Small, isolated by the sea, but economically powerful, it was just the sort of place for a 30-year-old man from Boston to make his mark.

But what mark? And why Nantucket? A letter that Samuel H. wrote in 1859 sheds some light on these questions:

> In April 1817, I visited Nantucket for a sad and sacred purpose; remained a year; returned to this my native place [Boston]; and in 1819 was induced to adopt Nantucket, as the future residence of myself and my two motherless children. (Written in Boston, 5 February 1859, and quoted in Samuel H. Jenks' obituary in Nantucket's newspaper, *The Inquirer*, of 30 September 1863.)

To decipher this letter and its mention of going to Nantucket for "a sad and sacred purpose," we have to step back to Samuel H.'s life at Boston. His pursuits there as a young adult are not particularly clear. He is said to have been in commercial business. But, he also pursued a young lady named Lydia Grose Williams, daughter of James Williams of Boston whom he married on 14 June 1812, most likely at Boston. Lydia and Samuel had a daughter, Lydia Maria, born probably at Boston on 05 May 1814. Lydia Maria would live well into adulthood and die in 1858. Her mother was not so fortunate. She died at Boston on 25 Jun 1814, most likely of complications from Lydia Maria's birth.

On 28 January 1816, Samuel H. Jenks married for the second time at Boston, this time to Lydia Stevens, daughter of Capt. Dennis and Phebe (Arthur) Stevens, formerly of Nantucket. On 16 February 1817, Lydia bore a daughter, Maria Louisa, but all was not well. On 17 May 1817, Lydia died at Boston of typhus. On 13 July 1817, just two months later, the baby also died. As Lydia's Boston death record makes clear: "Her remains was carried to Nantucket & was there interred" (Ancestry.com, *Massachusetts, Town Vital Collections, 1620-1988;* see Genealogy section). In fact, both mother and daughter are buried at the Prospect Hill Cemetery on Nantucket. Although Samuel H. is a bit off in his chronology in his letter of 1859, it is clear that this was the "sad and sacred" purpose which brought him back to Nantucket as an adult. What he did during the year he stayed there in 1817 is not known.

As the 1859 letter recorded in *The Inquirer* states, Samuel Haynes then returned to Boston, "my native place." Back at Boston, he strengthened his acquaintance with Eliza Williams, whom sources note as the sister of Lydia Williams, his first wife. Samuel H. and Eliza married, he for the third time, on Nantucket on 23 September 1818. The 1859 letter states that sometime in 1819, Samuel H. and Eliza moved permanently to the island. Their first child, William Alfred, was born on the island on 29 August 1819. So, the letter's contents to the contrary, Samuel H.'s children did have a mother, or rather a stepmother, when they moved to the island. What was the "inducement" that brought them there?

While there is no certain answer to that question, I suspect it had something to do with William C. Coffin, of that famous Nantucket family. William C. was of the generation of Samuel H.'s father and would play a major role in Samuel's life on Nantucket until William died in 1835. A barber and wigmaker by trade, William C., like most Nantucketers, was also involved in the financial deals related to the whaling business. He was financially influential enough to serve as a member of the Board of Directors of the newly formed Nantucket Bank. A Congregationalist, a Mason, and a Federalist, he was often a major political thorn in the side of his Quaker, largely non-Federalist, neighbors. He was among those who arranged the treaty with the British during the War of 1812. He pushed for changes in the structure of the "Proprietary," the landholding scheme set up by the original settlers. For a number of years, William C. had also been agitating for the establishment of a public school system on the island, in accordance with a Massachusetts law adopted in 1789, and resisted by the Quaker establishment since then. In 1795, the Nantucket Bank of which he was a board member was robbed of a substantial amount of cash, around $20,000, a major crime on little Nantucket. Some of his fellow bank board members and the chairman, Quakers and non-Federalists, accused William C. of orchestrating the robbery in which, it became clear over the years, he was not involved in the least. (See Philbrick.)

So perhaps it was William C. Coffin who, seeing a bright young man who could play a role in the island's fragile educational system and a potential ally in the fight for public schools, induced Samuel H. to relocate permanently to Nantucket. Or, perhaps, Coffin simply asked him to set up a private school that his own children could attend given the lack of public schools. That Samuel H. was a school teacher in his earliest years on the island, we learn from a short note in *The Inquirer*:

> 'Franklin School'—S.H. Jenks, having relinquished the superintendence of the above seminary in coincidence of other avocations, recommends to the encouragement of his former patrons, his successor MR. WILLIAM C. STARBUCK. (Nantucket Atheneum - hereafter NA, *The Inquirer*, 14 January 1823)

This "other avocation" was explained in the previous issue of the weekly *Inquirer* on 7 January 1823 in an editorial notice: "the present editor has assumed also the publication . . . pledged to no political faction, no religious sect. . . . A discriminating public will not see us starve, if we deserve a living—and if we forfeit their countenance, we shall fall contentedly." The "present editor," and now owner, was Samuel H. Jenks. As for William C. Starbuck, mentioned in the note in *The Inquirer*, he would be a principal associate of Samuel H. Jenks throughout his life on Nantucket.

At least one earlier attempt at a regular newspaper on Nantucket having failed, a man named Joseph Melcher had established the weekly *Inquirer* that was first issued on 23 June 1821. As noted in that edition, the first page was to be devoted to religious intelligence and moral extracts; the second page to foreign and domestic news and literary materials; the third page to shipping news and advertisements; and the fourth page to poetry and advertisements. "The publisher will studiously avoid taking any share in local or party politics." Annual subscription: $2.50.

The press was already an important business in America. With no other public media available in that day and age, the newspaper was seen as a key vehicle of tying the various parts of the new country together. The Federal government, under its first Postmaster, Benjamin Franklin, a former printer and publisher, assured that postal rates for newspapers were low, subsidized by much higher rates for letter mail. With few books in print, it is not surprising that Melcher's paper carried literary content. All the papers of the time did. The papers were seen as a primary vehicle for sustaining and improving literacy. (See Michael and Edwin Emery p 111.)

Melcher's profession of political neutrality to the contrary, it had not taken long for the political forces in the country, even in the earlier Colonial era, to note how the press could be used to promote a certain point of view and to support certain interests. As Daniel Walker Howe writes:

> Improvements in communications had perhaps even more far reaching consequences [than improvements in transportation]. For example, they would greatly facilitate the development of mass political parties in the coming years [after 1815]. It is no accident that so many leaders of these parties would be newspapermen; or that the largest source of political party patronage came from the Post Office. (Howe p 41)

Boston had many newspapers and undoubtedly, from a young age, Samuel H. was familiar with them. He had also likely seen their use for political purposes that had been a tradition at Boston dating back at least to the revolutionary days when people like Sam Adams regularly used the press to savage the British colonial government for its latest faux pas. No doubt, Samuel H. had also seen the influence of the press on the political struggles in the post-Revolutionary War period, as Federalist editors like John Fenno, Noah Webster, William Cobbett, and Benjamin Russell fought, sometimes in person, with anti-Federalist writers such as Phillip Freneau and Benjamin Franklin Bache (Ben Franklin's grandson). The press as an arm of various political forces in America was already well entrenched. As we will see, regardless of how Samuel H. learned this lesson, there is no question that he learned it well.

How Jenks originally got into the newspaper business on Nantucket is not clear. But, by late 1822, he was already editing *The Inquirer* since its masthead read: "Published every Tuesday by Joseph C. Melcher, State Street, Nantucket, Mass.—edited by Samuel H. Jenks." Clearly, Samuel H. was in the editor's chair when the paper printed this unusually extensive death notice:

> In this town on Tuesday last, Mrs. Eliza Jenks, aged 21, wife of Mr. Samuel H. Jenks, and daughter of Mr. James Williams of Boston, after a brief but

agonizing illness which she endured with indescribable patience and firmness. Amidst her most trying sufferings, her mind remained [indecipherable word] by the approach of inevitable death and she resigned her breath with that composure and confidence which results from a life of virtue, and a reliance on the impartial, the unbounded, the universal love and mercy of a kind FATHER WHICH IS IN HEAVEN.

Her unconscious little children are thus deprived of a most fond and devoted parent, and her husband is again bereaved of an inestimable companion; having now within a few years consigned to the grave three endeared partners whose ages average only nineteen years! Truly has he drunk deeply of the cup of bitterness.

[followed by a tragic poem, probably written by Jenks himself] (NA, *The Inquirer*, 27 August 1822)

Eliza had died giving birth to Eliza Haynes Williams Jenks, my ancestor, leaving Samuel H. with three small children. Samuel H., however, would not stay without a wife for long. On New Year's Day, 1823, he married for the fourth and final time. His wife was Martha Washington Coffin, the eighth child of his friend and associate William C. Coffin and his wife, Deborah Pinkham. Samuel H. and Martha's house was a gift to them by her father. The closeness of the senior Coffins to their daughter and son-in-law is demonstrated by their two houses, still sitting side by side today on Union Street in downtown Nantucket. Martha proved to be made of tough stock. She survived the birth of eight children, a number of whom lived to adulthood and, evidently, she became one of Samuel's right hands in the newspaper business. Martha outlived Samuel H. by nearly 25 years; she died at Boston in 1887.

So, in 1823, with a new wife, and the ownership and editorship of *The Inquirer* in hand, Samuel H. was poised to carve his name in Nantucket history. Some would approve of that name; others would have quite a different opinion. The changes in *The Inquirer* in 1823 under Jenks are obvious: less religion, more history, more politics, and sharper rhetoric. As early as 28 January 1823, Jenks was berating the town for not allowing enough space for everyone who wished to attend the annual town meeting. His even-handedness and generosity toward fellow newsmen of a different political persuasion are already evident when he refers, in February, to the "lugubrious snivelings of the Boston Recorder." While he may have made snide remarks about the *Boston Recorder*, Jenk's editorial pen in *The Inquirer* of the 1820s was not as sharp on national issues, political, and otherwise, as it would become in the 1830s and beyond. There was more editorial focus on issues at the state and local level, especially the issue of public schools for Nantucket.

Generally, those with a Federalist orientation, like William C. Coffin and Samuel H. Jenks, supported their Federalist brethren on the mainland who had enacted the State law that mandated that every town with a population of over 5,000 must have a public school. Nantucket met the population requirement, but ever since the enactment of the law in 1789, the town had refused to honor it. Many of the Quakers on the island were not in favor of public involvement in education. Many did not want to send their children to school with non-Quakers. Other Quakers thought that education should focus on practical skills, like those needed to sail a whaleship, and they were concerned that the more liberal education envisioned by their opponents could have a negative impact on manning the ships which were Nantucket's lifeblood.

Part of the pro-public school argument was that the schools that did exist were private and were supported by private funding that was, primarily, for those who had the means to pay—whaleship owners and captains among them. The argument ran that those that did not have the means did not send their children to school at all, so that these youngsters had nothing to do but get into trouble on the streets of the town. Samuel Jenks speaks of the debate in his previously quoted letter of 1859:

> Educated as I have been under the free school system of Boston—a system made universal throughout the State, by long-standing and positive legal enactment, I was astounded and grieved to find that Nantucket, with a population of some 10,000, should have taken advantage of her necessarily tolerated exemption from certain other burdens [possibly a reference to the exemption of the Quakers from military service due to their pacifist beliefs], to set at naught the laws requiring every town to furnish instruction, without cost to children of all classes. I sought to arouse the people, through newspapers (such as they were) and at town meetings, to a sense of their duty, and of their legal liabilities. I met with repeated rebuffs in the old town hall. Some of the primitives thought they had already 'good enough' schools (meaning the charity schools). Others, the friends [sic], declared they had schools of their own, and would not mingle their children with those of the world's people. Others again ridiculed my motion for an appropriation for public schools, by denouncing it as a 'Boston notion.' I was voted down thrice as an officious intermeddling 'stranger and coof.' (NA, *The Inquirer, 30 September 1863*)

In 1825, as the debate on public education on the island heated up, Jenks raised an editorial proposition that, "The minds of the rising generation are public property." In 1826, he continued on the public school theme, arguing against allowing any particular group (such as the Quakers) to set policy related to schools, and stating as specious the idea that going to school would empty whaleships of their crews.

The editorializing on the school issue reflected a political debate on the subject that occurred over a period of years in the 1820s at town hall meetings and among the selectmen that composed the town government. The debate continued until 1827. In that year, several events occurred that forced Nantucket's hand. First, the Massachusetts legislature revised the education law of 1789, imposing financial sanctions on any town that did not comply. Secondly, the pro-school lobby on Nantucket, prodded by Jenks and no doubt, William Coffin, engineered an indictment against the town for violating the state's education law. Faced with legal action and the possibility of financial penalties, the town selectmen finally capitulated, and funds were voted for a public school system for the first time.

While all of this was proceeding, another set of events related to schools took place in 1827. As a speck of an island in the Atlantic, Nantucket was almost entirely dependent on its seagoing fleet for its livelihood and trade in essential commodities such as foodstuffs. As noted, it was a significant bastion of Tory sentiment before and during the Revolution. It is not surprising, therefore, that during the colonial period, some Nantucketers would join the British navy. One such Nantucketer was Isaac Coffin, who not only joined the British navy, but became an admiral and a baronet, thus, Admiral Sir Isaac Coffin.

Evidently, Sir Isaac's rather senior role in the British navy throughout the revolutionary period did not prohibit him from returning to the now independent United States. Having done quite well for himself, he returned to Nantucket for a visit in 1827. Since he had no children of his own to whom he could bequeath his estate, he was hoping to fund some sort of legacy on the island. Sir Isaac, evidently, spent quite a bit of time with William C. Coffin who enlisted Samuel H. Jenks to squire the Admiral around the island. As Jenks put in his 1859 letter: "I took the gouty old hero [not to most Americans of the time, I assume] in a chaise to Siasconset." This small village was the Nantucketers' place for a quick get-away from the cares of the island and, no doubt, their rather smelly, whale oil-infused port town. The Admiral raised a couple of ideas for a legacy, such as building an actual physical monument to himself or establishing an Episcopal church. Jenks told him that few would come to look at his monument and even fewer would attend his church since he (Jenks) was probably the only Episcopalian on the island. Instead, Jenks proposed that Sir Isaac endow a *free* school, suggesting to the Admiral that: "You will thus benefit your numerous kinfolk, and their grateful posterity, while you effectually perpetuate your name." Jenks continued: "He (the Admiral) at once adopted the suggestion, entered upon the preliminary details, and I felt avenged in my struggles with the town."

Thus came into being, the Admiral Sir Isaac Coffin's Lancastrian School, "Lancastrian" being a style of instruction that was less rote and more experiential in character than most modes of instruction of the time. As made sense on Nantucket, the school had a fair emphasis on nautical skills. For a time, there was even a training ship called the *Clio* which travelled as far as South America on a voyage or two with young Nantucket boys as its principal crew. The *Clio* was not a particular success. The school itself, however, supported by a substantial endowment by a British Admiral named Coffin, was a great success. It became an incubator for new ideas in education and a training ground for a number of the teachers and administrators who would staff the Nantucket public school system. In the early 1900s, it became the public system's vocational training center. The substantial brick building that was built for the school after the Great Fire of 1846 still stands.

And since it was a Coffin school, it was free, at least to descendants of that original Nantucket Coffin, Tristram. Most Nantucketers of this period could still find a genealogical path back to Tristram since he had quite a few children and, by the time of the Coffin school, myriads of descendants. Children though, like those of the "coof" Samuel Jenks, before he married his fourth wife, Martha Coffin, would not qualify. So, Samuel H. wrote the Admiral a letter on 17 May 1827, which reads in part:

> I do not wish to trouble you with trifles; but I have to ask one favour, the granting of which will gratify me exceedingly, if consistent with your plan—if otherwise, I would by no means urge it.
>
> I have four children, three of whom are related to the Coffins only through their mother-in-law, my present wife, the daughter of Wm. Coffin, Esq. These, I should be happy to place, if possible, in 'Admiral Sir Isaac Coffin's Lancastrian School'—for several reasons: vis the principal teacher is my wife's brother, Wm. Coffin Jr.—the Seminary is located in my vicinity—while the

Free Public Schools (established since your visit to this place) are both at a great distance from my residence. . . . [The balance of the letter provides the names of the Jenks children who would attend and describes the beginning days of the school itself. The letter ends as follows:] Please pardon the presumption of this petition—and, as in duty bound, will ever pray—Your very obt. servant, Sam. H. Jenks (NHA, MS 99)

This favor was granted. Thus, after the great struggle to establish the public schools on the island, one of the principal protagonists placed his children in another institution. That did not prevent Jenks from praising the results when the new public schools went into operation:

On Monday last, two of the large public schools recently established by vote of this town, were opened for the admission of scholars. . . . Upon the benefits and blessings of a general diffusion of learning, we need not amplify. The time has come, when bigotry and parsimony can no longer impede the march of intellect. The spirit of liberality is awake, even in this place; and will, we confidently hope, magnanimously acknowledge and satisfy the claims of justice and humanity. (NA, *The Inquirer*, 9 June 1827)

The debate over the establishment of public schools was over. But this would not be the last time that Samuel H. Jenks would find himself in a major years' long argument involving the school system. The next time would come in the 1840s, when he found himself in quite a different, and ironic, position from the "spirit of liberality" he invoked in 1827.

All through the early 1820s, *The Inquirer's* national political tone under Jenks, while sharper than under its founder, Joseph Melcher, remained fairly muted. This may reflect the period, as the Federalist movement per se had largely spent itself, and those advocating its position of a strong, more activist Federal government had yet to coalesce into any new effective political body. In October of 1823, Jenks seemed to favor a third presidential term for James Monroe. After Monroe decided not to run, then Jenks ran a set of letters that supported a variety of other candidates including Henry Clay, John C. Calhoun, and John Quincy Adams. In a famous back-room deal, Clay made Adams President in exchange for the role of Secretary of State, the clearest stepping stone to the White House at that time. Andrew Jackson, their opponent, vowed revenge. In the election for President in 1828, Jenks equivocated in an editorial in *The Inquirer* of 5 May 1827: "We are far from acknowledging that John Quincy Adams and Andrew Jackson are the only men, to whom the magistracy of the Republic can be safely entrusted." He was sure, however, that some of their allies were, indeed, strange bedfellows, or, as he put it: "The doctrine is, let us coalesce and go snacks in the loaves and the fishes."

Even if he wasn't too sure about which candidate to pick for President, he remained perfectly clear about those in the world of journalism whom he favored or disfavored, even in the Federalist camp. There was Mr. Charles King of the *American and Advocate* in Washington, D.C., "whose stately style of scribbling reminds us of a mud-scow . . . ." Jenks also had a good word for, "Messieurs Gales and Seaton of the National Intelligencer. . . . Those prosing weathercocks [weathervanes], it is true, have written many a reader to sleep" (NA, *The Inquirer*, 27 October 1827). The two "prosing weathercocks" also published *The Register of Debates*, the precursor to today's *Congressional Record*.

Several other state and local concerns repeatedly appeared in Jenks' editorials in the 1820s, including the cause of eliminating automatic incarceration for debtors who could not pay their bills. But nothing seemed to catch his attention and pen as had the public schools debate. Perhaps being a bit bored or looking to expand his own entrepreneurial and political horizons, Samuel H. decided to try his hand elsewhere. One source had him as editor of a New York City newspaper for a brief time in 1824. But by the end of 1827, Jenks was off to Boston as explained in a letter from William Coffin to Sir Isaac Coffin, dated 09 December 1827:

> Your friend, my son-in-law S. H. Jenks has removed to Boston to edit a new daily paper called the Evening Bulletin. The first number I will forward to you, likewise one of the last Inquirers, which paper he continues at Nantucket, under care of a very smart man by the name of Thornton, from New Bedford. (NHA, MS 99)

The *Boston Evening Bulletin* was, at least at that time, a pro-Jackson publication. But, as the 1830s progressed, Jenks' politics and his editorial content became increasingly aligned with the causes long espoused by the Federalists and National-Federalists that came after them. Over the course of the decade, he moved his newspaper and his politics in line with the successor party to Federalist interests, that of the Whigs. As he did so, whatever claim he may have made to some sort of political neutrality in his writing ended as Jenks became not only a newsman with a definite political agenda, but a politician himself.

Jenks' peregrinations along the east coast in this period are not easily followed. What I was able to learn of them comes largely from newspapers of the day, particularly the Whig organ at Baltimore, the *Baltimore Patriot:*

> *May, 1830:* Mr. S.H. Jenks, late of the Boston Bulletin, has obtained a clerk-ship in the State Department in Washington. (AHN, *Baltimore Patriot,* 11 May 1830)

> *April, 1831:* We learn with pleasure, that Mr. Samuel H. Jenks, late editor of the Boston Bulletin, has been engaged as editor of the Evening Journal of New York. . . . He is a ready writer, sufficiently satirical for these evil times, and the master of more quaint phrases, and nine-cornered words, than any body else we know of.—We have broken several lances in the course of the long and arduous wars of this continent, and we now welcome him as an ally in the same til-yard. (AHN, *Baltimore Patriot,* 11 April 1831, quoting the *N.Y. Com. Adv.*)

And what is this "til-yard?" That is explained in a subsequent edition of the *Baltimore Patriot* on 25 April 1831, in an article entitled, "Confession of error:"

> Mr. Jenks, formerly editor of a respectable *Jackson* paper in Boston, called the 'Evening Bulletin,' has secretly taken charge of the editorial department of the New York Evening Journal. The address of Mr. Jenks to the patrons of the Journal, on commencing his editorial duties, is honorable to his own frankness, while it reads an admonitory lesson to many who recently agree with him but have not the courage to avow it. We subjoin one or two paragraphs:

> In common with thousands—perhaps hundreds of thousands, of his fellow-citizens, the subscriber cherished a confidence, founded upon the reputed personal integrity of President Jackson, that the Government, under his guidance, will be well and honestly administered. With this expectation, he entered cheerfully at the commencement of the existing Administration, into its support. So soon, however, and so often, as he noticed a deviation from the line of *political* rectitude, he straightway spake of it, freely, as one friend would warn another against the commission of any *moral* wrong.—For this freedom he was clamorously denounced by a certain faction of brawling demagogues and selfish placemen at the East, who had succeeded in worming themselves into favor with the Government, and had become creatures of this or that Minister, as the case might be, to whom they were indebted for sustenance. . . .

> The sceptre has been nearly wrested from the hands of him who desired to wield it acceptably to the People, and is now attempted to be swayed by a

quack 'magician,' who employs it as a divining rod for his own aggrandizement. (AHN, *Baltimore Patriot*, 25 April 1831)

Martin Van Buren, Jackson's Vice President, was known to his opponents as, "the Little Magician." In the balance of the article quoted above, Jenks continues to express, "strong feelings of respect for the abused veteran," Jackson himself, while stating that the hopes for Jackson's administration had been, "most sadly and grievously disappointed," primarily by the actions of Van Buren and his associates.

Jackson was the leading Presidential figure of his era. A Democrat in the Jeffersonian tradition, he was opposed to a central bank that seemed to him a creature of moneyed Eastern interests. He also favored a hard currency rather than "paper rags," as they were sometimes known, and he was not disposed to use Federal resources to expand public infrastructure. When states attempted to assert a right to "nullify" Federal law, however, as South Carolina did during Jackson's second term, Jackson moved vigorously to thwart such action. Some of his opposers simply disliked Jackson's policies. Others disliked his tendency toward an imperious style of governance, sometimes reflected in political cartoons that depicted Jackson as "King Andrew I."

Some of Jenk's still equivocal attitude toward Jackson comes through in the editorial viewpoint expressed in *The Inquirer* in 1832, which was rather more neutral than one might expect regarding Jackson's re-election bid, and approving of Jackson's efforts to beat back the South Carolina nullifiers. But by 1834, with Jenks, evidently, back in person in the editor's chair of *The Inquirer*, it is clear that the paper is now a full-blown Whig organ. Under the headline "Stratagems," Jenks opines:

> The Tory party [the Democrats] are determined to play a deep and desperate game for the next presidency. Some of the most shrewd of the leading gamesters have already begun to exhibit their skill of legerdemain. The object is to divert the attentions of their antagonists from the real point of view—the elevation of Martin Van Buren. (NA, *The Inquirer*, 8 October 1834)

By November of that year, Jenks was in the political fray himself as the nominated Whig candidate from Nantucket for the Massachusetts State Senate. On November 5th, as the sole editor of the sole newspaper in town, he invited anyone who wished to discuss political issues of the day, including his nomination, to speak up in the paper, reserving the right of "simultaneous reply," and requiring, "assertion, argument and fact, rather than idle interrogatory, intemperate declamation or personal abuse." One reply spoke of the "Monster Bank." (Jackson had recently vetoed the reauthorization of the second national bank, a key political issue of the day). Jenks, using his right of "simultaneous reply," characterized this as a "vapid response." There is no question though that the voters on Nantucket had swung around heavily to a Whig point of view, at least at this level of local politics. The *Baltimore Patriot* tells the tale:

> SAMUEL H. JENKS, Esq. the editor of the Nantucket Inquirer, has been elected to the state senate. The vote stood, Jenks (Whig) 633, Mitchell (Jackson) 65—a majority worthy the character, abilities and services of the successful candidate. (AHN, *Baltimore Patriot*, 18 November 1834)

From then on, there was no equivocation. The politics of Samuel H. Jenks and Nantucket's only newspaper were clear; they both spoke for the Whigs, and in no uncertain terms. As for his view of his personal situation on the island, this was probably best expressed in a letter to one of his Boston associates, Naham Capen, in June of 1833:

> I am rubbing along here between wind and water, endeavoring by rigid economy and hard fisted industry to find food, lodging and raiment for my numerous dependents—and a tough job do I have of it. If I can do this, I suppose I ought to deem myself fortunate, after so many cuffs and buffetings about this rascally world. Poverty is my portion and my destiny of that I am satisfied, and I bend my back to the blows of fate.
>
> This place (in reply to your inquiry) will please you amazingly for a few weeks or months' residence. We have fine air and everything comfortable. Pray <u>come and see us</u>. Take the stage to New Bedford—then the steamer to this place. The jaunt will be pleasant, and your visit, I will assure you, agreeable and happy. You can have fine rides, fishing excursions, squantums [picnics] and good society. We have 7000 people, 5 churches, 3 bands, and all that. Pray come, and bring Mrs. C., without fail. (NHA, MS 133)

Politician, Newsman and Postmaster

In 1834, the Whigs had the votes on Nantucket. As a national political party, they were the logical successor to the strong national government philosophy of the early Federalists; however, an even stronger motivation for many who came to call themselves Whigs was a dislike of Andrew Jackson. Jackson was a polarizing figure. Those who supported and adored him were strong Democrats. Those who came to dislike him intensely—anti-masons, states-rights advocates,

nullifiers—became Whigs whether they were interested in strong national government or not. A number of these Whigs dearly wanted to become President themselves, especially Henry Clay of Kentucky and Daniel Webster of Massachusetts,
towering Congressional figures of their day. One was a southern slaveholder and
the other a northerner with, for the most part, a non-slaveholding constituency.
Even John C. Calhoun, the nullifier of South Carolina, dallied with the Whigs
for a time. All of these fractures in the Whig framework would become evident
as the 1830s progressed, and they would pose a dilemma for newsmen, like Jenks,
who were trying to represent their party's interests in the press, while looking for
the most worthy candidate to support for President against Jackson's anointed
successor, Van Buren. (See Holt on the history of the Whig Party.)

In late 1835, *The Inquirer* reported the nomination by the Massachusetts Whig
convention of Daniel Webster for President. But there were many such nomina-
tions of many different men throughout the country, splitting the party until a
compromise candidate began to emerge in 1836. Only in October of 1836 did
Jenks and *The Inquirer* begin to swing behind that candidate, William Henry
Harrison. Jenks devoted space to castigating his fellow newsmen at Boston for
not favoring the Whig cause. But, while Nantucketers voted for Whig candidates
in overwhelming numbers, an improving national economy, and the Whig's lack
of national cohesion assured Van Buren's election.

At the state level, since Jenks was in the Massachusetts Senate, he reported
regularly in *The Inquirer* on what was happening at Boston, including the debate
over whether to abolish imprisonment for debt. This became a signature issue for
Jenks. In 1834, the state legislature passed a law that stated the there would be no
imprisonment for debts contracted after the 4th of July, 1834. But, if the debt was
contracted earlier than that, imprisonment was still possible. Jenks worked in the
legislature to repeal that provision and, eventually, succeeded.

At the local level, Jenks also found the time to serve on the Nantucket School
Committee. In 1834, the Annual Report of the School Committee found its way
onto the front page of *The Inquirer*. No local issue consumed more print in *The
Inquirer* at the time though than the attempt to diversify Nantucket's economy.
As an island, part of that economy was based on the coastal and Atlantic ship-
ping trade. But overall, the economy was based primarily on one product, whale
oil. There were those, like Jenks and his usual partner in local issues, William
C. Coffin, who saw economic diversification as important. Manufacturing of

textiles was becoming the centerpiece of the Massachusetts economy. Why not on Nantucket?

The product that Coffin, Jenks, and a number of others hit on as their means of diversification was, of all textiles, silk. Article after article in *The Inquirer* promoted silk production as the wave of the future for Nantucket, from the planting of mulberry trees and the raising of silk worms, to the processing of the raw silk and the manufacturing of silk cloth. Why these gentlemen opted for silk is not clear; nevertheless, Jenks and others (not William Coffin who had died in May 1835) eventually raised the capital to establish the Atlantic Silk Company in late 1835. The company imported state-of-the-art equipment for the plant, hired workers, and got into production using imported raw silk in 1836. The plant had the second power silk loom in the world. Thousands of mulberry trees were planted on the island. The venture lasted until 1844 and then collapsed totally. By then, the Nantucket whaling industry was also on the way out, and with the failure of silk, no other industry was in sight to replace it. The principal of diversification had been right, but this particular source of salvation was fairly dubious from the start.

Beyond the local island issues and national political news, other national and international news was always printed in *The Inquirer*. This news frequently was picked up from other papers, which thanks to Ben Franklin's foresight, continued to circulate free of charge to newspaper editors around the country. In January of 1835, an article was reprinted from South Carolina discussing a resolution introduced in the state legislature asking the Governor to request information from the "U.S. Executive" as to the, "authority by which the General Government has assumed to erect certain fortifications in the harbor of Charleston." Whatever answer the South Carolinians got, it did not stop the construction of Fort Sumter, the attack on which in 1861 would announce the beginning of the Civil War. In April of 1836, *The Inquirer* picked up a story coming from the "ill-fated country" of Texas about the: "desperate, bloody and cruel combat . . . that resulted in the slaughter of the garrison in the fort at Bexar [the full name of this military fortification was the Presidio of San Antonio de Bexar, better known today as the Alamo] . . . Col's James Bowie and David Crockett are among the slain—the first was murdered in his bed, to which he had been confined by illness—the latter fell, fighting like a tiger."

Another frequent subject of national and local news were disease outbreaks. From these disease reports, it is clear that health conditions in the United States of the 1830s were worse than what is found in most developing countries today. In July of 1832, it was cholera raging in New York and Detroit, as well as Quebec City and Montreal. In 1840, it was smallpox on Nantucket itself. In 1836, sickness found its way back to a family that disease had frequented so many times over the years. In late May, Jenks apologized if his editorial content hadn't been up to par: "we must beg the indulgence of our friends, until peradventure the cloud shall have passed out of darkness, and dissolved in the hope of returning sunshine." The cloud did not pass. On June 1st, *The Inquirer* announced, with another poem probably penned by his father, the death of Francis Henry Jenks, aged 18 months. The next child in the Jenks family would also be named Francis Henry. He managed to escape the scourge of killer diseases and live to adulthood.

The State Senate seat he held passed from Samuel H. Jenks after one term, when the district was enlarged to incorporate Nantucket with part of the Cape Cod mainland. In addition to his senatorial term, Jenks was twice elected as a Representative from Nantucket to the Massachusetts House in the late 1830s, as a Whig, of course. The Whigs on Nantucket, in general, and Jenks, in particular, having learned their lesson from the last presidential election, got behind William Henry Harrison a bit earlier than they had done last time around. Thanks in large part to an economic downturn that had plagued Van Buren during almost his entire term, the "Little Magician" lost his bid for re-election. On 14 November 1840, under a banner headline, "Most Glorious News," *The Inquirer* heralded the election of Harrison as President with these gracious words: "Van Burenism, Loco-focoism [a term used to denigrate the Democrats], and the whole family of corruptionists, whose misrule, for twelve long years has cursed the land, are now passing away, before the WHIRLWIND OF REFORM, into the regions of disgraceful oblivion."

By April 1841, after nearly a decade of faithful service to the Whig cause in the state legislature and in his newspaper, Jenks obtained his reward from the largest of all sources of public patronage at that time—the Post Office. On April 3rd, *The Inquirer* announced: "A CHANGE, with the present number of the *Inquirer*, the business of its publication passes into other hands," namely those of Samuel's son, William A. Jenks. Not discussed in this article, but elsewhere on the same page is the reason. Under a list of Appointments by the General Government to the office of Deputy Postmaster is: "Samuel H. Jenks, Nantucket, Mass, vice James Mitchell, resigned."

Although this was a piece of patronage that might have come his way eventually, Jenks had already expressed an oblique interest in the position. In a letter to Col. Charles K. Gardner, First Assistant Postmaster General and Auditor of the Post Office Department in the Van Buren Administration, Jenks called for the replacement of the incumbent postmaster. It is written in Jenk's usual understated style:

> I love my country, and cannot bear longer, without some countervailing effort, to participate in the degradation which this portion of it has endured for upwards of eight years in the person of this detestable subordinate. Doubtless his accounts with the department are sufficiently straight. He is well aware of the consequences of deficiency in that respect. But to the people among whom he is placed, there is not a more obnoxious person existing. (NHA, MS 133)

Written at the time from a Whig journalist to a Democratic political appointee, the desired outcome had to await the arrival of a Whig administration some three years later.

By 7 April 1841, however, *The Inquirer* was announcing the death of President Harrison on April 4th. The news had been brought to the island by steamship the previous night. Harrison died of pneumonia having served in office for only 30 days. This elevated John Tyler to the Presidency—a Virginia states-righter who disagreed with the Whigs on many fundamental parts of their platform, and who was almost as effective at thwarting their attempts to implement their program as any Democrat. This change, however, did not alter Harrison's appointment of the new Postmaster for Nantucket.

By the end of 1841, major changes took place regarding *The Inquirer*. For reasons that remain unclear, Samuel H. Jenks sold the newspaper to Hiram B. Dennis who also became editor. Perhaps it was a matter involving personal finances; perhaps his son did not wish to continue in the editor's chair; or perhaps Jenks was not allowed to hold a private company while holding a Federal government post. Evidently though, in the sales agreement with Dennis, Jenks agreed that he would not take an editorial position again for some period of time. This agreement would come back to haunt him in the future.

Despite his role as Postmaster, Jenks also maintained his close connection with the Nantucket schools that he had helped create and continued to serve on the

School Committee when so elected. While there is little in the public record about Jenks' tenure as Postmaster, there is a great deal concerning his involvement with the schools. The debate concerning those schools would consume him, and the island as a whole, for the next five years.

The Great Nantucket School Integration Struggle

The long fight to establish public education on Nantucket ran roughly parallel in time with the strengthening of the abolitionist movement in Massachusetts and on Nantucket. As the 1840s approached, it became clear that a new fight was brewing on the island between some of the original public school advocates who were still well represented on the School Committee, and those, including many prominent Nantucket abolitionists, who felt that the Nantucket public school system should be racially integrated. This issue would become a cause célèbre that would, ultimately, divide families, social institutions, political parties, and governing institutions on the island. The school integration debate, and actions by both sides in that debate, would rage on Nantucket until 1846. (See White's *A Line in the Sand* on which much of the following narrative is heavily dependent.)

By 1840, there were over 500 "persons of color" on Nantucket. Some of them were the descendants of slaves owned by earlier generations of Nantucketers, including Quaker families, members of whom were now ardent abolitionists. Some of those persons of color had come to the island because of the employment it provided in the whaling business. Some of them were descendants of the inhabitants who predated the arrival of any European on the island. Like many others on Nantucket, for lack of a better solution, they had set up their own private school in the early 1820s that supported their own educational needs. This school was known among many as the "African School." On Nantucket, this institutional division along racial lines was prevalent in almost all social institutions, including churches and even the abolitionist movement itself. So, when the public schools were first established, this same model was followed. A grammar school was set up in the general vicinity of the section of Nantucket called, "New Guinea" in order to serve the colored population; students at the other schools were all white.

In 1838, a high school was finally opened on the island, but there was only one such school. So, inevitably, the question arose, what was to happen when a colored student was ready to go to high school? No one had to wait long. Eunice Ross, a pupil who had shown great talent at what had become known as the York Street School, the school for black students, passed the entrance level exam for the new high school and was refused entry, bringing the issue of integration of the entire system to a head.

In 1840, the chair of the School Committee was none other than Samuel H. Jenks. He and others, such as his longtime associate in political and educational matters, William C. Starbuck, were dead-set against school integration. They argued, vociferously, in the usual Jenks style, that everyone, black or white, was legally entitled to an education, and that the system that Nantucket had established provided just that. True, the races were separated in the schools, but the educational content was equal, according to Jenks and Starbuck. Behind this legalistic argument were fierce feelings that "amalgamation" of the races, particularly the ultimate amalgamation of man and wife, was simply not acceptable.

On the other hand, the integrationists argued that the schools were separate, but not equal, with the Eunice Ross case being prima fascia evidence. They also argued that education at the York Street School was not on par with the other schools for whites. The dedicated abolitionists in the crowd, having seized on this issue, were not about to let it go. Their opponents felt the same.

While these opposing forces battled mightily on the School Committee itself and at Nantucket's annual town meetings, the bulk of the island's population remained ambivalent. This attitude was reflected in the annual elections of the School Committee, which tended to produce contrary results virtually year after year. One year, the integrationists would have a majority and would begin to move toward integration. The following year, the anti-integrationists would rise to the top and undo what had been done the previous year. This general ambivalence reflected the prevailing national attitude toward abolition. No major political party—Whig, Democrat, or otherwise—espoused it. Consequently, the press, with radical exceptions like William L. Garrison's Boston-based *Liberator*, did the same. While there may have been few on Nantucket who opposed the abolition of slavery per se, the continued segregation of nearly every social institution on Nantucket showed the general unease among many regarding the concept of racial integration.

In 1842, while several abolitionists were elected to the School Committee, the majority of those elected, including Jenks' key ally, William C. Starbuck, were anti-integrationists. The abolitionists then turned to the annual town meeting to press their case, and, in fact, succeeded in getting a motion passed that favored their position. On the following day, however, with a larger crowd in attendance,

that motion was reconsidered and voted down. It was not simply the white abolitionists who were upset with this result; the black citizens of Nantucket reacted
as well. Their address was published in *The Islander*, a Democratic newspaper,
the first serious political counterpoint to the Whig *Inquirer* on the island. *The
Islander* began publication in April 1841. An excerpt from the black citizens'
address of 1842:

> Resolution: That whereas the laws of this Commonwealth, in reference to
> the privilege of education in our town schools, make no distinction in relation
> to the complexion or symmetry of its inhabitants, it is therefore the judgment
> of the oppressed portion of the citizens of Nantucket, that it is their right, and
> they ought to claim, and do desire to enjoy, among other rights, the right of
> having their youth educated in the same schools which are common to the
> more favored members of the community.
>
> . . . hoping the day is not far off distant, when the good sense and Christianity
> of this republic will proceed to make its distinctions in Society on just and
> reasonable grounds, and not according to the color of their skin, and when
> the common proverb of distinction shall be, Mentem non frontem hominis
> spectato. (NA, *The Islander*, 12 March 1842)

Samuel H. Jenks used his old bully pulpit, *The Inquirer*, to editorialize nega-
tively on the content of such addresses until he sold the paper. The vitriol flowed,
with the owner/editor of *The Islander*, Charles Hazewell, entering the fray and
giving as "good" as he received:

> It may be that there are men who would not have noticed the attacks of the
> editor of the Inquirer, and have rested their defense on the ground of his notori-
> ous habits of blackguardism, his superlative meanness, and his utter inability to
> act in a courteous manner, or to write in a courteous tone. . . . To convince the
> public that we feared him not, we were compelled to inflict on him a summary
> punishment, which, if we may judge from his writing, told most effectively.
> *(The Islander*, 19 May 1840)

The Islander, in December of 1841, remarked on the editorial change at *The
Inquirer* when Jenks sold the paper to H.B. Dennis. Hazewell gave his congratu-
lations by stating that the Whigs would have a better paper—"a happy change."
As for Jenks, he was now reduced to making his views known and debating his
opponents through letters to the editor, in both *The Inquirer* and *The Islander*.
Almost always, these letters were penned using pseudonyms, like "Z" and "P."

The authors might debate each other for months at a time on any given issue in the op-ed pages of the local press.

In 1843, the townspeople voted in an abolitionist majority on the School Committee. This group included Cyrus Peirce, a highly respected educator who was Samuel H. Jenks' brother-in-law, having married Harriet Coffin, a sister of Samuel's wife, Martha. Despite this close family connection, clearly, these two did not see eye to eye at all on the integration issue.

The new School Committee majority immediately pushed in the annual town meeting for a vote to integrate the schools. After a huge amount of back and forth on the issue, the citizenry voted to postpone all action on this issue until the next year. The integrationists persisted in moving forward. The anti-integrationists, led by William C. Starbuck, tried to push the abolitionists off the Committee for not obeying the will of the town. This also did not succeed. So, with their majority intact on the Committee, the abolitionists proceeded to integrate the schools. They altered the boundaries of each of the schools and invited all children, regardless of race, within those boundaries to attend the school in their area. On 18 March 1843, *The Islander* came out in full support of this position, noting that the School Committee members wanted to close the York Street School and move the pupils to other schools. *The Islander* noted that the Town Selectmen were opposed to this action and wanted the School Committee to resign. *The Islander* avowed that the Committee had the right to act independently: "Many a measure which has had but a small claim of success when first advanced, has been indebted to its final triumph to the brutal opposition of its enemies, who forgot their manhood in their manner of manifesting their hatred to the cause of human advancement" (NA, *The Islander*, 18 March 1843).

That was to be the last word from *The Islander* on the subject in its final issue. Nantucket was a small place, and heavily Whig at that. The Democratic organ just was not able to survive. In 1844, the townspeople pronounced their judgment on the actions of the previous year's School Committee. Seven of the eight previous abolitionist members of the Committee were voted out. The anti-integrationists were given a strong majority, which included Samuel Jenks who again became chair of the Committee. Just as quickly as the previous Committee had moved to integrate the schools, the new committee took action to re-segregate them. The abolitionists tried to stop them at a special town meeting, but they did not succeed. Three of the most outspoken abolitionists still on the Committee resigned in protest. The Committee then redrew the school boundaries, reopened the York Street School, and moved all the black pupils back to that school. This was done publically by School Committee members appearing at each school, singling out the black pupils, and telling them that they were no longer allowed to attend that school, but must return to the York Street School. One of those directly involved in this process was Jenks. The accounts of what exactly was said that day, as given in the Nantucket press by Jenks and others, were undoubtedly shaped by the viewpoints of the writers toward the whole integration debate. There is no doubt, though, that it was a thoroughly unpleasant set of events that resulted in near violence and provoked an unexpected response. The black population of the town immediately boycotted the entire public school system. The abolitionists helped set up a schoolroom for them in the center of town that some attended. The School Committee, expecting that the boycott would not last long, kept the York Street School open and the teacher employed. He ended up teaching a handful of white students who found it convenient to attend there, and did so for quite some time since the boycott lasted all that school year and into the next.

By 1845, the abolitionists and the black community recognized that they were not going to succeed through either the School Committee itself or through the town meeting process. There was simply too much opposition on the island. So, they went off-island, to the Massachusetts legislature and the courts, closely following the same pattern that had been used by Jenks, William Coffin, and their associates 20 years earlier in the push for public schools on the island. Altogether, the black community and the white integrationists sent four petitions to the legislature, including one from Eunice Ross, who requested redress due to her exclusion from the Nantucket High School. Having been advised that they could not succeed under the existing Massachusetts law in getting the Nantucket schools integrated, they asked for a new law. The anti-integrationists responded with two petitions of their own, but in vain. The Massachusetts legislature approved a new law, Chapter 214 of the Acts of 1845—An Act Concerning Public Schools, which reads:

> Any child unlawfully excluded from any public school, which such child has legal right to attend, or from public school instruction, in this Commonwealth, shall recover damages therefore, in an action on the case, to be brought in the name of said child by his guardian, or next friend, or any court of competent jurisdiction to try the same, against the city or town, by which said school is supported. (quoted in White p 112)

This new law not only clarified that any child could attend any public school they had a legal right to attend, the law also had financial teeth. The town could be sued for damages if it did not comply.

To complete the similarity with the actions taken to bring public schools to Nantucket in the 1820s, only a lawsuit was needed. It was not long in coming. Absalom Boston filed a suit against the town on the grounds that his daughter, Phebe Ann, had applied to attend one of the public schools in June of 1845, and had been refused. Undoubtedly, she had applied to attend one of the all-white schools. Absalom Boston was one of the leading black entrepreneurs on the island. Among other accomplishments, he was a successful whaler, with his own ship and an all-black crew. A special town meeting was held to determine how to handle this suit. The abolitionists introduced a motion that Boston drop his suit if the town would allow Phebe to enter the school for which she was qualified. The answer was no. There was discussion of arbitration, but this motion was tabled. The only decision taken was that the School Committee itself would make the defense against the suit.

As 1846 rolled around, having exhausted the letter-to-the-editor approach to the school integration and other political issues, Jenks, with William C. Starbuck as publisher, initiated yet another new newspaper, *The Warder*. This started a brand new brouhaha with the new owner/editor of *The Inquirer*, Edward W. Cobb, who argued that Jenks' agreement with H. B. Dennis when he bought *The Inquirer* prohibited Jenks from becoming an editor of another paper. The usual vituperative exchange between the two editors ensued, but *The Warder* went forward.

In the very first issue of *The Warder*, Jenks took the integration issue straight on under the headline, "The True State of the 'Colored' Question." He quoted Wendell Phillips, a leading Massachusetts abolitionist who had noted, "the attempt made last year at Nantucket to exclude colored children from the school to which they had been admitted the previous year." Jenks commented: "The writer, being manifestly unable to treat on his subject from his own knowledge, must of course been furnished with the raw material of this fabricated slander, by some of the sanctimonious Ranters in our own midst, who are continually prating the same nonsense and calumny" (*The Warder*, 3 January 1846).

Jenks went on to say that everyone knew that "we" (the School Committee and the town selectmen) were providing enough money for all children, including the colored children to go to school. He argued that the school that had been established for colored children, until the integrationist actions of the last year, was, "equal in every respect to the other town schools for children of similar age and capacity."

Jenks argued that the integration of the schools that occurred in 1843 was, "plainly intended to facilitate the grand catastrophe of practical amalgamation," and, "that the public was thoroughly disgusted." He stated that the School Committee elected in 1844 worked to undo this "amalgamation" so as not to, "set at defiance the express will of their constituents." On February 11th, Jenks printed in *The Warder* the School Committee's report for the previous year that reads in part: "During the past year, in accordance with standing votes of the town instructing them in the premises, the Committee has educated the colored children by themselves, so far as has been practical. The additional cost of this arrangement has not exceeded $800." An interesting statement since the black boycott of the public schools was still ongoing. This would appear to be an attempt to show the townspeople that it didn't cost very much to run a separate school for blacks, and thus avoid the dreaded amalgamation.

Regardless of Jenks' attempts to keep the debate going and prevent the re-integration of the schools, it was not to be. The population in general, and the town selectmen, in particular, were no doubt well aware of the new law on the Massachusetts books, and had undoubtedly grown tired of the continuous debate over the integration issue that had been at the forefront of every town meeting for at least five years. In the 1846 School Committee election a "throw-the-bums-out" attitude prevailed once again among the electorate. All thirteen previous members of the Committee were defeated and the abolitionists were elected in force. With a strong majority of pro-integrationists, the new Committee moved within a week of their election to re-integrate the schools. The Bostons dropped their suit. The Committee summed up its actions in its annual report for 1846 as follows:

> On the first entrance day of the past year, a large portion of the children then composing the York Street School, together with a number who had for some time been deprived of educational privileges, applied for admission into the several Public Schools in the section where they severally resided, and were duly admitted. (quoted in White p 103)

And in July of 1846, it was no longer the supposed catastrophe of integration, or amalgamation, or the lack thereof, that held the town's attention. A catastrophe of another sort altogether engulfed Nantucket—fire. *The Warder*, which was the only paper to survive intact, carried the story under the following headline: "Awful Calamity—One Third of our town is in ruins. About [$]1,000,000 of Property Destroyed." *The Warder* reported:

> Buildings were blown up [deliberately, to try to stop the blaze], but the fiery elements seemed to have gained the ascendency, and for hours it appeared as though all human efforts to stop their destructive progress would prove futile. A scene of devastation meets the eye, that beggars description. Many persons have lost their all. . . . It is estimated that between 300 and 400 buildings have been destroyed. . . . It is very remarkable that no lives were lost; two or three were injured more or less severely. (NA, *The Warder*, 15 July 1846)

Clearly, this was a stunning event for the relatively small community. A committee of seven members, chaired by Samuel H. Jenks, was set up to investigate the facts and to see what improvements could be made to the fire department. The committee's findings, written by Jenks, were not flattering to the townspeople, noting that the prevailing attitude seemed to be, "save himself who can," with the rich hiring laborers to save their property while the laborers lost their own. Just as the long debate over bringing public education to Nantucket had come to a definitive end in 1827, so the debate over the integration of schools was now over. Nantucketers turned to other issues, including the physical rebuilding of their town.

Return to Boston

The story goes that Samuel H. Jenks was off-island when the fire occurred and that his wife, Martha, worked the next day to put out a broadsheet about the disaster in its immediate aftermath on the only workable printing machinery in the town. (See for instance Grace Brown Gardner's account in "Fifty Famous Nantucketers," published by *The Inquirer* on 25 February 1950.) Whatever the truth of that story, no actual copy of the broadsheet has been found. As noted, *The Warder* did print the story of the fire soon after its occurrence, and Jenks made a remarkable map showing the devastation of the town, house-by-house and business-by-business. He also continued to participate in the Whig politics of that year when the party was split into factions created by the fight over abolition and the school integration debate.

At a Whig convention held on Nantucket in September 1846, which included at least his "Union" faction, Jenks was once again nominated as a candidate for election to the Massachusetts House. As reported in *The Warder* of 18 September 1846: "The latter gentleman, at his own request, was excused from serving, by reason of his contemplated removal from town; and W.C. Starbuck Esq., was substituted in his stead." The anti-school integrationist Starbuck won state office, but so did several abolitionist candidates. This "contemplated removal" of the Jenks family was to Boston. Perhaps it was a move that was planned even before the fire broke out. Times had been tough. In the second edition of *The Warder* on 3 January 1846, Jenks had referred to himself at one point as, "the late Postmaster of Nantucket, who had just been punished by President Polk for the crime of being a Whig." As to the newspaper business, this had always been a difficult money-making proposition, especially in the relatively small town of Nantucket. Further, while clearly maintaining an influence in the town given his longstanding prominence in journalism and politics, Jenks had also undoubtedly made plenty of enemies from the initial brouhaha over establishing public schools, and particularly from the bruising debate, and his own actions, regarding school integration.

Perhaps Jenks was simply tired of being the perpetual outsider, the one with "Boston notions," a "coof." Boston had always been his alternative home. He had spent considerable time there over the years editing various newspapers and as a member of the state legislature. In fact, the public excuse for the move from Nantucket was his assumption of yet another newspaper editing job in Boston. This new occupation was noted in a piece entitled "Hon, S. H. Jenks" in *The Mirror*, another new newspaper on Nantucket, written by one of Jenks's owner/ editor rivals, John Morrissey, a fellow Whig:

> It is with extreme pleasure that we notice this gentleman's resumption of the chair editorial, as one of the editors of the Boston Daily Star, a Whig paper. Long, long years have we known him, and ever found him to be a MAN. As an editor he ever stood high, and his writings were always extensively copied throughout the country. It would be a waste of words to eulogize one so well known in this community; but we cannot refrain from this public expression of one who, while holding some views adverse to our own, we always greatly respected and esteemed. (*The Mirror*, 9 January 1847)

One might question the use by Morrissey of the word "eulogize" from a Freudian perspective. I suspect that he was probably at least a bit relieved to see the Hon. S. H. Jenks off to Boston.

When exactly the Jenks family made the move is not clear. But, by 1850, Samuel H. and Martha, along with many members of their extended family, and a family named Park, were living in Ward 12 at South Boston (Ancestry.com, *1850 U.S. Census, Boston, Massachusetts*).

Evidently, the work as editor of the Boston Daily Star did not last long since the 1850 census record shows Samuel H.'s occupation as, "Broker." Boston City directories also show Jenks as an insurance executive, a notary public, and a justice of the peace. Interestingly, in 1853, he was the President and Director of the Shawmut Mutual Fire Insurance Company, and in 1854, he was a Director of the Traders Mutual Fire Insurance Company. (See Ancestry.com, *U.S. City Directories*.)

He also never gave up his interest in schools. According to his wife, he had three major goals in his life, all of which he accomplished: the creation of the public schools on Nantucket, the abolishment of imprisonment for debt in Massachusetts, and the creation of a girls school at Boston. It is not certain, but the Boston school in question may be a Girls' High School that was established at Boston in 1852. Jenks also proved constitutionally incapable of staying out of school politics. A directory for the Boston government in 1850 shows Samuel Jenks as a member of the Boston School Board representing the Twelfth Ward (Ancestry.com, *U.S. City Directories*). I am uncertain how long he served on the Boston board. Evidently, he wasn't so tired from bashing heads with fellow school board members on Nantucket as not to do it all over again in Boston. As a politician, he was also a Whig delegate to a convention to rewrite the Massachusetts state constitution (Ancestry.com, *U.S. City Directories*).

On a personal level, even while at Boston, there was no escape for the family from the specter of illness and death that had haunted it for so many years. In 1858, Samuel Haynes Jenks Jr., who, with a wife and two small children, was still living with his parents at the time, developed a fever and died two days later (NA, *The Inquirer*, 26 January 1858). Yet, another blow to a family that had received so many. Before his death, Samuel H. Jenks himself would witness the death of three wives and seven of his twelve children, some as infants or young children, but others as adults with children of their own.

Samuel H. died on 23 September 1863 at South Boston. He was born in the promising year of the promulgation of the country's new Constitution. He died as the country tore itself apart during the Civil War. Jenks was eulogized at Boston, and later, in the Nantucket press that noted, "his family and friends have cause to lament the loss of one of no ordinary caste" (NA, *The Inquirer*, 30 September 1863). His wife, Martha, who outlived him by nearly a quarter of a century, took every opportunity to keep his legacy alive, particularly, the creation of the public schools on Nantucket. Apparently, she had less to say, at least that has survived, about the school integration crisis. Her own views on that crisis are unknown as far as I have been able to determine. I wish she had said more about Samuel H.'s role in founding a girl's school at Boston.

In 1932, the Nantucket newspaper published an article entitled, "Opening the New Volume," which discussed the beginnings of the newspaper business on Nantucket and spoke of Samuel H. Jenks' role as editor and owner of *The Inquirer*. Atop the article is a portrait clearly drawn in the latter years of Jenks' life: an older gentleman, dressed formally, still with a full head of white hair, posed pensively in profile, as if thinking back on his long life full of personal and professional struggles. A few years ago, as my son and I sorted through a box of assorted bits and pieces of memorabilia left by my grandmother, we came across a black-bordered octagonal pin containing a small version of this same portrait. In the Victorian era at the end of Samuel H. Jenks life, this pin most likely was prepared for and worn at his funeral.

<u>Change and Persistence</u>

Physically, Nantucket quickly recovered from the devastation of the Great Fire of 1846. Within six months, nearly the entire downtown was rebuilt; however, all was not well on the island. Samuel H. Jenks and others had the right idea, but the wrong product, when they tried to diversify the island's economy with silk. The whale fishery was doomed. The move of the whaling fleet to the Pacific required bigger ships. Bigger ships required deeper harbors. The natural bar at the mouth of Nantucket's harbor became a barrier to these ships. For a few years, the Nantucketers got by with ingenious locally built versions of floating dry docks called "Camels" which were used to float large ships over the bar. But in the long run, this solution proved impractical. Whaling moved largely to the coastal port of New Bedford.

Samuel Haynes Jenks
Courtesy of the Nantucket Historical Association,
item no. 1996.0016.030.

With whaling on the way out, owners and sailors of Nantucket ships were in the market for other work. The Gold Rush of 1849 in California provided the soonest opportunity. Many a prospective miner, from Nantucket or elsewhere, sailed to California on Nantucket whaleships which, never to make another voyage, rotted away in the backwaters of San Francisco Bay. Like many one-product economies, the island found no easy replacement for whaling. By 1875, the island's population had declined to 3,200. Eventually, new visionaries reconceived the island as a tourist resort which would play heavily on the supposed romance of the whaling ships and the wealth they produced, largely represented by the houses of the richest of the whaleship captains. Other elements of that earlier life simply disappeared: the ships themselves, the incredibly arduous work, and the smell of an entire industry based solely on the fat of the world's largest living mammal. (See Philbrick on this period of Nantucket's history.)

A number of key aspects of Nantucket life in the heyday of whaling persist, however. With its beginnings thanks to Samuel H. Jenks, William C. Coffin, and others, the public school system created on the island in the 1820s of course still continues. Eventually, even Admiral Coffin's Lancastrian School became part of the public system, serving for many years as the vocational training center, harking back to the school's original focus on experiential learning.

That public school system has remained integrated since the remarkable success in the 1840s, of the forward-looking Nantucket abolitionists, people of color on the island, and others with an interest in greater racial equality. In this case, Samuel H. Jenks held and reflected a widespread opinion of the day that "separate" was preferable when it came to schooling and other matters. Over a hundred years' later, racial integration in schools and elsewhere was still being debated and fought over, and not just in the South, but at Boston and elsewhere in the North. While the victorious Nantucket integrationists were clearly very much ahead of their time, just as clearly, Samuel Jenks was ultimately on the wrong side of the debate on this issue.

Undoubtedly, Jenk's most enduring legacy on the island is Nantucket's newspaper, *The Inquirer,* which merged with its principal rival in 1865 to form *The Inquirer and Mirror under* John Morrissey's leadership. It is still published on a weekly basis as it has been almost continuously since the 1820s when a "coof" from Boston made the local paper well known all up and down the eastern seaboard. Samuel Haynes Jenks is largely forgotten now by the general public, but in his day, he was well remembered for good or ill by those who encountered his "nine cornered words" which he wrote in *The Inquirer* as one of the country's leading practitioners of the art of sanguinary journalism.

CHAPTER 4

THE LAND SPECULATOR:
RICHARD THAYER

In the 1960s, my father suggested that I apply to attend high school at Thayer Academy in Braintree, Massachusetts, a town located just south of Boston. The Academy was a legacy of Brigadier General Sylvanus Thayer, who was Superintendent of West Point from 1817 to 1833, and is credited with substantially strengthening that institution. At the time, I was neither interested in Thayer Academy nor had any idea that our family was actually related to the Thayers of Braintree. The life of the highly esteemed General Sylvanus was unknown to me. Nor did I know that one of his ancestors, and mine, had become infamous in Braintree during the late 1600s when he seemed to claim all of the town as his own personal property.

The Thayer Connection

Once I became interested in genealogy, our family's link to the Thayers of Braintree became known to me almost immediately. The main work had been carried out by the premier family historian in my mother's family, her cousin, Barbara Bates. Her work, in turn, was based in part on the extensive genealogical record of the Thayers of Braintree already compiled by others.

In 1874, Bezaleel Thayer published the first multi-generational study, or "Memorial" as he called it, of the descendants of the first two Thayers in Braintree, the brothers Thomas and Richard. In 1907, Tomas Thayer Ojeda, a Chilean descendant of the Thayers, attempted to reconstruct the successive Thayer family groups who lived in Thornbury, Gloucestershire, England, prior to the immigration of some of these Thayers to New England. In 1934, Luis Thayer Ojeda wrote a multi-generational study of William Turpin Thayer of Bellingham, Massachusetts, which also touched on the Thayer family's roots at Thornbury. Later, the early Thayers at Braintree were documented by Waldo Chamberlain Sprague in his major study of the early families of the town. This collection is now housed at the New England Historic Genealogical Society and made available on-line through the Society. Most recently, the Braintree Thayers have been extensively documented by Patricia Thayer Muno in a continuing series of volumes entitled, *A Comprehensive Genealogy of the Thayer Family of America*, which includes a particular volume focused on the descendants of Richard Thayer. (See the Sources section for details.)

Based on these many sources, the descent toward my current-day family from the original Richard at Braintree runs through the next two successive Richards, followed by John, and then Micah. Born in 1723 at Braintree, Micah Thayer married Mehitable French in 1748, French being another common Braintree surname. In 1776, their daughter, Mehitable Thayer, married John Tower of the Tower family of Hingham and Weymouth. This union produced, among others, Alexander Tower who marred Selah (also known as Celia) Pratt in 1808. Their son, Isaac Pratt Tower, went on to marry Susan Snow whose life is among those documented in Chapter 5 of this book. (The Genealogy section for this chapter provides further detail.)

The first of the Thornbury Thayers to appear in New England was Thomas, who is found on the records of Braintree when he received 76 acres of land on 24 February 1640 (Pattee, p 30). In 1641, Thomas was joined by his brother, Richard, and his eight children, following the death of Richard's wife, Dorothy (Mortimore), at Thornbury in January 1640/41. Richard bought four acres of land on what became Elm Street at Braintree, about one-third mile east of Thomas' homestead and near the Monatiquot River. He was also made a freeman of the Massachusetts Bay Colony in 1641 (Sprague's Braintree, cards 4617 and 4618).

Richard remarried in 1646 to Jane, widow of John Parker of Boston. In the latter half of the 1650s, Jane sold her house at Boston and land at Brookline, and went back to England with several of her children from her marriage to John Parker. Sprague assumes that Richard went with her. Jane appears to have died shortly after arriving in England around 1660, since not long thereafter, Richard married, for a third time, to a Katherine of whom little is known (Sprague's Braintree, card 4617; Suffolk County Deeds, hereafter SD: 3:148 and 2:303).

What is known, definitively, is that in 1660, both Richard and Katherine were in the English colony of Barbados where Richard went into the mercantile trade, shipping products such as sugar and cotton to his sons in Massachusetts for sale there. Court documents show that several of his children were involved in this trade, either in Barbados or Massachusetts (Suffolk County Court Records, hereafter SCR: 424, 455 and 828). There is no indication that the elder Richard ever returned to Massachusetts. He died at St. Michael's Parish, Barbados, no later than 1663. It is not clear how long the family carried on the trade from Barbados after Richard the elder's death, but his wife, Katherine, continued to live on the island and died there in 1687 (Sprague's Braintree, cards 4617-18; Smith, p 373; Sanders vol 1 p 350).

Among the eight children the immigrant Richard brought to America was his eldest son, Richard, who was baptized at St. Mary's Church, Thornbury, Gloucestershire, England, on 10 February 1624/25 (Faxon, NEHGR, vol 60 p 285; Smith, p 373). It is Richard, the younger, who is the principal subject of this portrait. The reason for this focus is simple. This Richard generated an almost continuous litany of litigation and controversy throughout his life, creating a paper trail that can still be examined, as he worked to acquire, by whatever means necessary, one of the most valuable commodities of the day—land.

Land in the Early Days of the English Colonies in America

The earliest English explorers and settlers in America, taking a cue from the Spanish who preceded them, came looking for riches, among them gold and silver, and a quicker route by way of the fabled Northwest Passage to another treasure trove, the spices of the Orient. In the earliest days of the first two English colonies to survive in America, Jamestown and Plymouth, land, as a commodity of value, was an afterthought. The Massachusetts Bay Colony, in which Braintree came into being, was another matter.

Jamestown was a corporate venture from the start, a company town. Everyone worked for the London-based Virginia Company that owned everything, including the land, at least from the English perspective. The original colonists were entitled to shares in the Virginia Company, to be redeemed after seven years of work. Profits were to be earned by the Company from minerals found, timber harvested, and manufactures created—all to be exported back to markets in England. As discussed in Chapter 5, Jamestown struggled mightily during its first several decades. Its settlers did not find a river to the Pacific that they initially believed to be close at hand. No precious minerals were found and no manufacturing developed of any great value.

One particular product, though, proved to be a success—tobacco. Slowly, it dawned on the Virginia colonists and their backers that the land itself was of paramount importance, particularly if that land were owned by individuals.

Gradually, the Company began distributing some of its land to individual colonists. Then they hit on the idea of franchising the product, offering large tracts of land, known as "hundreds," to the wealthy in England, in exchange for their promise to send the needed people and implements to work the ground. With the success of these privately financed estates, fueled by tobacco, a wildly popular product in England, the future of Virginia was assured (Horn and Wooley).

Plymouth of 1620 fame was, at heart, a religious venture whose leadership initially decided that all lands and material would be held in common for the good of the community. This lasted about three years. At that point, Governor William Bradford recognized that self-interest was a key to promoting financial growth. Growth was imperative since the merchant financiers, with whom the Pilgrims had cut a deal to support their expedition to the New World, had to be paid. In 1623, every Plymouth family received an acre of land per individual in their family unit. As Bradford put it:

> The experience that was had in this common course and condition, tried sundry years and that amongst godly and sober men, may well evince the vanitie of the conceite of Plato's and other ancients applauded by some of later times; that the taking away of property and bringing in community into a commonwealth would make them happy and flourishing; as if they were wiser than God. For this community (so far as it was) was found to breed much confusion and discontent and retard much employment that would have been to their benefit and comfort. (Bradford pp 120-121)

In 1627, the commonly held livestock was also divided among the Plymouth households for their own use and profit. Somewhat ironically, the arrival of the Puritan colonists in 1630 at Boston and vicinity set the stage for a decade of relative financial prosperity at Plymouth. Like any newly arrived group, the Puritans had initial difficulties in growing sufficient crops and raising enough livestock to meet the demand of their substantial numbers. The subsequent inflation in prices in the 1630s, particularly for corn and cows, allowed the Plymouth colonists to reap substantial financial benefit as individuals and families. From that point forward, the principal of individual ownership of land and other assets, and the profits to be gained from them, were well established at Plymouth.

The Massachusetts Bay Colony (called hereafter Mass Bay) was also established with strong religious principles at the forefront. There would be, however, no communal ownership of property. The principle of private ownership within the

Colony was well entrenched from the beginning. Unlike early Jamestown and Plymouth, the Mass Bay leadership had already thought carefully about the question of land, and the fact that there were already people with a claim to it—the Indian inhabitants who lived in what became the New England states. Governor John Winthrop, a trained lawyer, asserted the principle of *vacuum domicilium*, meaning that if the land had not yet been brought under European-style cultivation, it could be legitimately taken and "improved." And if the Indians were to assert their rights, then the Mass Bay folk could make "reasonable composition" with them, "that wee may avoyde the least scruple of intrusion" (Wilson pp 83-84). In the first 50 or 60 years of the life of the colony, a lengthy series of "reasonable compositions" were made with the local Indians to assure that the colonists had a legal right, at least from the English point of view, to the land they settled on.

So within no more than two decades of the beginning of English colonization of America, corporate and communal forms of land ownership were laid aside in favor of private ownership. Throughout the colonial period and beyond, land would become the major driving force behind the expansion of the initial European settlement, and later the American settlement of North America. Land was bought or stolen (or both, simultaneously) from its original Native American inhabitants and given in huge tracts to English aristocrats and rich merchants in exchange for promises of settlement. Land was also acquired by those at the other end of the social and economic hierarchy, those who would have had no hope of ever owning a square inch of land in Europe. It would become a principal source of wealth in the colonies, and also a source of an equally amazing amount of dispute and litigation, well recorded in the courts of both Plymouth and Mass Bay colonies. Richard Thayer did his level best to keep up with all those who were attempting to acquire this key commodity. In one instance, the citizens of Braintree even thought he was laying claim to the entire town.

Richard Thayer—Real Estate Holder and Land Speculator

Richard Thayer, the younger, got off to an early start in the real estate business at Braintree, thanks to his father. When Richard, the elder, married Jane Parker of Boston in 1646, he decided that he no longer needed to retain his Braintree holdings along the Monatiquot River. This area was one of the original concentrations of settlers in the town. The elder Richard had expanded upon his original four acres by buying additional land and housing from his neighbors—Moses Paine,

John Niles, and Dermon Downing. In 1648, he sold all of this for 40 pounds to his eldest son Richard. This would be the beginning of the younger Richard's real estate empire. Like his father, he continued to expand on his original purchase by buying additional land from neighbors in the Monatiquot River area. In 1663, he bought five acres of land from John Gourney and eight acres of land from George and Katherine Aldrick (or Oldredge). In 1667, he bought roughly 35 acres from Lyonell and Ellinor Wheatly. (On these transactions, see SD 5:455-460.) Some of the financial resources he used to buy these lands may have come from his share of the profits from the family's Barbados trading operations.

His initial acquisition in 1648 from his father put the younger Richard in a good position to marry. This he did on 24 December 1651, to Dorothy Pray, daughter of Quinton Pray, an ironworker who lived near the Thayer homestead. What was this ironworker doing in Braintree?

The Company of Undertakers of the Ironworks in New England, the brainchild of John Winthrop, Jr., was established in the mid-1640s. It was the first attempt in Mass Bay to produce and market locally-produced iron implements. Its operations covered several different locations in the Colony. As we have already seen, one of these ironworks operations was on the Saugus River near Lynn, Massachusetts, where Joseph Jenks, the progenitor of the Jenks family discussed in Chapter 3, was active. The other principal location was at Braintree. The Ironworks business failed in 1653 amidst allegations of financial mismanagement. The deposits of bog iron, the source material for the Ironworks, may also have been insufficient to sustain the Braintree operation. That failure set the stage for the next attempt by Richard Thayer to expand his growing real estate holdings. (On the Ironworks, see especially Hartley, as well as Bates, Holly, and Sprague.)

The proprietors of the Ironworks purchased or had allotted to them by the Colony several pieces of land to carry out its tasks at Braintree. While there has been much debate over the years regarding the precise location of some of the original Ironworks operations at Braintree, it is clear that nearly 3,000 acres of land were acquired north of the Monatiquot River to provide the timber need-ed to fuel the company's furnace and forge. When the Braintree branch of the Ironworks failed, some of this land and the associated dam built to support the company's forge as well as other structures were made available for sale, enticingly close to Richard Thayer's other real estate holdings along the Monatiquot.

One of the major investors in the Ironworks was Thomas Savage, a Boston merchant. At various times, he also held a number of significant positions in the Mass Bay government including representative from Boston to the Mass Bay Court, Commissioner of Boston, and Assistant to the Governor. He was also a leader in the Ancient and Honorable Artillery Company of Massachusetts, which he commanded in the Colony's initial response to the Indian uprising now known as King Philip's War. He was clearly a formidable member of the Mass Bay establishment. In 1653, Savage helped precipitate the bankruptcy of the Ironworks Company by calling in the debt owed him from his investment. (On Savage's life and his role in the Ironworks, see Park and Hartley.)

Seeing a great chance to profit from the Ironworks collapse, Richard Thayer bought Ironworks property from John Paine (sometimes spelled Payne), yet another merchant of Boston. On 12 September 1667, Paine and Thayer signed a deed that not only describes the purchase, but which also shows that convoluted verbiage in legal documents has a long history in this country:

> [J]ohn Paine of Boston, merchant, in consideration of a valuable sum of money . . . hath given granted bargained sold aliened enfeoffed and confirmed and by these presents do fully clearly and absolutly give grant bargain sell alien—enfeoffe confirm unto this said Richard Thayer his heires and assignes for ever, one dwelling house and coale house orchards dam with the lands adjoining thereto on the north side of the River called by the name of Manaticote, part of it formerly in the hands of Quinton Pray otherwise known by the name of the Iron works at Brantery. (SD 11:309)

The problem was that the history of this land, after the Ironworks collapse, was very complex. The title to the land that Thayer bought from Payne was murky, a common problem involving land transactions in the early days of the colony. Thayer sued and won a judgment against Payne in 1675, which required him to perfect the title (SCR 1885). Payne, however, never took action. This failure to perfect the title opened a path for Thomas Savage to make a claim over the land that Thayer had bought.

Following the financial collapse of the Ironworks Company, Savage and William Payne, John Payne's father, had acquired much of the Company's property, including its assets at Braintree. What is known of this joint acquisition seems to indicate that there was never any clear delineation regarding which man owned which assets of the former company. Taking advantage of this ambiguity, and knowing of the unresolved problems with Thayer's title, Savage made his own claim to the land that Thayer had bought from John Payne (Hartley pp 266-67). In March of 1681/82, Thayer actually got a writ of attachment for 500 pounds against Savage after arguing that Savage's attempts to gain control of the land had no legal basis. Savage's answer to Thayer's complaint was so thorough that the final verdict by the Suffolk County Court that reviewed the case was that Thayer's errors and mistakes related to this case had attainted the jury. The previous verdict was nullified. (On this case, see SCR 2053.) Savage got most of the land. Thayer's dream, of expanding his real estate holdings by buying former Ironworks property at Braintree, had come to naught at the hands of a powerful Boston merchant and politician.

In these early days of the Colony, however, there was other nearby land to be had. The town of Dorchester had been established in the first years of the Mass Bay Colony. By the 1650s, like many such early settlements, it had become over-crowded. The Dorchester selectmen then made arrangements with the Colony to expand into adjacent land in the vicinity of what was known then, and now, as the Blue Hills. As the land near the Blue Hills was allocated among members of the Dorchester population in 1657, a 500-acre plot "in a convenient place" came into the possession of Captain Roger Clapp (or Clap) of that town (Massachusetts Archives Collection, hereafter MAC: 37:372a). There was a problem, however; Josiah (or Josias) Wampatuck, the principal Sachem of the Massachusett Indians in this area, had also signed a document for the lease of a parcel of land on the south side of the Blue Hills for 100 years. The lessee was Richard Thayer (MAC 30:72). The land Thayer had leased was evidently part of the same parcel recently awarded to Roger Clapp.

Once again, Thayer was in a tangle over real estate with another prominent fig-ure in the Mass Bay Colony. Roger Clapp was at various times one of Dorchester's representatives to the Colonial Court, and he held other positions in Dorchester's local government. His major claim to fame, though, was as Captain of the Castle, a key defensive fortification on an island in Boston Harbor that still bears that name. Clapp was Captain of the Castle for 21 years. Neither he nor Thayer was interested in relinquishing his claim to the Blue Hills land. (See Strong on the life of Roger Clapp.)

Captain Clapp had enough clout to assert his control over the Blue Hills prop-erty. That action prompted Thayer to seek another document from Wampatuck.

This document of 24 October 1666 deeded the land to the Crown of England, for the benefit of one Richard Thayer with the idea being that royal power would trump colonial governance (MAC 30:131). But, to assure that this action would go nowhere, the selectmen of Dorchester engineered the signature on a new document, on 10 December 1666 that confirmed the sale of the Blue Hills land by the Indians to the selectmen of Dorchester. This sale included the land granted to Roger Clapp. The signatory on that document was the selfsame Josiah Wampatuck. In return, the Indians received a 6,000-acre plot in the Blue Hills as their own (MAC 31:24-28). So it appears in the deed. Other sources, however, indicate that this land was set aside by Dorchester in an arrangement with the Rev. John Eliot as one of the original "praying towns" for Indian converts to Christianity. Evidently, Wampatuck and Eliot had rather differing views on the purpose of this land, often called Ponkapoag.

This war of deeds settling nothing, it was time to resort to the courts. In 1678, Ephraim Tincam (or Tinkham) gave testimony that he saw Josias Wampatuck sign, seal, and deliver to Richard Thayer the deed to land in the Blue Hills (MAC 30:133). In 1680, Clapp accused Richard's son, Nathaniel, of trespassing, cutting down grass, and carting off hay from the Blue Hills land. Nathaniel was found guilty (MAC 37:373). In 1683, "Old Hahawton," a member of Wampatuck's council, along with other Indians, made a deposition stating that Richard Thayer had badgered Wampatuck into leasing him the Blue Hills land, referred to in this document as Clapp's Farm. The Indians stated further that Thayer knew it was Dorchester's land when he signed the deed (MAC 30: 275a). Wampatuck was no longer able to refute this statement having been killed in 1669 while leading an attack in New York against one of the Massachusett Indians' powerful enemies, the Mohawks. Even in his last will and testament of 1691/92, Clapp was still complaining of Thayer's interference with his Blue Hills property (MAC 37: 375-378).

As if these disputes were not enough, Richard Thayer was also experiencing significant financial problems. In 1663, and again in 1667, Thayer mortgaged the land he had acquired from his father and others, including the Ironworks land, to yet another Boston merchant, Simon Lynde. With his failure to gain clear title and access to the Ironworks and Blue Hills lands, Richard was not able to earn the income needed to pay off the mortgages. So, the land stayed in Lynde's hands. Evidently, Thayer continued to reside on his own land—as a tenant. (See SD 5:446 and 7:236.)

These events set the background for a trip to England that Richard Thayer made in 1682. His frustrations with his failures on the real estate front had reached the point that he decided to put his grievances in a petition to the English Crown that, as Sprague notes, "so alarmed the Braintree inhabitants that they sent a petition to the throne of England in rebuttal." The Braintree citizens were alarmed since they thought Richard's petition might possibly give him ownership of the town outright if it were approved. There were other Mass Bay residents who were no doubt up in arms, as well, since they were named specifically in this petition—Thomas Savage and Roger Clapp.

Thayer's Petition to Charles II and Braintree's Response

Early on in my family history search, I came across a book in an antiquarian bookstore in Georgetown, Washington, D.C.: *The History of Old Braintree and Quincy*, by William S. Pattee, MD. For some reason, the medical profession seems to have made a specialty of creating town histories in the second half of the 19th-century. Pattee's book is typical of the genre. Knowing that my ancestry was full of Braintree families, like the Thayers, I bought the book. In a section on "Land Troubles," Pattee devotes a number of pages to the brouhaha over Thayer's claims, which begins as follows: "A certain Richard Thayer, in 1682, laid claim to all the territory of the town of Braintree, by virtue of a surreptitious Indian Deed; he petitioned the King of England and obtained a hearing" (Pattee pp 40-41).

If the whole petition had been based on some fraudulent document, it is unlikely that there would have been any hearing. But the "Indian Deed," as it came to be know, was, and still is, real enough. After a detour through the Adams family archives, the Deed was turned over to the Braintree Town Clerk's office in 1858 by Charles Francis Adams. The Deed is now found in a vault in the Town Clerk's office, having been set at some point in time in an ornate wooden frame.

The 1660s seems to have been an era for setting down in writing the land transactions that had been made with the Indians in the preceding decades. Some 20 years before the Braintree deed was written, the original proprietors of Braintree had purchased the land for the town from Kickquatabut (or Chickataubut) and Sagamore John, the chief Massachusett Indian leaders in the area originally settled by the Mass Bay colonists. There was no written record of the original purchase. As the Braintree residents put it in their "remonstrance" to the King regarding the Thayer affair: "[a deed] was not thought so necessary unto Indian Conveyances until of later time" (Pattee, pp 48-49). So, in 1665, the Braintree leaders signed what would now be called a quit-claim deed with the omnipresent Wampatuck, son of Kickquatabut, and his council members: Daniel Squamog, Old Nahaton, William Manunion, Job Noistenns, Robert—alias Mamuntago, and William Hahatun. Eight Braintree residents are named in the document as acting on behalf of the town of Braintree in that original sale, including, when it comes to real estate, the ubiquitous Richard Thayer. Wampatuck signed a similar deed in the same year involving the Town of Hingham.

This "Indian Deed," between Josiah Wampatuck and his council members and the Braintree townsmen, was an insurance policy, as the Braintree citizens asserted in their remonstrance to Thayer's petition, "done to confirm the English title by writing." But in his petition to Charles II, Richard Thayer appears to treat the deed as a sales document with himself among the principal buyers. This is not surprising since, in a sense, it can be interpreted that way. Money did change hands. For his signature on this deed, Wampatuck received twenty-one pounds, ten shillings and the right to hunt and fish on the land he was giving up, "provided he do the English no harm."

In his boldly worded petition to the King, Thayer argued that Braintree itself was not really part of the Mass Bay colony at all since the colony had illegally swallowed up the town, "under pretense of an imaginary line [that] enlarged their southern boundary." Then Thayer got to the heart of the matter. By an order of a General Court, the colony, "have disposed of a great part of yo'r Peticoner's land by Capt. Thomas Savage and Capt. Clapp, now or late inhabitant of Boston."

Thayer then went on to state that, for many years, he had "been disturbed in his possessions by said Savage and Clapp," and had to defend his ownership in court, using as evidence, "His Enroled Deed from the said Wampatuck Josias." Thayer stated that the Mass Bay courts had not allowed the Deed in evidence, thus, he had appealed: "to yo'r Majesty in Councill, to the end he might obtain a fair Tryall for his said Land." But that, too, was also refused by the Mass Bay courts.

According to the petition, Thayer had come to England three years prior to this current action to put his case before the King, but was dissuaded by the colony's agents in London since they argued that he could make a new appeal to get his land back.

Yo'r Pet'r according forebore his prosecution here and returned again for New England, when, instead of restoring him, they have lately granted judgement and execution against yo'r Pet's Lands and Plantation, and have thereby dispossessed him and his wife and family of their Estates, to his bitter Ruin, without yo'r Majesty's Royall Justice and favor vouchsafed to him.

Thayer went on to make the same argument found in the document by which Wampatuck granted the disputed Blue Hills land to the Crown of England, "in favor of Richard Thayer." If the boundaries of Mass Bay didn't really include Braintree (and by implication, other lands like the Blue Hills), then the only power that could adjudicate disputes involving this land was the Crown. Therefore, Thayer argued, he had a legitimate right to request that the Crown itself redress his real estate grievances against those Mass Bay interlopers, Savage and Clapp. (For Thayer's petition, see MAC 3:34 and Pattee pp 41-43.)

On 8 December 1682, the Privy Council acted on Thayer's petition:

The King's Most Excellent Majesty in Councill, upon reading the Peticon of Richard Thare, of Braintry, in New England, complaining of the Colony of the Massachusetts Bay, for wrongfully dispossessing him of a large tract of Land in that Country, which he and others long since purchased of an Indian Sachem, on the pretence that the said Land is within the limits of their Charter or Grant, as in said Peticon is more largely expressed.

It is this day ordered by his Majesty in Councill, that a copy of the Peticon be given to the Lords of the Committee for Trade and Foreign Plantations, who are to examine the application thereof, and to report to the board how they find the same, together with their Lordships' opinion and his Majesty will declare his further pleasure. (MAC 3:34; Pattee p 43)

The Committee for Trade and Foreign Plantations wasted little time and met on this matter on 25 January 1682/83. Thayer must have been ecstatic. This Committee included: "Lord Hooper, Lord President, Earl Sunderland, Earl of Clarendon, Earl of Craven, Earl of Conway, Earl of Rochester, Lord Vic. Fauconberg, Lord London, [and] Lord Dartmouth." Now, here was a group a tad more powerful than the likes of Savage and Clapp. On 2 March 1682/83, the Committee made a recommendation in Thayer's favor. The Lords of the Council for Trade and Foreign Plantations, replying to the King and the Privy Council, recommended, that the petition be received, the town of Braintree ordered to produce an authentic copy of the Indian Deed, and that: "the government of Massachusetts Bay be also obliged to give notice to the Defendant[s], Thomas

Savage and Capt. Clapp, of said appeals, and to send to the Board such papers and Records as shall be necessary for the full decission of the Case." The King, in council, accepted the recommendation. (Documentation related to these actions can be found at: MAC 3:34; Pattee, p 44-5.)

Naturally, these developments sent the town of Braintree into a tizzy. Two town meetings were held that covered this subject: one on 5 March 1682/83, and another on 17 July 1683. At the first meeting, the attendees voted that all those who legally owned land in the town had a proper right to it, "notwithstanding any expression in the Indian Deed from Josiah Sachem." At the second meeting, a committee was created consisting of the town selectmen, Caleb Hobart and David Crosby, asking them to send an authentic copy of the Indian Deed, "according to his Majesty's order; and to consider and to doe what may be conducable for the Towne's safety." (On the town meetings, see Pattee p 41; Bates pp 20 and 22.)

In addition to sending a copy of the Indian Deed, the Braintree citizens sent a "remonstrance," a formal rebuttal of Thayer's claims, to the King (Pattee pp 46-52, citing Mass Historical Society Collection, Fourth Series, vol V p 104). While couched in the obsequious politesse by which all monarchs of the day were addressed, the remonstrance is, nonetheless, very clear as to what the Braintree inhabitants think of Richard Thayer and his petition, as this portion of the document shows:

> We do profess ourselves (upon reading and hearing a true copy) to be surprised with astonishment at the impudence and presumption of said Rich. Thayer, in dareing to approach the Royal presence for aud[i]ence with a complaint made up and composed of *notorious untruth* and *falsehood*, under which we do relieve ourselves only by the consideration of his character and condition, whereby he is notoriously known in New England to be a person too likely to be the author of such a composure, wherein he boldly and most impudently speaks that which will appear incredible, and impossible in reason to be believed when his falsehood therein shall be detected, and the truth declared, which we shall hereby endeavor to do truly and fully.

The Braintree petitioners made it clear that Richard was simply not a person of worth about whom the King should be troubled or concerned. They admitted that Richard was a citizen of the town who came there in 1641 with his father, who did manage to obtain four acres of land in, "a remote and obscure part of town." But to drive home what rascals these Thayers were, the petitioners noted: "The grantor, yet living with us, now saith he is not paid for it to this day."

The petitioners debunked Richard's claim regarding the Indian Deed, stating that Wampatuck Josias was then an old man, in his "nonage," under guardianship, and incapable of selling anything. First, this statement raises the question of the initial value to Braintree of Wampatuck's signature on the document. Secondly, if Wampatuck Josias was so decrepit in 1665, how did he manage to lead a major attack against the Mohawks in 1669 in which he died? Despite having noted that Wampatuck was incompetent, the Braintree petitioners still thought the Sachem not enough of a fool as to have sold the town outright to Richard Thayer, or any of the other townspeople listed in the Indian Deed. The Braintree petitioners argued that Wampatuck knew the actual sale of the town lands had been made years earlier, and that the land was worth far more than the twenty-one pounds, ten shillings that he received for signing the 1665 deed. The petitioners emphasized, "It cannot be imagined that we betrusted Richard Thayer to buy both ourselves and our children out of all lands and possessions, and so out of the world."

As to Richard's assertion that Braintree was a no-man's land falling between the boundaries of the Mass Bay and Plymouth colonies, and thus, subject to the rule of neither, the remonstrance asked why then, as a citizen of Braintree, had Thayer used the Mass Bay courts to adjudicate his many cases and disputes? A fair question.

This remonstrance or rebuttal was signed by 134 people from about 90-100 families from Braintree and surrounding towns; but, the citizens of Braintree weren't done yet. They sent yet another remonstrance, this one, "To Our Honored Agents, Joseph Dudley and John Richards, Esqs" (Pattee pp 52-54 citing the Mass. Gen. Hist. Register vol XIX p 53). Since the townspeople were no longer addressing His Royal Majesty, the tone became considerably blunter:

> By what (this Mr. Thayer, as your honors please to call him) is buoyed up, wee cannot see, but hee looks like a little Soveraigne here, before the power be in his hands. And of a mushrome, hee's swolne in conceipt to a Coloss, or giant of State, and dreams of a Dukedome or province, since as first essay hee hath gotten a Maister-shippe. . . . Whose cards, had they been good, hee had the less need of cheating, fraud and falsehood to help him out.

The Braintree citizens end this particular letter with the following:

> The same clemency that hath appeared in our Sovereigne, to lend an eare to a single complaint, wee hope will not be stopt at the petitions of many hundreds living, and thousands unborne, for the continuance of our wonted liberties, according to our ample charter by the Royall James and by Charles the first of blessed memory, and by our present and most celebrated Sovereigne continued, and which wee have never violated. Wee cease not day nor night to pray for his Royall p'son, our great defender under God, and for his most Honorable Council. Neither do we forget your honours, our faithful advocates, but begge the most high to secure your persons, succeed and prosper your consultations, dispatch your affaires, and hasten your returne, that thousands who at your departure disbursed floods of tears, may once at length embrace you with an ocean of joy.

In many respects, it is surprising that Richard Thayer's attempt at involving the Crown in resolving his land troubles went as far as it did. But his timing was propitious, and I suspect, premeditated. It was clearly no secret that Charles II, King of England, whose father had lost his head to the Puritan revolution in England some 33 years earlier, was no lover of the Puritan government of the Massachusetts Bay Colony. It also seems highly likely that any well-informed person would have known that there was a movement afoot in England at this time to revoke the Mass Bay charter and replace the government of the colony with a new Dominion of New England to be headed by a governor to be appointed by the Crown. So it seems Thayer chose his moment carefully, and the Crown responded, initially, as he had hoped. It notified leading members of the Mass Bay establishment that their actions, even those ratified by their highest courts, were under review, and requested that they show cause as to why those decisions shouldn't be abrogated.

I believe that Thayer never had the least expectation of gaining possession of Braintree outright. He knew very well that his wasn't the only English name on the Indian deed of 1665. Surely, he also knew the border disputes between Mass Bay and Plymouth Colony had long been resolved and that Braintree did not really fall into a no man's land between the two. What seems likely is that he was hoping for a much narrower ruling that would void Mass Bay's judgments regarding his specific land cases with Savage and Clapp and, at the most, award him the land in dispute outright, or at the least, call for a retrial of the cases under a new Crown-controlled colonial government.

In the outcome, Thayer got nothing out of his petition, although no one has yet actually found any final judgment rendered in the case. The last word we have from the Crown was given on 16 February 1682/83, when it was noted:

> His Majesty, in Councill, was pleased to approve thereof, to receive and admitt the appeal of the said Richard Thayer, and it was therefore ordered that the whole matter be heard at this board the first Councill day in Michalmas Term next, and that the matter be finally determined. (MAC 45: 187-188; Pattee pp 45-46)

Richard Thayer certainly did not end up owning the Town of Braintree, nor did he receive any relief regarding his complaints against either Savage or Clapp. While the English Crown and its Committee for Trade and Foreign Plantations would have most likely wished to render a judgment in favor of the plaintiff, they knew that they needed, at a minimum, a solid legal basis for doing so. The remonstrances prepared by Braintree, and the point-by-point refutation of Thayer's claims by the Mass Bay Colony's agents in London, dated 25 January 1682/83, systematically demolished Thayer's case. This was true despite the fact that one of those agents, Joseph Dudley, was sympathetic to the changes in the Colony's system of governance favored by the Crown. Dudley and his fellow agent, John Richards, were members of the Mass Bay establishment and no doubt knew both Savage and Clapp personally. They were not about to let the less than sound arguments of a small-time real estate speculator from Braintree undermine the social order in New England. The structure of governance might eventually be altered, as indeed it was, but not to the disadvantage of the Savages and the Clapps, as well as the Dudleys, of that era.

Aftermath

In the final analysis, the petition to the King of England produced nothing for Richard Thayer. So he returned to Braintree, but he never gave up the fight for either the Ironworks or the Blue Hills land, even after his principal antagonists were both dead.

Thomas Savage died in 1681/82, firmly in possession of a great deal of Ironworks lands, including much of what Richard Thayer had purchased from John Payne. Thayer finally managed to obtain some redress in this case by suing the administrator of John Paine's estate and winning a judgment against the estate (Sprague's Braintree, card 4620). But such a resolution was not enough for Thayer.

There were other claimants to the Ironworks land, the London-based "adventurers," the merchant financiers who had, according to their account, financed lands, buildings, mills, etc., worth many thousands of pounds and had lost a great deal of their investment when the Ironworks Company failed. Evidently, some of these people did not feel that their interests had been satisfactorily served in the dissolution of the business. So in June of 1685, James Dowy of London, Esquire, and Samuel Baker and Joseph Lyndson of London, Gentlemen, leased to Richard Thayer their interest in: "lands, waste grounds, woods, farmes, stock, etc. for one thousand years commencing from the feast day of the Nativity of St. John the Baptist last past." The yearly rent: "one peppercorn to each of the three bargainers upon the 5th day of May every year" (SD 16:42). This appears to be a frivolous piece of paper in many respects. But, once again, there appears to have been forethought given to the politics of the time that might have been turned to some advantage by Thayer.

By this time, the Dominion of New England had, indeed, come into being. The old Mass Bay charter was supplanted. The first president of the new council of the Dominion was Joseph Dudley, the same person who had acted as an Agent in London for the colony when the controversy erupted over Richard Thayer's petition to the King. By the end of 1686, a Royal Governor of the new Dominion had been appointed, Sir Edmond Andros. Among many other changes, Andros wanted to move away from fee-simple ownership of land and to establish a system of quit rents with the proceeds going to the Crown. He was proposing to review all previous deeds so that he could establish the new rents on these lands. Surely, such a review could have possibly played into Thayer's hands. (For the history of this period, see Brown and Tager pp 47-48; Muno p 279.)

This review of deeds, however, and many other actions taken by Andros did not endear him to the existing Mass Bay establishment. In 1689, King James II of England, who had succeeded Charles II in 1665, was overthrown by the Protestant William of Orange. When this became known in New England, the old magistrates of Mass Bay formed a "Council for the Safety of the People," deposed Andros, reinstalled the previous governor—the now 86-year old Simon Bradstreet—and restored the Mass Bay charter (Brown and Tager pp 47-49). So, in the final analysis, Thayer's ploy, like his petition to Charles II, gained him nothing, due this time to the changing circumstances surrounding the English throne.

As for the Blue Hills land, Roger Clapp died in 1691/92, so it was left to his widow, Joanna, and his son, Samuel, to continue the fight, which they prosecuted vigorously. They sued a whole contingent of Thayer family members in 1692 for trespass and other offenses, like burning the hay crop. Among the records from this case is an affidavit from one of Clapp's workers stating that he came upon a Thayer burning hay on the Blue Hills land. When asked why he was doing that, the Thayer in question replied that since it was his hay, he had simply decided to burn it. The Thayers lost the case (MAC 37: 375-78).

The Massachusetts Bay records also include a June 1750 petition by a group of Thayers, "proprietors of a tract of land lying on the colony or patent line run between the late colonies of Massachusetts Bay and New Plymouth in 1664." The Thayers called for settlement of an ownership dispute between themselves and other claimants. The dispute focused on whether the land actually was located in Plymouth or Suffolk County. The Thayers argued that the land had been annexed to Suffolk County, was purchased by the petitioners from an Indian Sachem called Josiah, and had been in their possession since 1668 (MAC 46: 221-3). Given the date of acquisition mentioned in the petition, it seems unlikely that this is the Blue Hills land long in dispute between the Thayers and the Clapps. Whatever land was involved, the Thayers were still pushing similar arguments to those used in Richard Thayer's petition to Charles II, undoubtedly, with the same result. The old Indian deeds had been out of favor for some time as a legal basis for making land claims. The Crown's man, Governor Andros, just before he was deposed in Massachusetts in 1689, stated in another case that Indian deeds were, "nothing worth if at all . . . no more worth than the scratch of a bare's [sic] paw" (MAC 35: 169).

As for Richard Thayer's original family holdings along the Monatiquot, Richard left his family with a legal mess. Sprague states, however, that Thayer's family was able to regain ownership of at least some of this land, by paying off the debt owed on the mortgages held by the heirs of the Boston merchant, Lynde (Sprague's Braintree, card no. 4621).

The story, as far as Richard, himself, is concerned, finally comes to an end with his death in 1695, recorded at Braintree. Despite the fact that he must have made quite a few enemies given his raucous career in the land business, he continued to live in the town. In the early days of the Mass Bay Colony, you might have found yourself expelled for what was considered religious heresy. But, trying to gain a financial or commercial advantage through the courts, or even by a rather out-rageous appeal to the Crown of England, remained within the bounds of legally permissible behavior. Richard stayed on. Either he or the family arranged for his burial in the old Hancock Cemetery in what is now, Quincy, along with many an Adams and other notables and non-notables of Old Braintree. At least in this one instance, this piece of Massachusetts real estate is one to which Richard Thayer still has claim.

Final Thoughts

First, should anyone believe that the litigious nature of American society is of recent origin, this review of Richard Thayer's real estate business in 17th-century Massachusetts thoroughly dispels that notion. He and his adversaries, and many more like them, made full use of the courts at every possible opportunity. In

Richard Thayer's gravestone located in the Hancock Cemetery,
Quincy, Mass.
Photo by the author.

fact, going to court appears to have been the contact sport of the era. If you lost the game on any given day, then you could always look forward to the next round in court to possibly give you the victory—and, if not this year, or even this generation, then perhaps the next. Clearly, when it comes to fighting it out in court, no matter how large or trivial the matter, there is nothing new under the sun in this country.

Secondly, you don't have to be a saint to be remembered. Sometimes, it is those whose lives were not so uplifting and exemplary who so enraged their neighbors that they responded by suing them in court or excoriating them in letters to the authorities of the day, ultimately preserving a record of their doings and their character in the process. Such is the stuff of family histories. There are heroes in many families, like the upstanding Sylvanus Thayer, whose deeds are rightly recorded. Then there are the odd, the outrageous, and the villains as well. Richard Thayer was no villain, but much of what he did in trying to protect his real estate interests falls under the categories of the bold and, at times, the outrageous. As such, he has earned a place, along with the upstanding and the virtuous, in the annals of his numerous descendants.

CHAPTER 5

MAN OF THE TEMPEST:
STEPHEN HOPKINS

Very early on in my research, it became clear that my family's lineage, on both my mother's and father's sides, contained lines that stretched into the early history of English colonization in New England. There were Thayers, Pratts, Frenches, Towers, Fernalds, and Jenks, whose histories took the family's roots back to the days of the Massachusetts Bay colony, and the early settlements of Maine and New Hampshire. But some lines, as always happens, ended at that infamous term in family history, the "brick wall." Such was the case with Susan Snow. The genealogies in chapters 1 and 2 of this book trace the more recent history of my mother's family to Nancy Ann Tower, wife of William Wood, and introduce Nancy Ann's parents, Isaac Pratt Tower and Susan Snow. The historian on my mother's side of the family, Barbara Bates, had long ago shown that Isaac Tower's history could be traced in a straight line to a John Tower who emigrated from England and ultimately settled in Hingham where he died in 1702. But for years, neither Barbara nor I could make headway on a very thorny question: who were the ancestors of Susan Snow? This chapter provides the answer to that question which ultimately led to Stephen Hopkins, a man who was at Plymouth in 1620 and earlier in his life, almost certainly, was at Jamestown in 1610.

The Missing Link

My first foray into the history of Susan Snow took me into one of the largest collections of genealogical data in the world, that maintained by the LDS Church. Information in this collection showed that Susan Snow was connected to a family of Snows from central Massachusetts, one of whose branches became prominent in the LDS Church and included one of its presidents, Lorenzo Snow. Susan's particular line led back through her father, Asa Snow, and his wife "Mrs. Snow." This ambiguous marriage left me with an uneasy feeling that this reading of the Snow history, at least as it pertained to me and my own extended family, might not be correct.

When I came into possession of the documents on my mother's family compiled by her Aunt Grace, I had a few journalistic clues to the solution of the puzzle. First, was a five-generation picture that includes, as the eldest, Susan (Snow) (Tower) Leach. This photo was from the local newspaper, the *Brockton Times* (of Brockton, Mass), and is noted in Chapter 2. Second, was an article from the same paper, printed around the same time, devoted to Susan Leach's 89th birthday that stated she was born on 22 December 1822 at Lyman, New Hampshire, and was one of five children of Ara Snow and Pemelia (sic) Briggs. Another set of clues came from *The History of North Bridgewater, Plymouth County, Mass, from its First Settlement to the Present Time* by Bradford Kingman, published at Boston in 1866 (p 641). Here I found the family of Ara Snow, son of Nathaniel, who "came from Douglas, Mass," and Ara's wife, Pamelia, daughter of Jacob Briggs of Norton. The family group lists six children, of whom the last is Susanna, born 22 December 1822, who married Isaac Tower of Braintree.

So, it was clear that Susan (or Susanna) Snow was not linked to the Utah Snows, but to some other Snow family. Who were these Snows? Why was Susan born at Lyman, New Hampshire, a remote (for the time), small town in the White Mountain area of New Hampshire?

I had found many graves of Susan's (or Susanna's) brothers and sisters, and her parents, Ara and Pamelia, all in the same Brockton, Massachusetts, graveyard, the Union Cemetery, not far at all from the grave of my mother's father, Leon Pennell. It was clearly a family plot, but there was no stone for Susan. I expected to find that Susan's death had occurred at Brockton. A search through some *Brockton Times* microfilm, however, turned up a very brief announcement in the 14 October 1912 edition about the death of Mrs. Susan Leach, age 98, on 13 October 1912 at Rockland. While her age was off by a decade in this announcement, it led me back to a death record in an LDS church collection of Massachusetts Deaths, 1841-1915. The image of the original death record showed that Susan had been living with her daughter, N.A. Wood, at Rockland at the time of her death, and that her birth occurred at Lyman, New Hampshire, in 1822 to Ara and Pamelia (Briggs) Snow. This record stated that she was, indeed, buried in Union Cemetery at Brockton, no doubt with the other Snows of her family.

Meanwhile, other searches identified a long line of Snows stretching back to Cape Cod, and eventually to Plymouth, ending with a Nicholas Snow who came to Plymouth on the *Anne* in 1623, only three years after the original landing in 1620. These early days have been extensively documented. That documentation revealed the connections between these Snows and other members of the Plymouth Colony, including the marriage of Nicholas Snow, the first of the line in this country, to Constance Hopkins. Constance was a Mayflower passenger, who came over in the company of her father Stephen, her stepmother Elizabeth, her brother Giles, her half-sister Damaris, and most remarkable of all, her half-brother Oceanus—a very descriptive name for a child born at sea as the *Mayflower* made its voyage from England to New Plymouth.

When it comes to the early descendants of the Stephen Hopkins family, the gold standard is actually a set of "silver books," so called for their silver covers. This is the series *Mayflower Families, Through Five Generations* by the General Society of Mayflower Descendants. The sixth volume, third edition of that set, published in 2001, provides the material on the Stephen Hopkins family. There are thousands of names in that volume, but the ones relevant to this discussion are: Stephen Hopkins himself; his daughter Constance and her husband, Nicholas Snow; their son, Mark, born 1628, and his wife, Jane Prence, daughter of a governor of Plymouth Colony, Thomas Prence; their son, Nicholas, born 1663, and his wife, Lydia Shaw; and their son, Nathaniel, born 1697, and his wife, Elizabeth Eldridge. Among Nathaniel and Elizabeth's children is Nathaniel Snow, born 1735 at Rochester, Mass, a small town just north of Cape Cod. This Nathaniel married Azubah Nickerson of another well-known Cape Cod family.

So, the question remaining was whether it was possible to link Nathaniel and Azubah (Nickerson) Snow with Ara Snow and his wife Parmelia Briggs, the parents of Susan Snow. It is Nathaniel and his wife Azubah who took their family out of southeast Massachusetts and brought them to New Hampshire, via central Massachusetts. By profession, Nathaniel was a surveyor, and what better place for a surveyor than on new lands just being settled. The family migrated first from Rochester to the town of Douglas in central Massachusetts. A property deed at Douglas in 1761 conveyed land from Josiah (no surname given) to Nathaniel Snow of Rochester (Worcester Registry of Deeds, Book 48, p 40). Further references to a Nathaniel Snow at Douglas are given in the *History of the Town of Douglas, Mass. through 1878* by William Emerson, published at Boston in 1879. Emerson states that Douglas formed its revolutionary era Committee of Safety and Correspondence on 11 March 1776 with Nathaniel Snow as a member, and that a Nathaniel Snow was also a Selectman of the town.

Assuming that this is the same Nathaniel Snow that bought land at Douglas in 1761, then the family may have resided in the area from as early as 1761 through at least 1776. There are six known children of Nathaniel and Azubah: Ara, Azubah, Jerusha, Mahala (or Elizabeth), Nathaniel, and Ono, and possibly, one other, Ezra. The approximate dates of their births, ranging from 1762 to 1775, would indicate that they may all have been born at Douglas or environs. For whatever reason, there are no vital records extant of these births at Douglas. Kingman's book, however, shows that Ara, son of Nathaniel, came from Douglas, Mass. On 19 December 1863, Ara Snow died, aged 96 years, 7 months, 12 days, as recorded in a brief announcement in the *North Bridgewater Gazette* of Tuesday, 29 December 1863. The Massachusetts vital record for this death at Brockton (North Bridgewater in 1863) shows that Asa (or Ara) Snow, died of old age, at 96 years, 7 mos, 13 days. His place of birth is listed as "Douglas (Inc ?)," and his parents are listed as Nathaniel and Azubah. This definitive linkage of Ara to his parents in a vital record is the last missing link in the chain of thirteen generations from this author to Stephen Hopkins.

By the late 1780s, New Hampshire records show that Nathaniel Snow and his family moved on from Douglas to northern New Hampshire (Hammond pp 190-193, Kilbourne p 60, and Welsh pp 34-35). The 1810 U.S. Census places Azubah Snow at Bethlehem, New Hampshire, as a widow, thus presumably, Nathaniel Snow died in that area prior to 1810. The Baptist Church of Bethlehem listed Azubah as a member in 1822. No other known record documents her life after that date (Beals pp 233-236).

The children of Nathaniel and Azubah continued to live in the region for a time, and some of them settled there permanently. Ara appears frequently in the early town and tax records of Bethlehem, and then moves on to Lyman, New Hampshire, sometime after 1810. An 1814 inventory of residents lists Ara, as well as Calvin and Sylvester Briggs, brothers, whose father, Jacob, applied for a Revolutionary War pension at Lyman in 1818. It is highly likely that Jacob had a daughter who was also living in the area at that time, Parmelia (or Pamelia). It is also highly likely that Ara Snow and Parmelia Briggs were married in one of these towns in the White Mountains of New Hampshire around 1810, although no record of that marriage has yet been found. Eventually, there would be six children of this marriage: Pamelia, Ara, Thomas Hale, Jerusha, Jacob Cheney, and Susan (or Susanna). The town records of Lyman, New Hampshire, confirm that at least four of Ara Snow's children were born in New Hampshire: Pamelia at Bethlehem, and Ara, Thomas H., and Jerusha, all born at Lyman (*Records of the Town of Lyman, NH*, p 136). Jacob Snow's Civil War records (National Archives) indicate that he was born at Lyman in 1821. As noted, Susan's death record states that she was born there also, in the following year of 1822.

No later than 1830, the elder Ara Snow and wife, Parmelia, both originally from Massachusetts, moved south again with many members of their family, eventually coalescing around what is now Brockton, Mass (U.S. Census, 1830, North Bridgewater, Mass). Finally, the parents, many of the children, and other members of the extended family were buried in the family plot at the Union Cemetery at Brockton. Given this convoluted path, it is not surprising that the connections between these Snows in a graveyard at Brockton, their progenitor, Nicholas, who came to Plymouth in 1623, and Nicholas's connection to the Hopkins of Plymouth, were lost to later generations such as my own. What do we know about this Hopkins family into which Nicholas married?

<u>Two Stephen Hopkins or One?</u>

The existence of a Stephen Hopkins and family on the Mayflower and at New Plymouth in 1620 is well documented. The existence of a Stephen Hopkins as a member of the Third Supply group headed to Jamestown in 1609 is also a known fact. The question is, are these two Hopkins one and the same?

The religious dissidents who formed the core of the *Mayflower* company were no more prepared to be colonists and live off the land on their arrival in America than the settlers at Jamestown in 1607. Many of the families in the initial group to arrive at Plymouth had spent over ten years in Holland, attempting to escape persecution from the established church in England and its governmental supporters. They were not explorers or soldiers. Many of them earned their living in Holland as weavers. So, it is not surprising that they should take along with them a number of "strangers" or "Londoners," those not of their religious persuasion, but who had needed practical skills for use in the new settlement. They recruited men like Miles Standish, who was a soldier by profession and knew how to organize people and materials for the defense they reckoned they would need. The well-known John Alden was a cooper. Stephen Hopkins was also a stranger. Why did they include him and his family in their company? Most likely because he had an even rarer set of skills. A trail of largely circumstantial evidence links the Stephen Hopkins of Plymouth Colony to the Stephen Hopkins of the early days of the Virginia Colony via the famous wreck of the *Sea Venture*, the flagship of the Third Supply voyage to Jamestown. If this is the case, then Hopkins already knew something of the life of a colonist in the New World and, most likely, had had some dealings with the local inhabitants of the land, the Native Americans. Such a man would, potentially, be of great use as the Pilgrims set out on their voyage in 1620.

The case for Hopkins of Jamestown being the same man as Hopkins of Plymouth has been taken up by a number of well-known genealogists. Caleb Johnson supports the case in his article, "The True Origins of Stephen Hopkins of the Mayflower," published in the American Genealogist, vol 73 (July 1998) and in his book, *Stephen Hopkins, Here Shall I Die Ashore*, pp 143-159. John D. Austin, in *Mayflower Families Through Five Generations—Stephen Hopkins Family*, p 1, states: "Stephen [of the *Mayflower*] was undoubtedly the man of that name who served as minister's clerk on the vessel *Sea Venture*, which sailed from London 2 June 1609, bound for Virginia." Robert Charles Anderson, in his 2004 book, *The Pilgrim Migration*, notes that Caleb Johnson's discovery of Stephen Hopkins family at Hursley, Hampshire, England, "strengthens the argument that this was the same Stephen Hopkins who was the minister's clerk on the vessel *Sea Venture*, which met with a hurricane in 1609 while on a voyage to Virginia" (Anderson p 274).

The most compelling evidence of the connection for me is how the Pilgrims made use of Stephen Hopkins once they reached America, which is documented by his contemporaries, Bradford and Winslow of Plymouth Colony. On nearly every early encounter with the Native Americans, Hopkins was present. It is Hopkins and Standish who first greeted the Sachem Massasoit when he made his first appearance at the colony. The Indian, Squanto, lodged in the Hopkins home on many of his frequent visits. Hopkins and Edward Winslow made the first trip to meet Massasoit in his home village of Pokanoket, as is quite amusingly described in the book known as *Mourt's Relation* (see Sources, Chapter 5). Most telling, I believe, is Edward Winslow's account, as recorded in *Mourt's Relation*, of Hopkins' identification of a device (an Indian snare) found by the Pilgrims on their very first trip ashore near Provincetown. According to Winslow, no sooner had Hopkins finished his explanation of the device than William Bradford blundered into it and became the object lesson that proved the correctness of Hopkins' words. Why would the Pilgrim leadership make such use of Hopkins in their relations with the Indians and how would he know about this type of Indian trap unless he had some prior knowledge of Native American life? And, where would he gain such knowledge if not at Jamestown? To me, it is Hopkins' actions in the first several years at Plymouth that are the best evidence that he is the same Stephen Hopkins who, a decade earlier, was at Jamestown. (See Johnson.)

Stephen Hopkins—Beginnings

The most recent research by Caleb Johnson shows that Stephen Hopkins was baptized on 30 April 1581 at Upper Clatford, Hampshire, England, the son of John and Elizabeth (Williams) Hopkins. The family moved from Upper Clatford to the city of Winchester where John Hopkins died in 1593. Nothing of any substance is known about Stephen's childhood after his father died when Stephen was age 12. He resurfaces in the town of Hursley in Hampshire where his daughter, Elizabeth, was baptized in 1605, with the record showing Stephen's wife's name as Mary. In 1606, Stephen and Mary baptized another child, Constance (sometimes called Constanta), and in 1608, they baptized a son, Giles, both at Hursley. Records show that shortly after Giles' baptism, on 19 May 1608, Stephen's lease on a manor in Hursley was revoked, and the family was put in a tough spot. What to do? (On the Hopkins family in England, see Johnson pp 161-171.)

When next we hear of Stephen Hopkins, he is in Bermuda in late 1609. The chain of islands we call Bermuda wasn't known then as the blue skies-sandy beaches island resort of today. Rather, it was an uninhabited series of small islands in the Atlantic, some 600 miles off the North American coast, with a ferocious reputation, often called the Isle of Devils. Hopkins was there as a result of the shipwreck of the flagship of a total of nine ships, known as the Third Supply, on their way in 1609 to the Virginia Colony's Jamestown settlement. Stephen's presence as a member of the Third Supply on the *Sea Venture*, and his role in subsequent events on Bermuda, is attested to by one of the chroniclers of that voyage, William Strachey, a "gentleman" and writer who would become for a time the Secretary to the Council of the colony at Jamestown.

The Virginia Company of London and the Settlement of Jamestown

England was a slow starter in the race to discover, document, and colonize the New World. All the Europeans of Hopkins' time knew that the Spanish, following in the wake of Columbus, had found fabulous wealth in gold and silver in Central and South America. But, although they laid claim to all of it, the Spanish reach on the still largely unexplored landmass to the north stopped at Florida. The French were making inroads with a series of explorations much further north and had the beginnings of settlements in what is now eastern Canada.

The English did know a bit about this territory, however. By the mid-1500s, they were regularly sending fleets of fishing boats to the Grand Banks of the northern Atlantic. Those trips put them in touch with Newfoundland. The soldier and adventurer, Sir Humphrey Gilbert, had letters patent from the English Crown to set a colony in this northern territory; he sailed with a fleet in 1583 to claim Newfoundland for England. No permanent settlement took place and Gilbert, and his ship, *Squirrel*, were lost on the return voyage. Gilbert's half-brother, Sir Walter Raleigh, made another attempt at colonization, this time at a more tolerable latitude, on Roanoke Island in present-day North Carolina. Famously, the inhabitants of Roanoke were found to have disappeared en masse when ships returned to resupply this little outpost.

These early settlement efforts were underwritten by wealthy members of the English aristocracy with the permission of Queen Elizabeth I. Elizabeth, however, was no great enthusiast. Thus, none of these ventures were undertaken or financially backed by the Crown itself.

A different mood prevailed following the death of Elizabeth in 1603. The Scottish James VI became James I of England. He made peace with the Spanish, thereby putting out of work a great many soldiers and sailors who had been for many years employed in fighting Catholic Spain and Ireland on behalf of Protestant England. So, a ready-made source of tough, battle-hardened leaders and troops was on hand to support a renewed colonizing effort. The merchant class, many of whom had been enriched by their efforts in the East Indies and elsewhere, now had capital of their own to back new ventures. James I was also somewhat more favorably disposed than Elizabeth had been toward such risky ventures, although no more ready to financially underwrite them.

In April 1606, King James granted a royal charter that created two joint-stock companies, the Virginia Company of Plymouth and the Virginia Company of

London. The Plymouth group was backed in particular by Sir John Popham, at various times Speaker of the House of Commons and Chief Justice of the Queen's Bench. In 1607, this group attempted a colony at the mouth of the Kennebec River in what is now the state of Maine, known either as the Sagadahoc or Popham Colony. This venture, however, did not survive a year. The Virginia Company of London, backed by powerful merchants such as John Smythe (not to be confused with Capt. John Smith), was more successful or at least more persistent.

By December 1606, the London group had readied a fleet of three ships, the *Susan Constant*, the *Discovery*, and the *Godspeed*, destined to plant a colony in the Chesapeake Bay area. Their departure was delayed by bad weather until February, but they managed to bring 104 settlers to the Chesapeake on 26 April 1607. The colonists found a small neck of land up what they named the James River that flowed into the western shore of the bay. This location appeared easily defensible and had deep water near it so that the English could dock their ocean-going vessels right next to the settlement. The ground, however, was also swampy, and the ground water brackish, which would cause them no end of problems in the future. In fact, for the next fifteen years at least, the settlement would see dissention, disease, hunger, famine, and death at levels that would make living there a major challenge in the best of times, and in some years, an outright horror.

Why was this attempt at colonization so often bordering on disaster? First of all, there were huge conflicts over the colony's purpose. The merchants and aristocrats who put up the money were looking for quick financial returns. If the Spanish had found gold and silver in Central and South America, why not in North America? Perhaps just beyond the Appalachian Mountains that could be seen not far from the coast, lay the fabled passage to India, a quicker route to the Spice Islands of Asia. Much time and many lives in the early days of the colony were spent searching for that gold, silver, and a passage to India, to no avail. When it became apparent that such riches were just not to be had in any quantity in eastern North America, then what? There were timber and other natural products that might do. Exploiting such natural resources at a commercial level would have required a labor force far beyond that which could be financed in the colony's early days. So, if commerce and trade were not sufficient justifications, then there were geopolitical and religious reasons as well. If the "naturals" in the area could be converted to England's prevailing form of Christianity, then a good excuse for the colony was the creation of a Protestant bulwark of English and

Native Americans against further incursion northward by the dastardly Spanish Catholics. This panoply of purposes, and, above all, the search for quick profits, would lead to confusion and disaster in the colony's early years.

One small problem with the idea of converting the "naturals" was that, for the most part, they weren't having it. The Native Americans residing in that part of the Chesapeake Bay area in which the English had landed had recently confederated under a strong leader, Wahunsonacock, known to the English as Powhatan. In the first years of the colony, these "naturals" may have seen the English as a good potential source of labor on *their* behalf, or simply hoped that they would tire of the place and go home. When that did not happen, then they sporadically made their best efforts to make the English colonists' lives miserable by restricting their access to local food sources, and on several occasions, made a concerted effort to wipe them out. An Anglo-Native American Protestant alliance against Catholic Spain in North America was not to be.

Food was a constant problem for the colonists. In the early days, those who came out to Virginia did so to get rich from all the minerals or other valuable materials they would find. They did not bring sufficient farming equipment to produce enough food to support themselves when their imported food stocks began to run out. Also, their labor force initially consisted of many "gentlemen" who didn't know one end of a hoe from another, and who had no interest in learning. The military men who often led them, and the sailors who brought them, didn't know anything about farming either. The colonists' idea was to trade with the Indians for needed food, and if they didn't play ball, to extort food from them by force. Was it any wonder that the Indians would often retaliate by undermining the settlers' meager efforts at agriculture? To boot, the colonists arrived in the initial year of a severe seven-year drought that created food shortages for everyone, Native American and English colonists alike.

So, the settlers were constantly battling the natural environment and were frequently battling the Native Americans in the neighborhood. The largest problem, however, was that those in leadership positions were continuously battling each other. There were many close relatives of various earls and other members of the aristocracy who were recruited to go to Jamestown to make their fortune. Also, among the early leaders were many, like John Smith, who had literally fought their way into the ranks of the gentry by their military service to the crown in the Spanish-controlled Netherlands, or in Ireland. Then there were the admirals and captains of the sea, who were also a tough lot in their own right. Many of them like the well-known one-armed Christopher Newport, had spent many years as "privateers"— government-sanctioned pirates. They had little use for landlubbers of all stripes, including their military counterparts on the land. The origins and motivations of some of the first leaders of the colony are lost in a mist of suspicion and intrigue, some of it created on the ground in Virginia, and some generated by their powerful backers in England who had their chosen minions designated to the council at Jamestown that governed the colony's day-to-day business.

That council became the ideal administrative structure for disaster—seven men selected by the colony's backers in London who would select their own President. The members of the first such council were unknown until the original colonists arrived in Virginia. Some of the "gentlemen" not selected for the council thought they should have been, and did their best to undermine the work of those who were selected. Those selected bickered and fought with each other at practically every opportunity. On occasion, there would be a putsch. John Smith was at one time imprisoned and sentenced to be hanged by his successor as President and was saved only by the timely arrival of a ship captained by Christopher Newport. Newport evidently thought well enough of Smith, or poorly enough of those who had usurped his position, to save him. Later on, although no one knows really what happened, there is strong suspicion that some of his enemies arranged to throw a lighted match into the sleeping Smith's lap while aboard a boat, igniting his powder bag, severely injuring him, and forcing his return to England.

Due to all of these factors, at the time of the organization of the Third Supply fleet in 1609, the colony was slipping into the abyss. Near anarchy prevailed in the leadership. Food stocks were largely gone and the "naturals" had the Jamestown area blockaded. Those who attempted to leave the confines of the stockaded Jamestown fort were sometimes set upon and killed. Others managed to find their way over to the Indians who knew better how to live off the land. For those who stayed at Jamestown, the lack of food, fresh water, and resulting disease were rapidly carrying them off. The remaining settlers were reduced to eating their livestock, rats, and anything that moved. Finally, they resorted to eating some things that did not move anymore, the bodies of the dead. Like Roanoke before it, the colony was on the verge of vanishing. Where was the fleet of the Third Supply?

The Third Supply Fleet and the Wreck of the *Sea Venture*

By 1609, it was common knowledge that life at Jamestown was no picnic. Writings by John Smith and others were in circulation that spoke to the colony's deficiencies in no uncertain terms. The financiers of the venture, particularly the merchant class, had other writers who were painting a different picture. Corporate advertising is not a new art. Also, there were many of the clergy who were playing up the idea of saving the local population from their pagan ways as a worthwhile endeavor. While it was a tough sell in some respects, the idea of a new life in a new world was still enticing to many who were poor and destined to be always landless, or to the eighth son of an earl looking to make his own way, or to the true adventurers who could be enticed into the endeavor simply for the thrill of it. For such reasons, a fleet of nine ships was carrying about 600 colonists and a new round of supplies for the colony when it finally got underway on 8 June 1609.

The Colony's leadership in London had seen by this time that the council method of government was an abject failure. So, the London leaders had just appointed Thomas West, the Lord De La Warre, governor for life. Other business detained him in England, however. So the newly appointed Deputy Governor, Thomas Gates, was making the trip to lead the colony until De La Warre could make an appearance. Gates was of the soldierly class, having distinguished himself in the fighting in both Holland and Ireland. The Admiral of this fleet of nine ships was George Somers, a long-time leader in the British Navy, who had also served on ships in the East India Company. The Captain of the flagship, *Sea Venture*, was the old pirate, Christopher Newport, who had already made two voyages to Jamestown. For some reason, all of these leaders sailed on the flagship. Among the gentlemen on board were: the writer, William Strachey, who was expecting to write a book on the colony that would make his reputation, and get him out of debt; the new minister for the colony, Rev. Richard Bucke; and a man who came to play the role of Rev. Buck's assistant, reading scriptures and the like at services—Stephen Hopkins.

This fleet was to take a new, more northerly route across the Atlantic that would be faster, it was hoped, and would stay largely clear of the Spanish territories in the Caribbean. That route was being pioneered, as the Third Supply fleet assembled, by another veteran of cross-Atlantic voyages, Captain Samuel Argall. For nearly two months, the fleet made its way across the Atlantic in near perfect conditions with all nine ships usually within sight of one another. But as the ships collectively neared the North American coast, conditions began to change. Black, threatening clouds gathered, and on 24 July 1609, the fleet found itself in the midst of a major Atlantic weather phenomenon, called by the name of a Carib Indian god—a hurricane. Strachey referred to this as "a dreadful storm and hideous." By the 25th, Strachey wrote, "yet did we still find it [the storm] not only more terrible but more constant, fury added to fury, and one storm urging a second more outrageous than the former." The *Sea Venture* was towing a ketch, a small sailing ship, with about 20 crewmen and others aboard. Somers knew that in the raging storm, if the ketch went down, it could easily take the *Sea Venture* with it. He ordered it cut loose. No one ever saw this boat or its passengers again. All sails were struck as the helmsman did his best to keep the *Sea Venture* from turning into the wind and "turning turtle" which would be the end. (The story of the *Sea Venture* is from William Strachey's letter, "Wreck and Redemption of Sir Thomas Gates, Knight," circulated privately in London in 1610/11 and first published by Samuel Purchas in *Purchas His Pilgrimes*, London, 1625; reprinted by Johnson pp 175-220.)

In the midst of this disaster, the *Sea Venture* began to leak. By the time the leakage was discovered, the hold had five feet of water in it. Gates organized three crews of every able-bodied soul to man the pumps and bail fore, aft, and amid-ships. This was kept up constantly, with little or no food, most of which was soaked, and none of which could be prepared under these conditions. At one point, the entire ship was inundated by an enormous wave, but it stayed afloat. Still, the level of water in the hold increased and the ship began to list. So rigging, trunks, cannon, and whatever could be moved went over the side.

On the fourth day of this battle, with the ship still taking on water, and no way of knowing where they were, everyone was about to give up. Then, Somers, still at his post in command of the vessel, spied an anomaly on the horizon. He waited until he had a better view and then raised the shout—"land." On Friday, July 28th, with the storm finally abating, Somers, Newport, and the crew managed to ground the ship on a reef a half-mile off the coast of what is now known as St. George's Island in the Bermuda chain. Miraculously, the ship came to rest between two coral heads in such a way that it remained upright. If it hadn't, all would have drowned since no one of that day, including the sailors, knew how to swim. Instead, the sailors lowered the small boats, and all 150 men and women (there were a few on board) reached shore, as did the ship's dog.

The *Sea Venture* itself was a wreck, but passengers and crew were safe. One small problem, however—they were roughly 600 miles from the Virginia coast on a set of uninhabited islands that few mariners had ever visited because of their reputation. First, the fringing reefs were a lurking disaster for ships. Secondly, some of the birdlife made strange sounds that gave the islands a feeling of being haunted; thus, the name, the Isle of Devils.

These colonists and their leaders knew that there was almost no hope of rescue. So, if no one would come to them, then they would have to find their own way out. They reinforced one of the ship's small boats, making it as sea-worthy as could be and then dispatched it under the master mate, Henry Ravens, with six sailors and one settler in an attempt to reach Jamestown to get help. Those on Bermuda hoped that within a matter of several months, their rescue would be affected. Ravens, his crew and the little boat were never seen again. By November, the *Sea Venture* leaders recognized they must try another tack and actually build a ship or two of their own that would take them all off the island to Jamestown.

By this time, the disease of dissention that seemed to affect anyone who had anything to do with Jamestown began to raise its head among the members of this shipwrecked band who, one would think, would have cooperated as closely as possible in order to get off the island. The first incident was a fight among the sailors that left one man dead. Gates quickly condemned the murderer to death, which he later commuted. Thus, began a rift between Gates and the sailors, and possibly with Somers himself. Several other attempts at mutiny followed.

Why these rebellions? Gates had a writ to reach Jamestown and relieve it. He was a soldier, the Colony's new acting Governor, and he was bound to obey orders. But, first of all, they were not in the territory of the Virginia Colony. So, what authority did Gates, or the Colony, have on Bermuda? Secondly, everyone knew that the conditions at Jamestown were hard. (If they had known exactly how hard, perhaps these rebellions might have been prosecuted more vigorously.) Bermuda, on the other hand, turned out to be quite a forgiving place. It was relatively temperate. Fresh water was available. Further, the food stocks turned out to be tremendous: wild pigs left over from prior Spanish visits to the islands, innumerable types of fish, sea turtles, fruits, and birds of many kinds. One bird, the cahow, was the one that made the sort of cries that gave the Bermudas their haunted reputation. The colonists discovered, however, that with the right type of noises made, called "low-belling," these birds would walk right up to you begging to be dinner. So why leave? Why not claim this bounteous land for England and be the first colonists? Given the generally benign conditions, this was an enticing idea.

As it turned out, one of those who had such rebellious thoughts was Stephen Hopkins. In a long letter addressed to an "Excellent Lady," probably a hoped-for benefactor, William Strachey wrote of the wreck of the *Sea Venture*, and among other things, Hopkins' plot:

> Yet could not this [a previous plot] be any warning to others, who more subtly began to shake the foundation of our quiet safety, and therein did one Stephen Hopkins commence the first act or overture: a fellow who had much knowledge in the Scriptures, and could reason well therein, whom our minster therefore chose to be his clerk, to read the psalms, and chapters upon Sundays, at the assembly of the congregation under him: who in January the twenty-four, brake with one Samuel Sharpe and Humfrey Reede (who presently discovered it to the Governor) and alleged substantial arguments, both civil and divine (the Scripture falsely quoted) that it was no breach of honesty, conscience, nor religion to decline from the obedience of the governor, or refuse to go any further led by his authority (except it so pleased themselves) since the authority ceased when the wreck was committed, and with it, they were all then freed from the government of any man; and for a matter of conscience, it was not unknown to the meanest, how much we were therein bound each one to provide for himself, and his own family: for which were two apparent reasons to stay them even in this place; first, abundance by God's Providence of all manner of good food; next, some hope in reasonable time, when they might grow weary of the place, to build a small bark, with the skill and help of the aforesaid Nicholas Bennett, [a sailor involved in one of the earlier mutinies], whom they insinuated to them, albeit he was now absent from his quarter [a number of the rebellious sailors had left the colonists and were in hiding] . . . so they might get clear from hence at their own pleasures: when in Virginia, the first would be assuredly wanting, and they might well fear to be detained in that country by the authority of the commander thereof, and their whole life to serve the turns of the adventurers with their travails and labors. (quoted in Johnson pp 195-196)

Strachey was a great supporter of Gates. So it is no surprise that he was no advocate of Hopkins' point of view. In historical hindsight, however, it appears that Hopkins had it about right. Of course, having been informed of the plot, there was no way that Gates could let Hopkins' rebellion stand:

> [I]t pleased the governor to let this his factious offence to have a public af-
> front, and contestation by these two witnesses [Sharpe and Reede] before the
> whole company, who (at the tolling of the bell) assembled before a *corps de
> garde*, where the prisoner was brought forth in manacles, and both accused, and
> suffered to make at large, to every particular, his answer; which was only full of
> sorrow and tears, pleading simplicity, and denial. But he being only found, at
> this time, both the captain and the follower of this mutiny, and generally held
> worthy to satisfy the punishment of his offence with the sacrifice of his life,
> our governor passed the sentence of a martial court upon him, such as belongs
> to mutiny and rebellion. But so penitent he was, and made so much moan,
> alleging the ruin of his wife and children in this his trespass, as it wrought upon
> the hearts of all the better sort of the company, who therefore with humble en-
> treaties, and earnest supplications, went unto our governor, who they besought
> (as likewise did Captain Newport and myself) and never left him until we had
> got his pardon. (quoted in Johnson, p 196)

While Hopkins may have, "wrought upon the hearts of the better sort of the
company," it probably did not hurt that he was not an indentured servant or a
laborer, but most likely of the minor merchant class, well known to everyone
because of his reading of the Scriptures on the voyage. Whatever the reasons, the
pleas of the gentlemen of the company got him off.

While Gates eventually let Hopkins off the hook, he finally did carry out a
death sentence on one man of the higher class in the last of this series of mutinies,
when Gates recognized that he would lose his authority if he didn't enforce one of
his own edicts. Arguing his gentlemanly status, Henry Paine did manage to con-
vince Gates to alter his punishment from hanging to being shot. Strachey notes,
"and towards the evening he had his desire, the sun and his life setting together."

On to Jamestown

Gates had his writ. He would reach Jamestown. In the final analysis, Somers
agreed, although he had spent a fair amount of time surveying the Bermuda
islands, drawing a detailed map, and perhaps harboring ideas about staying there
himself. So while Gates and his crew labored on what would eventually become
the *Deliverance*, some 60 feet long and 20 feet wide at the beam, Somers and
his sailors built a much smaller vessel, the *Patience*. On these two little ships,
all the remaining colonists (a few had died there, including two children born
on the island) and crew set sail on the 10th of May, 1610, bound for Jamestown
more than nine months after coming to ground in Bermuda. There were three

exceptions—sailors who opted to take their chances on Bermuda. These three had been involved in one way or the other in the plots to stay on the island and they got their wish. Two of these sailors were later named to the governing council of the British colony on Bermuda. It took all of about two years before the London merchants and aristocrats managed to get a revised Virginia charter that encompassed Bermuda, and to create a settlement there, thanks to the wreck of the *Sea Venture* on its shores in 1609. George Somers' son was a principal mover in this effort.

Meanwhile, while work was going forward on Bermuda to get the castaways off the island, every other ship of the Third Supply, with the exception of the *Sea Venture* itself and the little ketch it had towed, reached Jamestown. Some of the ships were dismasted and some had experienced heavy loss of life. For the most part, however, these arrivals only compounded the colony's travails since most of the food they carried had already been eaten or was ruined, and most of the equipment was aboard the lost *Sea Venture*. Several of these ships returned to England with a number of would-be colonists. The bickering and dissension among the colony's leadership continued since Gates was in Bermuda, and with him, the fiat that would give him one-man rule over the colony. It must have been an incredulous sight for the remaining starving settlers of Jamestown, when Gates, Somers, Newport, and the balance of the *Sea Venture* crew and passengers, with very few losses, showed up on their doorstep on 23 May 1610.

The arrival of all these people, with little food and few supplies with them, only added to the likelihood of a greater disaster—starvation. In a matter of days, Gates, with his new authority as the Acting Governor, came to the only logical conclusion under the circumstances—abandon the colony. He would not sanction the burning of Jamestown though, and Gates was the last one on board the departing vessels to assure that this did not happen as they all left on the 7th of June. The plan was to sail up the North American coast to attempt a rendezvous with English fishing vessels that could help with feeding the departing colonists and getting them back to England. In one of the amazing coincidences that are a hallmark of early Jamestown, at the entrance to the Chesapeake Bay, they met another English vessel carrying, of all people, the new Governor of the Colony, Lord De La Warre, and a new group of settlers with new supplies. De La Warre ordered the return to Jamestown which, I suspect, may have hastened the deaths of a number of old settlers who had had their hearts set on returning to England after all the horrors they had experienced.

During the remainder of the first fifteen years of the colony, this pattern would be repeated continuously. More colonists and supplies would appear in ships out of England. Most of them would die because of the harsh conditions, disease, depredations from those whose land they took, and above all, poor leadership. In 1622, after a number of years of truce, the Native Americans under Opechancanough, who succeeded Wahunsunacock, staged a major coordinated attack throughout the several settlements of the colony that killed over 300 settlers and was clearly designed to wipe them all out. This attack, in fact, sealed the fate of the Native Americans in the Chesapeake region since it provided an excuse to take no quarter and push them off the land without mercy. Around this time also, James I decided to put the full force of the Crown behind the colonial effort at Jamestown and turn the venture into a royal one, assuring that it would continue and that more funds, people, and supplies would flow to the slowly expanding colony. Despite all the trials, hardships, and horrors, there was always someone new who was willing to risk everything to make something of themselves in this "new" land. Eventually, some, and then more and more of them succeeded.

William Strachey, he of the long letter concerning the wreck of the *Sea Venture*, thanks probably to the close relationship he had developed with Thomas Gates, stayed on at Jamestown for several years and became the Colony's Secretary. His letter concerning the wreck was sent back to England soon after his arrival at Jamestown. It circulated privately in London's elite circles and eventually came to the attention of the writers of the day, including one William Shakespeare. There is no doubt that Strachey's sensational letter is a source of one of Shakespeare's last plays, *The Tempest*. The play is set on an island following a shipwreck. *The Tempest* is replete with passages that tie closely with Strachey's narrative. It includes a drunken character named Stephano who plots with the savage, Caliban, and the jester, Trinculo, to kill Prospero, the master of the island, and seize it for themselves. Whether this particular passage in the play is based on Strachey's account of Hopkins' mutiny is unknowable, but there is obviously a strong resemblance. Eventually, Strachey returned to England, never to be a major writer. He died a pauper.

Stephen Hopkins also was not one of those who succeeded long-term at Jamestown. His time in the colony is not documented which is no great surprise.

Given his attempt at fomenting rebellion against Gates on Bermuda, he must have been somewhat of a *persona non grata*, at least among the gentry. On the other hand, he was clearly a tough sort who had survived a hurricane, and undoubtedly, the colony needed every able-bodied soul in these dark days to stave off further disaster. He probably participated in the frequent trips around the Chesapeake Bay to search for food or new areas for settlement. His actions later at Plymouth suggest that he had contact with the Indians surrounding Jamestown and became acquainted with their way of life. Perhaps he was forced to stay and work in order to earn passage back to England. Hopkins may have learned at some point that his wife, Mary, had died in 1613 and knew that his children would be at risk without him. So, eventually he returned to England, although precisely when is not known. We do know he was there by 19 February 1617/18 because on that date he married again, this time to Elizabeth Fisher, at Whitechapel, Middlesex.

Stephen and his family next appear in a home in London, ". . . just outside the London Wall on the highroad entering the city at Aldgate in the vicinity of Heneage House. In this neighborhood lived: John Carver and William Bradford of the *Mayflower* company; Robert Cushman, the London agent for the Pilgrims, and Edward Southworth, whose widow and sons later came to New England" (Austin p 2). Whether it was one of the Pilgrims themselves, like Carver, or more likely, one of their commercial associates, like Cushman, who initially asked Hopkins to make the trip, no one knows. Incredibly, after the disaster on Bermuda and the horror and travails at Jamestown, Hopkins accepted the offer to do it all over again, as one of the "Londoners" or "strangers," those who were not part of the Pilgrim congregation. But this time, he chose not to be separated from his family. All those in the family still living made the voyage: "Master" Stephen Hopkins (as he was called); his pregnant wife, Elizabeth; children from his first marriage, Constance and Giles; his daughter, Damaris, from his marriage to Elizabeth; and two servants, Edward Doty and Edward Leister.

The Pilgrim Community: England, Holland and the New World

The impetus behind the voyage of the *Mayflower* was totally different than the forces that drove the Virginia Company. The group which is now generally known as "the Pilgrims" were members of a single congregation of Separatists from Scrooby, Nottinghamshire, who wished to stand apart from the Church of England, which though Protestant in general orientation, still maintained a form of worship and religious practice that the dissenters thought was not justified by scripture. What they were after is beautifully expressed by one of the original leaders of the colony, William Bradford, "the truth prevail and the churches of God revert to their ancient purity and recover their primitive order, liberty and beauty" (Bradford p 3). Neither Elizabeth I nor, later, James I agreed with such sentiments and an environment of harassment and persecution ensued which drove this congregation under its minster, John Robinson, and several other congregations of separatists, to migrate to Holland.

The Scrooby congregation would spend a total of twelve years in Holland, which was more tolerant of religious dissent, particularly of the Protestant variety. These English, however, were still immigrants, not full citizens of the state. Like many modern-day immigrants, most of the work they could get involved long hours in textile production. Over the years, as Bradford notes, the hard labor took its toll on young and old alike. Further, they were living in an environment that, while tolerant of religious difference, was also tolerant of customs and practices that weren't very religious at all. After a number of years, the Pilgrim congregation was beginning to lose its young people who were drifting away. In essence, this small, tightly knit Separatist community was in danger of falling apart.

What to do? It was time to emigrate again. "The place they had thoughts on was some of those vast and unpeopled countries of America, which are fruitful and fit for habitation, being devoid of all civil inhabitants, where there are only savage and brutish men which range up and down, little otherwise than wild beasts of the same" (Bradford p 25). The leadership thought of the area, now known as Guyana, on the northwest coast of South America, but came to the conclusion that it was too tropical for the English constitution and too close to the Spanish for comfort. They knew, of course, about the Virginia Company and the colony at Jamestown, but they certainly weren't interested in Jamestown per se with its Church of England congregation and not very wholesome reputation, from their point of view. According to Bradford: "at length the conclusion was to live as a distinct body by themselves under the general Government of Virginia; and by their friends to sue to his Majesty that he would be pleased to grant them freedom of religion. And that this might be obtained they were put in good hope by some great persons of good rank and quality that were made their friends" (Bradford p 29). They did obtain two patents from the Virginia Company for a distinct colony, but ultimately, could use neither one because they settled far north of the Virginia Company's writ.

The other huge issue they faced was how to finance the expedition to get to North America and become a viable society there. The Virginia Colony was a speculative financial venture underwritten by some of the wealthiest merchants and aristocrats in England. It had royal approval, if not financing. This small band of religious dissenters had neither ready wealth nor royal patronage in hand. So, they had to find those persons, particularly among the merchant class, who would back them. Many of the early writings about Plymouth, like Bradford's, focus on the interminable wrangles between the colonists and their financial backers who were not always the most scrupulous in their dealings with the Pilgrims. It would take the Pilgrim leadership many years to finally settle the debts to the English merchants who had underwritten the venture.

Despite the wrangles over the financing, the Pilgrims left Holland in July of 1620 to return to England. By the 5th of August, they were underway to the New World in two ships, the *Mayflower* and the *Speedwell*. But the *Speedwell* began to leak and they had to put in for repairs twice. The second time, it was determined that the *Speedwell* could not continue. Bradford and others were of the opinion, which Bradford says the *Speedwell*'s Master later admitted, that the Master did not want to make this trip and created some of the *Speedwell*'s problems to assure that it didn't (Bradford pp 53-54).

The result was that the Pilgrims had to reduce the number of people making the voyage and cram as many people and supplies as possible onto the *Mayflower* which sailed again on September 6th with just around 100 colonists and the ship's crew. Their delayed departure meant that they would arrive in North America in winter which they knew was not the season to attempt to establish a new colony. As Bradford noted, "and for the season it was winter, and they that knew the winters of that country knew them to be sharp and violent, and subject to cruel and fierce storms, dangerous to travel to known places, much more to search an unknown coast" (Bradford p 62). The late departure created another problem that affected the Hopkins family directly. The baby that Elizabeth was carrying was born aboard the ship during the Atlantic crossing. This baby boy, Oceanus, miraculously survived what were clearly very difficult conditions for all the passengers on that journey.

On November 11th, land was sighted which turned out to be far north of where they had intended to land. It was Cape Cod in present-day Massachusetts. The company decided to turn south to attempt to sail, as Bradford said, to "Hudson's

River." But the driving winds and the fierce shoals off the outer Cape almost ended the voyage for everyone in the attempt. They returned to Cape Cod Bay and anchored near the tip of the Cape at what is now known as Provincetown.

Since the *Mayflower* had landed so far to the north, the leadership knew immediately it had a problem. It was not on land under the jurisdiction of the Virginia Colony. And the same muttering began to arise as occurred when the *Sea Venture* blundered into the Bermudas in 1609. It seems quite plausible that one of the voices that threatened mutiny then, threatened the same once again. Bradford doesn't name names, but he does describe the situation:

> [O]ccasioned partly by the discontented and mutinous speeches that some
> of the strangers amongst them let fall from them in the ship: That when they
> come ashore they would use their own liberty, for none had power to command
> them, the patent they had being for Virginia and not for New England, which
> belonged to another government, with which the Virginia Company had nothing to do. (Bradford p 75)

In the Bermudas case, the response to mutinous actions was a show of force by the authorities, leading to one man being shot by order of a court martial, several others being left on the island, and one, Hopkins, being reprieved from death by his own pleading and that of his associates. The Pilgrims were a religious body, not a commercial operation run largely by former military personnel. So the leadership took a very different approach. They drew up a document that has come to be known as the "Mayflower Compact," which states, among other things: "We whose names are underwritten . . . by these presents solemnly and mutually in the presence of God and one of another, Covenant and Combine ourselves together into a Civil Body Politic." Their response to this crisis of being beyond the pale of known governance was to create a new government. It worked. The men of the colony, Separatists and strangers alike, a few of the servants, but no women, signed the document on 11 November 1620. If Stephen Hopkins had any reservations, he put them aside and signed the document. (On the circumstances surrounding the creation of the Compact, see Bradford pp 75-6.)

With governance resolved, the main issue was a safe harbor and shelter. This brought to the fore, the "strangers," particularly Miles Standish, the soldier who was their military commander, and Stephen Hopkins, with his experience on the ground at Jamestown and environs. On 15 November, the first expedition set out by small boat to reconnoiter the area near Provincetown itself. The group included Standish, and as advisors: Bradford, Hopkins, and Edward Tilley. On this first trip, they spotted their first Indians and tried to run after them while armored, but trying to catch up with the unencumbered locals was not a winning proposition. On the way back to the ship they became "shrewdly puzzled," in other words—lost. Edward Winslow recounts: "As we wandered we came to a tree, where a young sprit [sapling] was bowed down over a bow, and some acorns strewed underneath. Stephen Hopkins said it had been made to catch some deer. So as we were looking at it, William Bradford being in the rear, when he came looked upon it, and as he went about, it gave a sudden jerk up, and he was immediately caught by the leg." So, one of the principal leaders of the Pilgrim group provided a live demonstration that confirmed Hopkins' knowledge concerning Indian techniques and practices (*Mourt's Relation* p 23). On the next trip, probably with many of the same actors, although they are not named, they met their first local inhabitants, the Nauset, who were not friendly, having previously made the acquaintance of European visitors who had treated them very badly.

These two forays convinced the group that there was no suitable area for habitation or good anchorage for the ship at the tip of the Cape. So, in early December they ventured across Cape Cod Bay to search for a better harbor, originally described by Capt. John Smith and supposedly known to at least one of the sailors of the Mayflower crew. The members of this expedition were: Capt. Miles Standish, John Carver, William Bradford, Edward Winslow, John Tilley, Edward Tilley, John Howland, and "three from London"—Richard Warren, Stephen Hopkins, and Edward Doty, as well as members of the ship's crew (Mourt's Relation, p 32).

The trip across the Bay and into what is now known as Plymouth Harbor nearly cost the men their lives as the weather worsened and broke both the boat's rudder and main mast. But, they reached the harbor on December 8th and, after some dispute on where to situate their new colony, declared this harbor area good enough, recognizing the lateness of the year and the deteriorating health of the passengers and crew alike on the ship. On the 16th, the crew brought the *Mayflower* safely into Plymouth harbor, and by December 25th, the Pilgrims were at work on the first shelter.

The story at this point in terms of mortality is quite similar to the story of the beginnings of Jamestown and is well known. In the middle of the winter, the Pilgrims could not build enough shelter to house everyone, so many stayed aboard the *Mayflower* along with the crew. In the sub-freezing temperatures of a New England winter, the cold and disease began to take its toll. Bradford describes it:

> But that which was most sad and lamentable was, that in two or three months' time half of their company died, especially in January and February, being in the depth of winter, and wanting houses and other comforts; being infected with the scurvy and other diseases, which this long voyage and their inaccomodate condition had brought upon them. So as there died some times two or three of a day in the foresaid time, that of 100 and odd persons, scarce fifty remained. (Bradford p 77)

Thirty years later, Bradford recounted the story of each family and what had happened to them, such as the Mullins family: "Mr. Mullins and his wife, his son and his servant died the first winter. Only his daughter Priscilla survived, and married with John Alden." (Bradford p 445). Three families made it through that first winter without losing a member. One of those was the Hopkins family.

On 16 March 1621, into the weakened camp of the English at Plymouth came an Indian sachem named Samoset speaking to them, to their amazement, in broken English. Samoset was from the coast of Maine and had had dealings with the English fishermen exploiting the rich fishing grounds of the Grand Banks off the New England Coast. He spoke of another local Indian named Squanto, who spoke better English, and who made an appearance a few days later. According to Bradford, he was the sole survivor of a tribe known as the Patuxet who had lived in the immediate area and who had been decimated by a severe disease outbreak that had hit the area in 1617.

With the arrival of the Indians, Stephen Hopkins was in his element. Squanto spent his first night at the Hopkins house. When the local sachem of the Wampanoag tribe, Massasoit, arrived a few days after the arrival of Squanto, Hopkins and Standish were sent to greet him. They arranged for a meeting with the newly appointed Governor, John Carver, who forged a mutually advantageous peace treaty with Massasoit. Unlike the Jamestown situation, the tribal groups around Plymouth were in a weakened condition due to losses from disease, and needed all the help they could get in defending themselves from more powerful nearby tribes such as the Narragansetts. Perhaps hearing directly from Stephen Hopkins of the consequences of antagonizing the Native Americans in the early days of Jamestown, and clearly recognizing the perilous state of his own organization, Carver's treaty with Massasoit called on the Pilgrims and the Indians under

Massasoit to come to the aid of the other when needed. This defense pact endured for over 50 years and allowed the colony to live in peace with its neighbors in that crucial early period. And it was Squanto, living at least on occasion in the Hopkins household, who showed the Pilgrims how to grow the local corn, where to fish, and the general lay of the land.

On 5 April 1621, the *Mayflower* sailed for England with its depleted crew who had not been any more immune to disease and cold than the rest. By May, the survivors of that first winter began to form a few new families, with men who had lost wives marrying women who had lost husbands. In July, Stephen Hopkins and Edward Winslow were off on a trip to visit Massasoit to assess how the other half lived and their relative strength. They caught up with Massasoit just as he was returning to his base at the village of Pokanoket. The Indian sachem was unprepared for their arrival. There was little to eat and a bed shortage. So, the sleeping solution was for Massasoit and his wife to share their bed, he and his wife at one end and Hopkins and Winslow at the other end. It became even more crowded when, "Two more of his chief men, for want of room, pressed by and upon us, so that we were worse weary for our lodging than for our journey." Despite the nocturnal singing (the Indians evidently sung themselves to sleep), the fleas and lice, the crowded sleeping arrangements, and not much food, Hopkins and Winslow succeeded in further cementing good relations with Massasoit and made it back to New Plymouth in one piece. (On the trip to Pokanoket, see *Mourt's Relation* pp 60-68.)

In the late summer and early fall of 1621, after the harvest, things were looking better for the fragile little colony. So, the governor, now Bradford, since Carver had died in April, declared a day of fasting and thanksgiving for their deliverance. He also sent out hunters to bring in some of the local waterfowl. Bradford devoted no more than a paragraph to this event in his writing. Edward Winslow, however, in a letter printed in *Mourt's Relation,* said that sometime in this same period, Massasoit appeared with 90 men, "who for three days we entertained and feasted." The Wampanoags shot five deer and, "bestowed on our Governor, and upon the Captain and others." Out of this scattered and brief correspondence are the beginnings of what now has become the national event known for its turkey with all the trimmings, largely bereft now of its original religious focus, although we continue to call it Thanksgiving.

The year 1623 produced several significant events for the Hopkins family. First of all, the leadership decided that each man in the colony, believer and stranger alike, should get their own acre of land, all things being held in common up to that point. The Hopkins got a total of six acres of land. It is interesting to note that the family's land bordered a grant made to the only Indian to receive land at

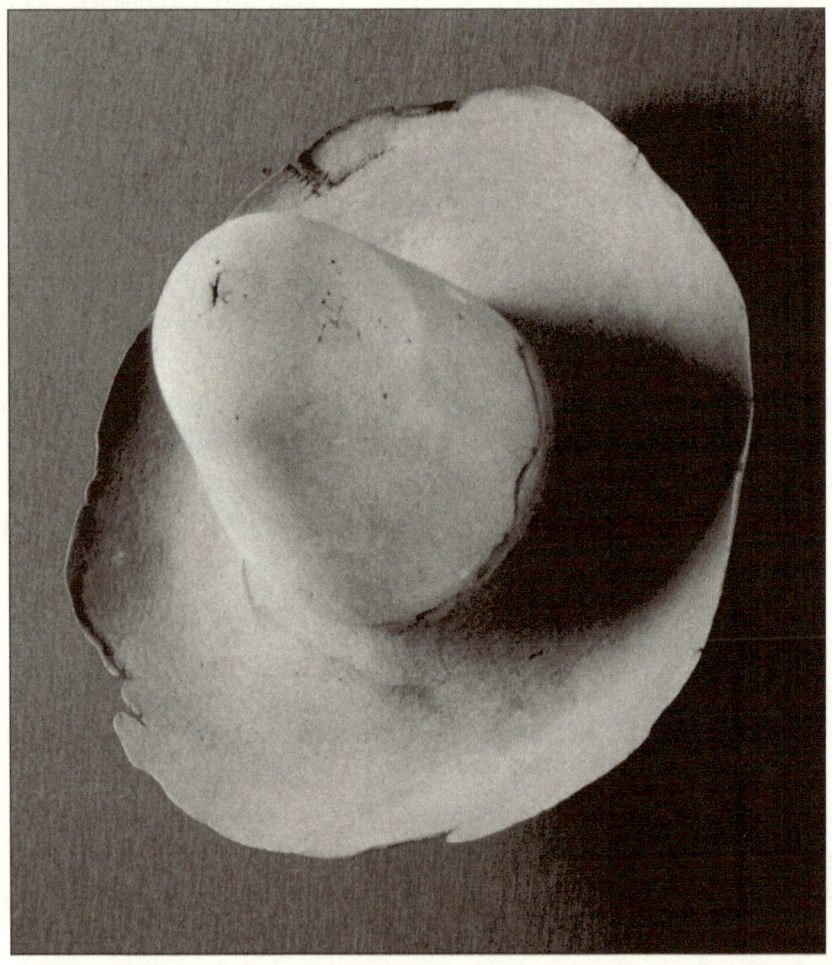

Made in England around 1615-1640, ownership of this beaver hat is attributed to Constance Hopkins.

Courtesy of Pilgrim Hall Museum, Plymouth, Massachusetts

that time, Hobomock, who had become one of the colony's most trusted Native American friends. Also, in that year the ship *Anne* arrived, bringing new colonists, including a young man named Nicholas Snow who may have known the Hopkins family back in England. Nicholas Snow was housed with the Hopkins, and, some time before 1627, married Stephen's daughter, Constance.

In 1627, the last of the communal arrangements was done away with by the Plymouth colony authorities. The cattle and other livestock were distributed among family groups, including the Hopkins. The Puritan migration to Massachusetts Bay that began shortly after that in 1630, increased demand for corn and livestock grown at Plymouth and brought a level of prosperity to the struggling colony that it had not known to date.

By this time, the period of the initial explorations and adventures were largely over, and while always a small operation as colonies went in those days, the Plymouth settlement was safe from the imminent threat of destruction. The key issues facing the colony were dealing with its rapacious financial backers in England, developing the trade and commerce needed to pay them off, and managing the day-to-day governance of the colony. Nothing is said of Stephen Hopkins' role with the former, but the records of the colony do tell of Hopkins' part in governance and matters on both sides of the law.

By 1632/33, Hopkins was one of seven men on the governor's council. Similar appointments were made through the year 1636. It is possible that he was involved in similar positions in earlier years, but if so, records of such appointments have not survived. The governor's council dealt with a variety of legal matters: hearing criminal cases, dealing with civil matters such as land transactions, and making new laws. In mid-1636, however, Hopkins was accused and convicted of beating and seriously wounding a young man named John Tisdale. The circumstances surrounding this event are not clear from the record, but his conviction on this charge marked the end of Hopkins' government service. (On Hopkins' life at Plymouth, see Anderson and Johnson.)

In fact from that point forward, Hopkins' dealings with the law were usually as the accused. Evidently, he had gone back into a trade that he probably had practiced back in England, running a shop from his home. And judging from the cases: allowing drinking in his house on the Sabbath, allowing folks to play shuffleboard, permitting folks to get drunk at his house, overcharging for "strong water, wine and beer," it is clear he was running a pub of sorts. He was convicted of most of these charges and had to pay fines. In 1638, Hopkins threw out of his household a pregnant maidservant, Dorothy Temple, who had been consorting with one Arthur Peach who was executed that year for his part in the killing and robbing of an Indian. She still had more than two years to run on her indenture to Hopkins and the court ruled that he had "to keep her and her child." Hopkins was so incensed with the maid, however, that he refused the court order, finally arranging a deal with another colonist to take her off his hands.

Like all the original settlers, and most who came later, Stephen Hopkins was involved in many land transactions over the course of his life at Plymouth, both buying and selling. He owned one of the first piers at Plymouth Harbor and was an investor in a 50-60 ton boat. He bought land on Cape Cod at Yarmouth and built a house there. In the end, though, he never moved from the original house he had built on Leiden Street at Plymouth, the first street laid out when the colony began. His days of seeking and rebellion had long passed; Plymouth had become home. He died sometime after 6 June 1644, likely in the house on Leiden Street, requesting in his will that he, "be buried as near as conveniently may be to my wife deceased."

The Hopkins Legacy

There is no doubt that the young Stephen Hopkins falls into that class of people we often call "adventurers," those who have some sort of a thrill gene in their system that must be satisfied. Today, you might find such people involved in extreme sports, becoming astronauts, or visiting the bottom of the Marianas Trench. In early 17th-century England, one of those thrills was the physical exploration of the "New World." A relative handful of people, including Hopkins, sailed for the Americas to see what they could make of themselves there. He survived the wreck of the *Sea Venture* on Bermuda, his own attempt at mutiny, and the terrible circumstances at Jamestown in the Starving Period in 1610. Then, when offered another opportunity, he chose to do it all over again, this time with a group of religious zealots who were at least as unprepared as the Jamestown colonists and much more poorly funded and supported. This second time around, Hopkins risked not only his own life, but that of his entire family including his pregnant wife, Elizabeth, for the adventure, and the land that went with it.

Unfortunately, what we know of Stephen Hopkins comes from others: Strachey, Bradford, and Winslow, as well as sundry colony and court records. The fact that Hopkins could read is documented by Strachey. But if he wrote anything, it has not been preserved. So Hopkins is seen only marginally, or by inference, perhaps even in a play by Shakespeare. Clarity about what Stephen Hopkins and a handful of others accomplished has also been lost, physically by the passage of time, and also by the human tendency to mythologize important events of the past.

The physical facts on the ground created by the early English adventurers have now largely disappeared. Original houses and fortifications at both Jamestown and Plymouth, built with prodigious physical labor by malnourished and ill men, disappeared long ago, although some remains are now reappearing thanks to current archeological efforts, particularly at Jamestown. While much has been done to increase our understanding of the appearance of the first settlements and what really happened during those early years, the facts of 400 years ago have been reshaped over time to form the myths and legends that we know so well today, legends such as the landing on Plymouth Rock and the "love" story of John Smith and Pocahontas. These myths remain well known and continue to hold more sway than the reality of what actually happened at both Jamestown and Plymouth.

But there is no doubt that in the waning days of 1620, and through the harsh winter of 1621 that killed half the little Plymouth colony's population, the physical and mental strength and perseverance of a few people, including Stephen Hopkins, assured the continued existence of that colony, and in Stephen's case, his own family as well. I also do not doubt, that whatever he did at Jamestown in 1610 and thereafter, despite the cloud that may have hung over him from the aborted mutiny on Bermuda, was in a similar spirit. In the process, he and a relative handful of others were responsible for the continuance of English settlement in North America over the first several decades of the 17th-century when it very much hung in the balance.

Progeny and descendants are another legacy left behind by Stephen Hopkins and his two wives, Mary and Elizabeth. He had ten known children and, most likely, two others whose names are not known. Some of them died in childhood, including Oceanus, the child of the Mayflower, who is not listed in the enumeration of Plymouth residents made on 22 May 1627. Some of Hopkins' children made it to young adulthood but never married, such as Caleb, who became a mariner and died at sea near Barbados. The last named child, Elizabeth, was probably mentally challenged, and one day simply wandered off and was never seen again. But, four of the Hopkins children—Constance, Giles, Deborah, and

Damaris—are known to have produced 37 children. (For further details, see the Genealogy section for Chapter 5.) Today, there are likely tens of thousands of descendants of this one man. I know now that I am among them. Some of you who read this piece are likely descendants as well. Even if you are not, it is still interesting to know a bit about this remarkable man and his role in the survival of the earliest permanent English settlements in North America, both of them.

CHAPTER 6

THE IRONIC ENIGMA:
THE SEARCH FOR THE MACDONALDS

On the wall in my family's study is an "Ahnentafel" chart, a genealogical map of our family that begins on the left side with the most recent generation (in this case, my children) and ends on the right side with the ninth generation. At the 6th generation, my wife and I have filled in nearly all of the 32 spaces on the chart with names such as Morey, Griffith, Sharp, Fernald, Covert and Heaton, among others, who lived for the most part in an arc extending along the eastern edge of North America from Maritime Canada to Tennessee and Kentucky. The only two names missing in the sixth generation are the MacDonalds, my family name. Why are they missing?

Several factors contribute to this gap, including a family break-up that occurred in 1899 that I recently learned about. One key reason for this lack of knowledge is simply that my grandfather, James Alfred MacDonald, was never asked the simple questions that would have revealed much about his immediate family and those who came before them. We didn't have to go far to ask. James Alfred spent the last four years of his life living with my family before he died in 1964. As a result, I have had to search for years for even the simplest genealogical facts: names, and dates and places of birth, death, and marriage. Many of these facts have yet to be found. So, quite ironically, the family for which I should be most able to construct members' portraits, like the ones in the foregoing chapters of this book, is the one about which I know the least.

The most recent MacDonalds on our Ahnentafel chart are obvious; they are my children and myself. The basic genealogical practice, when looking into a family's past, is to begin in the present. To wit, I was born at Boston in 1950. My parents told me so and I have the birth certificate to prove it. My family was living at Boston at that time because that is where my father came from, and where my mother was living prior to their marriage. Irving Francis MacDonald, my father, was born at Boston on 10 October 1922, one of three brothers, children of James Alfred MacDonald and Theresa Francis Fernald. I personally knew all of the actors in these two MacDonald generations previous to mine; they are part and parcel of who I am.

Irving MacDonald has already appeared in this book in Chapter 1. Unlike my mother, I really don't know much about his life as a child. As I've already noted, just because you live in the same home with someone for years does not guarantee that you know his or her prior history. I do know that my father grew up in the Dorchester area of Boston on Wrentham Street. It was the era of the Great Depression. As a young boy, he would often earn a few coins by lighting fires on the Sabbath for orthodox Jewish families in the neighborhood. As a teenager, he attended a trade school to learn cabinet making. At some point, a shop accident put an end to the possibility of that line of work. The Depression experience clearly left a lifelong impression on my father. Even years later, he was always concerned that whatever he had today might somehow be lost tomorrow.

Like his parents, my father was quiet and reserved. But he possessed a wry wit that was often on display in the company of friends. From the very beginning of their relationship, my mother called my father "Mac," and it stuck. Many of his long-time friends knew him by nothing else and were surprised to learn that his name was actually Irving.

Mac's story comes into sharper focus during World War II, the defining event for everyone of his generation. My father was not a teller of war stories; he never dwelled on his experience. Nevertheless, for two years plus he was in the "service," with the Army Air Corps 9th Photo Reconnaissance Squadron in India and Burma. This squadron included a group of pilots who flew the famous route over the Himalayas (the "Hump") to help support the Nationalist Chinese who were fighting against the Japanese in western China. These particular planes were equipped with cameras designed to take reconnaissance photos to track the movements of the Japanese. Mac's job was to develop those photos. The unit was first based in what is now modern-day Bangladesh. As the Japanese were pushed back out of Burma, my father's unit moved too, ultimately working out of Myitkinya, not far from the Chinese border. Mac was not involved in combat, but he served his country like millions of others of his generation in the epic fight of his time.

Some in this unit would make photography their life's work. In my lifetime, I cannot recall my father ever picking up a camera, even for a family photo. He did make a photo album during the war, as just about everyone else did, which is now in my possession. Mac's album contains some of the typical pictures that often fill such albums: buddies, camps, USO events, and in the case of my father's squadron, planes. His album, however, is dominated by pictures that one of his compatriots referred to as "local color." Clearly, Mac was fascinated by the people, the villages, the temples, and the local life all around him. He said that one day he would like to go back and travel across India by train from Bombay to Calcutta as his unit did when it first arrived on the sub-continent. Though my parents traveled a good deal, that particular dream was never realized.

Later, my father held a series of jobs in and around Boston until our family moved to Brockton, Mass in 1953. Several members of my mother's family worked as custodians in the school system there, and they encouraged my father to do the same, which he did. He worked in the Brockton schools for over 30 years and, despite my mother's entreaties that it was time to retire, he was working in a school just down the street from our home on the day he died. Stricken with a massive heart attack, he died on the spot on 05 August 1985 at the age of 62. No one got a chance to say goodbye to Mac, not even his wife of 37 years.

I see my father now in the bits and fragments of memory from my childhood: the curly haired young man in the military uniform, paired with the picture of my mother in her nurse's uniform and cap...Sunday afternoon trips to Plymouth when my mother was working the 3-11 shift at the hospital...the fishing boats unloading their catch of haddock and cod, and the salty taste of fried clams purchased from the take-out windows of the seafood restaurants along the dock... doing most of the work of building a set of model rockets, powered by CO_2 cartridges, for a science fair I entered...standing proudly with my mother and I, and the rockets, in a photo that made the local paper, the *Brockton Enterprise*... being out Monday nights with the candlepin bowling league and returning home every year from the annual bowling banquet with a trophy or two.

Over the years, my father accumulated a shelf-load of trophies. I've kept several, just as I've kept his sergeant's stripes from the war, a pocketknife, and an armload of wartime photos, mementos from a life now passed. But more important than the bits and pieces of stuff, I still feel the strength of his relationship with my mother, his dedication to his friends, many in our church, the First Baptist Church of Brockton, and his love for me. Those qualities have shaped my own life, along with my mother's great example of perseverance that I've already related.

James Alfred MacDonald, Irving's father, worked in Boston as a crane operator and in foundry operations according to what I've been told by the family. By the time I can personally recollect, James Alfred and his wife, Theresa, were living in a rented home on Whitfield Street in the Dorchester section of Boston. I remember the house distinctly because, for years, my Dad, Mother, and I would make the trip there on Saturday nights to spend the evening with my grandparents and eat supper, as we New Englanders always called it. There were always home-made baked beans, brown bread with raisins in it, and frankfurters. The beans, Boston's best, were cooked in a crock set in a metal oven-like box that in turn sat on the black, kerosene-burning stove. The kerosene sat in an inverted glass bottle near the stove. As it was consumed, it was sucked into the stove with a signature glug-glug-glug sound that, for some reason, is fixed in my memory along with the taste of the brown bread and beans.

Other than my grandparents' kitchen, the ground floor of the house was composed of a front parlor and another room used for storage. The storeroom, among many other things, held the stuff that I played with when we were visiting. In a small wooden keg were marbles and other bits and pieces of playthings that kept a young boy amused while my parents and grandparents visited. The parlor held the chairs where Grandpa and Grandma MacDonald sat in the evening. Alfred, as my Grandmother always called him, would smoke his ubiquitous pipe and Grandma would rock in her rocker as the evening passed. Other details of the room escape me now, but the pipe and the rocking chairs remain.

James Alfred was a man of few words as befitted his "Down-east" heritage. Like most young children, I paid little attention to what little he did say. But I do remember my grandfather's mild and quiet manner and his striking appearance: the full shock of white hair, the slight hook to the nose, and the high cheekbones that reflected the family story about an Indian in the family background. I knew that James Alfred came from Prince Edward Island in Canada. In fact, Richard Farnsworth's portrayal of Matthew Cuthbert in the Canadian Broadcasting Corporation's well-known film of Lucy Maude Montgomery's famous novel, *Anne of Green Gables*, fits my grandfather to a tee, right down to the flat cap. In his last several years, James lived with my family at Brockton until he died of cancer in 1964.

Theresa was about as reticent as my grandfather. She loved to go for drives with him and my parents once cars came into the family. Living in Boston as they did,

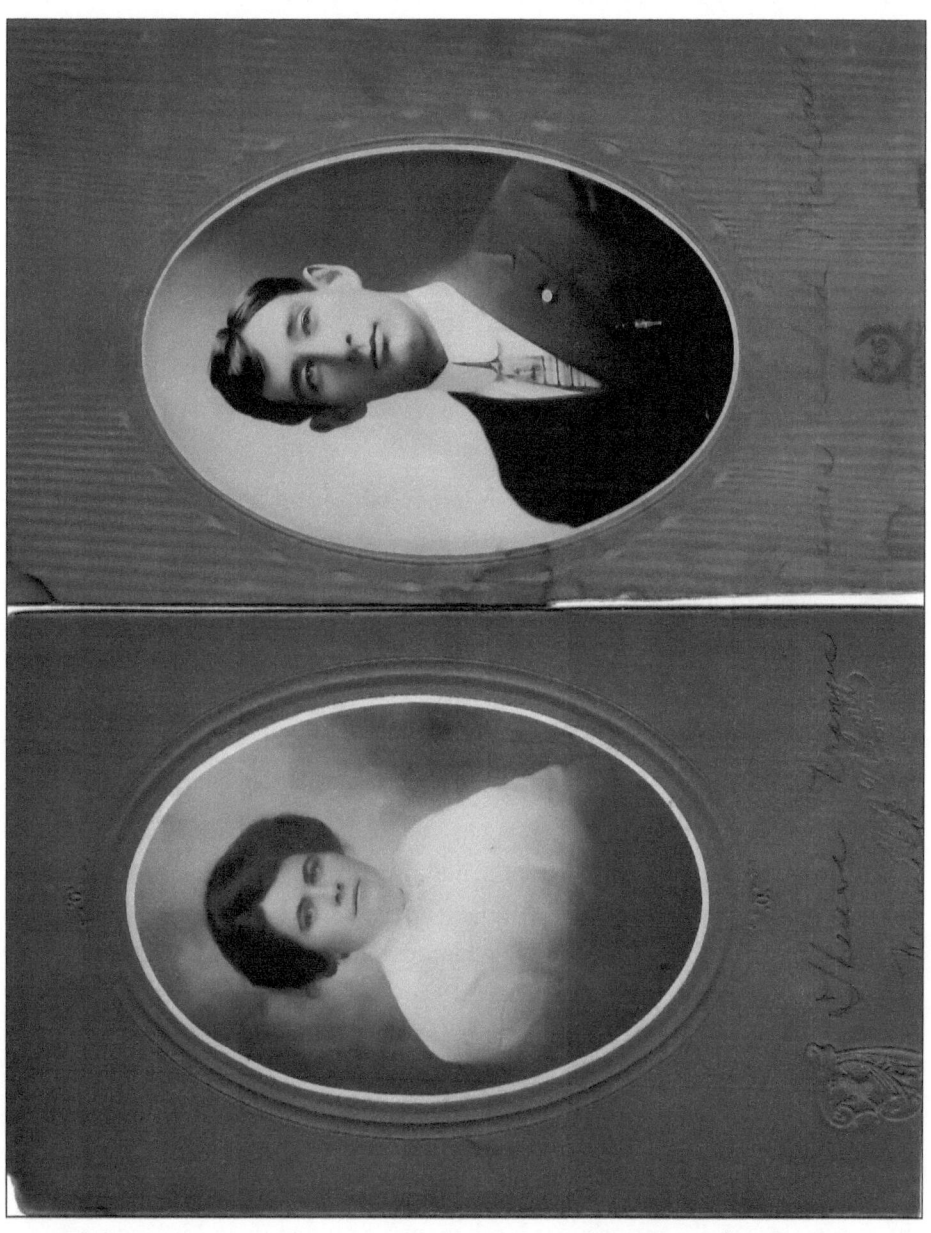

Theresa Frances (Fernald) and James Alfred MacDonald, about 1915.
Collection of the author.

there was little need, and little money, for cars until after World War II. Neither of my parents had a license to drive until the early 1950s. Like most women of her generation, Theresa handled the household affairs. In later years, she developed high blood pressure and diabetes that would contribute to her death in 1959. Her blood and heart problems most likely had a genetic base that she passed on to her children. Of her three boys, all would have heart problems, and two would die of heart attacks. None would see the age of 70.

By birth, Theresa was a Fernald. As I have previously related in Chapter 3, she was born to Daniel Fernald and Maria P. (Heaton) Fernald at Haverhill, Mass, on 24 January 1890, part of a family of Fernalds that extends back to the early history of colonial New Hampshire. Many of the descendants of this family still live in the same southern parts of Maine and New Hampshire.

From family knowledge, I knew that James Alfred and Theresa had married at Lee, New Hampshire, in 1915. A transcription of their marriage certificate from the town clerk of Lee revealed a trove of family information. It showed that James A., born on Prince Edward Island, was 28 years of age when he married on 10 November 1915. He was a box maker by trade, living at Nashua, New Hampshire. Theresa is listed as age 25, a housewife living at Lee, New Hampshire, who was born at Haverhill, Mass. Alfred's father is listed as David, a farmer from Prince Edward Island, and his mother is shown as Hannah E. Carr, a housewife from Prince Edward Island as well.

Why was James Alfred at Nashua making boxes? *The Nashua Experience: History in the Making 1673-1978* tells the story (see Sources - Chapter 6). Sited on the Merrimack River in southern New Hampshire, Nashua was one of the many mill towns in their heyday in the late 19th- and early 20th-centuries in New England. In the mid 19th-century, entrepreneurs financed the construction of the Middlesex Canal system along the Merrimack River that helped link Boston to Concord, New Hampshire, and all the towns in between. With this connection made, towns like Nashua could go into the manufacturing business in earnest. First and foremost were textiles. The Nashua Manufacturing Company, the first major textile operation at Nashua, was founded in 1823. Under various ownerships, it remained in business until the 1970s. Foundries were also important, making parts for the railroad and steamship industries, and a myriad of other forgings needed to support the growing industrial economy. Paper, boxes, spring water, and soapstone were some of the other businesses that developed and flourished for a time at Nashua.

A visit to the New England Historic Genealogical Society (NEHGS) at Boston produced a bit of evidence of the MacDonald family's time at Nashua. Looking through the NEHGS's set of town directories, the predecessors of today's phone books, I found James Alfred in several:

1916: McDonald, J Alfred, iron molder, h[ome] 3 Fifield Lane
1917: McDonald, J Alfred, iron molder, h[ome] 59 Bridge
1918: McDonald, James A, asbestos wkr, h[ome] 59 Bridge

In *The Nashua Experience*, there is a statement that ties James Alfred's presence on Fifield Lane with his occupation as a box maker as recorded in the transcription of his marriage certificate. "Another box-making firm moved to Nashua from Tyngsborough in 1890, operated by E.O. Fifield. He built a large shop on the corner of Taylor Road and the street was subsequently named after him." So my grandfather evidently worked for Mr. Fifield making boxes while he lived on Mr. Fifield's own street. The naming of the street was not enough to keep Fifield at Nashua, however. He eventually moved his business to Milford, New Hampshire. My grandfather also moved on, into the foundry business.

At the National Archives in Washington, D.C., I searched for evidence of any family members at Nashua in 1910. No luck. But I did find a fascinating snap-shot of an early 20th-century American mill town. So many nationalities: Irish, Lithuanians, Russians, Italians, Greeks, Turks, Norwegians, Germans, French Canadians and English-speaking Canadians, to name a sampling. Except for the Canadians and residents from other U.S. states, it is Europe in miniature, recreated in a small American town with something to offer which Europe did not possess in abundance at that time—jobs. There was also probably another attraction, the more evanescent freedom to say, do, and move as you pleased, opportunities that were also in scarce supply in much of class-bound Europe at that time.

A look at the U.S Census records of 1920 showed that the MacDonald family, including the oldest child, George A., had moved on to Boston, specifically, 115 Wrentham Street. The census record also shows James A.'s year of immigration to the U.S. as 1891, and he was still in the iron molding business.

So, like so many other workers in the mill towns of New England, James A. was an immigrant, in his case, from Prince Edward Island (PEI). As we will see, his father arrived first, looking for work in the late 1880s or very early 1890s. The availability of work brought thousands from Eastern Canada to the U.S. in the late 19th- and early 20th-centuries: French Canadians from Quebec and elsewhere; and those of primarily English, Scottish and other European heritages from the Maritimes—Prince Edward Island, Nova Scotia and New Brunswick. By 1950, those of French Canadian descent alone made up 50 percent of the total population of Nashua (*The Nashua Experience*, p 137).

One great source of information about immigrants is their naturalization records. I sought out James Alfred's records at the regional office of the U.S. National Archives at Waltham, Massachusetts, later to discover that my parents had the originals in their possession all along. The record is found in the Naturalization Records of Boston, 1906-1926, microfilm roll 81 from "Low" to "McGowen." On 16 July 1917, James Alfred declared his intention, in triplicate, to become a U.S. citizen on Form 2203 of the U.S. Department of Labor's Naturalization Service.

The first striking bit of information on this declaration is the name, James Alfred McDonald, not MacDonald. When I was a boy, I thought we had always been MacDonalds. I had thought the Nashua directory records were a mistake. Why this name change? The family scuttlebutt was that James Alfred never got along with his father. Was he so angry with his father that he chose to add the "a" to differentiate himself from the previous generation? Did he just like the look of that "a" in Mac? I also speculated that perhaps a clerk began the process by adding the "a" to the birth record of one of his sons by mistake. But a look at the birth record of James Alfred's first son, George, shows that the certificate was specifically modified in 1958 to formally add the "a" to make his name MacDonald. Whatever the reason, it is clear that James Alfred deliberately made us the Macs we are today.

The declaration of intent to become a U.S. citizen states that Alfred was an "iron moulder" in 1917, living at 59 Bridge Street at Nashua. That much squares with the Nashua town directory of 1917. His wife, Theresa, is listed. The declaration states that he emigrated from, "Charlottetown, P.Q. Canada on the vessel *Charlottetown*," arriving at the port of Boston in 1891. The petition concludes: "I am not an anarchist; I am not a polygamist, nor a believer in the practice of polygamy; and it is my intention in good faith to become a citizen of the United States of America and to permanently reside therein: SO HELP ME GOD."

James Alfred was four years old when he came to the States. Clearly, he came with an adult, most likely a relative. If so, how did they get to Boston? My periodic searches for the record of the ship that brought James Alfred to the U.S. kept turning up empty. I did learn, however, that there was no ship, *Charlottetown*, from that era plying the PEI to Boston route. In fact, my lack of success in corroborating the details in the immigration record made me begin to doubt the statements made in it. Had the record been invented to hide how my grandfather actually got to the States?

The advent of the Internet and on-line databases finally provided the answer. At the touch of a button or two, what once was hidden away in hard-copy records, microfilm, or microfiche in often hard to reach archives, is now available in digitized form on a home computer. So in December 2007, I typed James Alfred's mother's name, Hannah McDonald, into the powerful search engine of Ancestry.com and, finally, found the ship's record that I had long sought.

The ship's name was actually the *S.S. Indiana*. It made the voyage from Charlottetown, PEI via Halifax, Nova Scotia on 24 August 1891, and it docked at Boston Harbor. According to the passenger manifest, on board were Hannah McDonald, James Alfred, and two younger sisters. Other than the name of the ship, the information in my grandfather's naturalization record was confirmed. Further, the ship's record shows that the family came to America to meet relatives, most likely, James Alfred's father who had probably come ahead to find work.

In 1921, my grandfather made a formal petition for naturalization. By this time, he was still living at the Wrentham Street address at Dorchester with his young family. The petition says that James A. had lived in the U.S. continuously since 1913. Did he go back and forth to PEI prior to 1913? It's a possibility, but there is no evidence to support that. The witnesses to the petition were Charles W. Woodman, the husband of Theresa's sister, Elsie, and Clarence G. Fernald, Theresa's brother. Finally, on 3 April 1922, after renouncing allegiance and fidelity to George V, King of Great Britain and Ireland, and swearing to defend the Constitution and laws of the United States of America against all enemies, foreign and domestic, and after bearing true faith and allegiance to the same, James Alfred was admitted as a citizen of the United States.

So we know that James Alfred formally became a U.S. citizen. Whether he actually ever saw Prince Edward Island again after 1891 is not known, but it is clear that my grandfather's origins lie in that place. Over my lifetime, I've made three trips to the island. I went there first as a child of 11 with my parents. We were curious to see this place from where our MacDonalds, or McDonalds, came. Separated from New Brunswick by the Northumberland Strait, PEI is a province of Canada in its own right. Originally inhabited by local Indian tribes such as the Mi'kmaq, the English and French periodically exchanged the island between them during their long struggle for dominance in Canada. The English finally won out in 1763 under the Treaty of Paris, and the island which had gone by a variety of names, including Isle St. Jean, was renamed Prince Edward Island after King George III's son Edward who was the father of Queen Victoria.

To promote settlement, PEI was divided in the late 1700s into a series of "lots" that were granted to English private interests. These parties were supposed to pay quit rents and provide settlers for the island. For the most part, they did neither and were simply engaged in land speculation. The lot structure, however, formed the foundation for townships that exist to this day. From 1770 onward, small groups of settlers began to arrive, including a group of Catholic Scottish Highlanders who settled near Tracadie Bay, and a group of Scottish Protestant Lowlanders who settled around Malpeque Bay. There were about 800 Scottish settlers who arrived in 1803 under the sponsorship of Thomas Douglas, Lord Selkirk. This influx of Scots early in the history of English-speaking immigration to PEI continues to make its mark on the composition of the island's population to this day, and is often reflected in the Scottish heritage of many immigrants from PEI to the U.S.

Still largely rural in character, PEI is covered with a strikingly red soil, good for growing potatoes, which became a major export. There was little industry, however, which accounts for one of its most successful exports—its people—to the industrializing northeastern United States, and similar parts of Canada. Other than potatoes and people, the stories of Lucy Maude Montgomery, including the famous *Anne of Green Gables*, have been one of PEI's major exports. Written in the early part of the 20th-century, the "Anne" stories give a descriptive view of the island at that time. The books tend to portray PEI as a bucolic island paradise of sorts. Well, perhaps, if you were a Scot or some other northern European type who knew how to cope with winter's sub-freezing temperatures when the only heat would come from a wood-burning stove in the kitchen. In his book, *Them Times,* the PEI historian David Weale wrote a chapter entitled, "In Bed With a Brick," which includes a description of the bone-cold winter on the island at the time of my grandfather:

> In many of those old farm homes, the only warm place during most of the winter was in the kitchen; or, more precisely, that part of the kitchen nearest the stove. One woman recalled that in her home, even with the kitchen fire burning, the potato skins or 'jackets' on the kitchen table would sometimes be stiff with frost before the dinner meal was finished. . . . Going to bed required a hero's heart. Armed with a hot brick in a sack, or a granite stone in a knitted cover, or a piece of hardwood or a bag of salt or grain, or even the Eaton's catalogue warmed in the oven since suppertime, you screwed up your courage and headed upstairs to the bedroom. . . . Another memory I have of those frigid bedrooms is of the frozen-over chamber pot under the bed. There was a curious sense of childish conquest in directing a stream of steaming urine at a single spot in the ice until it punched through. If you had anything left, you started over again at a new spot. (David Weale, *Them Times,* pp 14-15)

Perhaps people went south to the U.S. just to warm up!

I recall little of the family trip to PEI in the early sixties. In my bedroom, I used to keep a very red rock that came from the island. The fishing trip with my Dad also remains vivid. The crew of the small fishing boat chummed for mackerel that swam in a fast and furious circle around the boat, bending our light bamboo poles almost in half as they hit the bait. There was half a barrel full of mackerel and cod at the end of the day. You could take home as much as you wanted. We looked around a bit for the family connections on that trip, but having discovered that seemingly a quarter of the island was named MacDonald—you could tell by the mailboxes—we gave up what seemed an insurmountable task.

As I renewed the search in earnest in the 1970s, I wrote to the PEI Division of Vital Statistics in 1977 looking for a birth record for my grandfather. The Division informed me that the registration of births for the province began only in 1906, too late for James Alfred, but the letter from Vital Statistics stated, "among some old baptismal records, we noted one for him." All I had to do was write to officials of the Free Church of Scotland on Prince Edward Island. In return, I received a handwritten copy of the following record: James Alfred, born to Donald McDonald and Hanna Carr on 03 May 1887. On 23 June 1889, Elias Roberts, an elder of the church, had baptized the boy at Albany, Lot 27.

I was pleased to have just one more little bit of substance to go along with the still-vague family stories.

But, why were the stories about the family so vague? One of those stories was that my grandfather, James Alfred, had run away from home as quite a young man since he did not get along with his father. The story went that he had had a bad time of it as he tried to survive by working for various farmers, most likely in the southern part of New Hampshire. As a consequence, his connection with the rest of his family was, for the most part, lost. It was a subject that, evidently, this very reticent "Down Easter" was reluctant to discuss. So, although Alfred lived at our house for the last four years of his life, as far as I know, no one ever asked him the most fundamental questions about his own life and that of his family. Did he have one or two sisters? What were their names? Was it his MacDonald grandmother who was supposed to be a Mi'kmaq Indian? What was the name of his grandfather? What did he know about the lives of his mother, his father, and his sister, or sisters, after their arrival in the United States? He may not have known all the answers, but whatever he knew, he took with him to the grave. Sadly, either these questions were never asked, or perhaps, never answered.

So, later, when I became the self-designated family historian, I found myself lacking the most basic information about the MacDonalds. As a result, facts that could have been learned from this key family source have taken me sometimes decades to discover, and in many cases, have yet to be found.

In the early 1980's, I recognized that my chances of visiting the island personally would be few and far between. So, with the recommendation of the PEI Heritage Foundation, I hired a professional genealogist, Beryl Barrett, to see what she could find concerning my MacDonalds on PEI. I still have the typed correspondence between Mrs. Barrett and myself. From 1980 to 1983 she followed numerous leads, attempting to unravel the mystery of the antecedents of James Alfred. She found a promising MacDonald family, but then discovered that they were clearly Catholic which didn't fit with my grandfather's baptism in the Free Church of Scotland. Members of another likely candidate family asserted that their Daniel had married so-and-so and that the couple had moved to Toronto.

Mrs. Barrett had better luck identifying the Carr family into which my great-grandfather had married. The most likely set of Carrs emerged, but the trouble was the presence of two Hannahs in that family, one a niece of the other. Which one married Daniel? But then, finally, a marriage license emerged, dated

17 April 1886, for a Daniel McDonald and a Hannah Carr, both of Tryon, PEI. Also, a record was found which confirmed part of that family story that James Alfred had at least one sister, possibly two. Mrs. Barrett found that when Elias Roberts baptized my grandfather, he also baptized Rachel Florance (or Florence), born 08 December 1888, daughter of Donald McDonald and Hannah Carr. Mrs. Barrett told me that in often pre-literate 19th-century Canada, little distinction was made between two names such as Donald and Daniel.

So, at last, some tangible information on James Alfred's parents and a sister came to light. But more like a glimmer. A marriage record, a baptismal record, but nothing more. What happened to the older generation, Daniel and Hannah? What happened to James Alfred's sister, Rachel Florence?

Eventually, I joined the PEI Heritage Foundation with its great focus on the island's family history and put my queries in their newsletter. On the MacDonald side, this brought no information whatever. But over the course of a couple of months in 1989, two letters arrived, both from relations of Hannah Amelia Carr, my great-grandmother. In short order, I had placed in my possession a huge amount of information on the family of Joseph Carr, Hannah's father. Joseph was the son of John Carr, who, with his brother Thomas, emigrated to PEI from England in the early 1800s. This Carr family is traceable for three more generations to a John Carr of Wilberfoss, Yorkshire, England. Arlene Sorenson, from whom I received one of these letters, was the daughter of Robert Carr, one of the several sons of Joseph Carr, and a brother of Hannah. A great collection of information, to say the least.

In 1992, I was finally able to make another visit to PEI to see what I could find for myself. I spent time at the Heritage Foundation and the Provincial Archives. Mostly, I was only able to confirm what Beryl Barrett and Arlene Sorenson had already found. In the Provincial Archives, thanks to a microfilm made by the LDS Church, I was able to see the handwritten record of the baptisms by Elias Roberts of my grandfather and his sister Rachel. They were in a diary where Roberts recorded all the baptisms of his career, his writing very strong and clear in his younger days and increasingly weaker and faltering as he reached the end of his ministry. Also, I obtained a copy of the marriage record of Daniel McDonald and Hannah Carr, celebrated on 24 April 1886, performed by Rev. I.J.S. Skinner, Baptist Minister of Tryon, PEI. Tryon is another small village adjacent to the aforementioned Albany.

While I was looking through the census records of the island, a couple of new items came to light. In the 1891 PEI census, in Lot 28, I found the Joseph Carr family (family number 249): Joseph, born in England, 61 years old; his wife, Elizabeth, 50 years old, born in Nova Scotia; three of their children, including Hannah, age 25; and Hannah's children, James A., age 3 and Rachel F., age 2. There was also another grandson of Joseph listed, with no name given, but listed as four months of age. The enumeration was done on 02 May 1891, indicating that this child was most likely born in January 1891. Was this unnamed child another child of Hannah's or a child of one of Hannah's sisters or brothers? Arlene Sorenson's family history work had not pinpointed the parents of this child; however, the aforementioned record of the arrival of the *S.S. Indiana* at Boston in August 1891 provided the answer. Two daughters of Hannah McDonald are given in that record, the aforementioned Rachel and another child named, Mary, aged one-half (six months). There can be little doubt that the unnamed child in the family of Joseph Carr in the 1891 Canadian census for Lot 28 is Hannah's second daughter despite the designation of the child as a "grandson" in the census record. After looking for so many years, my grandfather's family stood complete: Daniel McDonald and his wife Hannah Amelia Carr and their three children: James Alfred, born 1887; Rachel Florence, born 1888; and Mary, born 1891.

In 1993, we decided to make a family camping trip to PEI, where we were rained out, just as my family had been in 1961. Soon after we arrived on the island, we were sitting in Arlene Sorenson's home at the small village of Tryon, right in the very area where my grandfather was born, and his parents were married. We went over the records she had sent me, and I obtained more details. On an end table in Arlene's living room sat a grainy picture of Joseph, Hannah Amelia's father, an image of a farmer right out of *Anne of Green Gables*. Arlene said her own Aunt Katy, still living at the time of our visit, remembered as a child her father going to visit her Aunt Hannah. But, what became of Hannah, where, and when she went, Katy didn't know—and neither did Arlene. As for Daniel McDonald, the Carr family descendants had nothing on him. Another look through the archives, microfilmed church records, cemetery lists, old newspapers, and books, regrettably, produced nothing much new or concrete.

So Daniel's origins remain an enigma. He appears on the scene at Tryon, PEI, in 1866 as found in the records of his marriage to Hannah Carr. But where did he come from? The search is hindered by the fact that there were, and still are, a lot of MacDonalds on PEI. There was no law mandating the collection of vital records in Canada prior to the early 1900s. So, church records of births and deaths are, for this reason, a critical source. So far, I've not found a church record of the birth of Daniel McDonald or a marriage record for a set of McDonald parents for Daniel that would fit the bill. There are many such records for the Carrs. Why this difference between the two families?

One of the few claims my grandfather made about his MacDonald family was that he had an Indian grandmother. She would probably have been a Mi'kmaq from the region of Atlantic Canada and Maine. Daniel's mother, totally un-known to date, could certainly have been an Indian. But, if she were, what are the chances of finding any information on this woman?

In 1989, Arlene (Carr) Sorenson, my primary source of information on my Carr ancestors, wrote me a letter that told an interesting story about members of that family. Her Aunt Katy told Arlene that she remembered overhearing two of her mother's sisters talking one day, "when they didn't know that anyone was listening and saying 'Poor Kate' [referring to Catherine McLeod, wife of Robert Carr, one of my great grandmother's brothers]. Aunt Katy could never figure out why they would say that because she thought her mother was getting along fine. When she was older, she discovered that they were referring to Catholic Catherine having married a Protestant."

So, at this stage in the social life of the island, if it were nearly beyond the pale for a Protestant to marry a Catholic, then I suspect that an Anglo-Saxon-Mi'kmaq marriage or liaison would not have been well received either—probably, not an item for the church record books. I will, of course, keep doing what I can to find the MacDonald origins. But, clearing up the mystery of the MacDonald ancestry has proven to be no easy task.

Tracing what happened to Daniel, Hannah, and their family once they reached the States has proven an equally daunting problem. I know the basic history of James Alfred, of course. But, as for his parents and his two sisters, they have vanished just as effectively as the McDonalds before Daniel. To start with, all I had were stories, like the one of James Alfred running away from home at the age of twelve. There is another family story, vaguely remembered, about James Alfred trying to look up a sister (or two?), possibly in Rhode Island. By that account, things did not go well. Not long before she died, my mother told me that she remembered Theresa, James Alfred's wife, saying that she had met Daniel and hadn't enjoyed the meeting. Since James Alfred and Theresa met and married in southern New Hampshire in the early 20th-century, that would most likely place Daniel there as well.

Through 2013, my search of public records in the U.S. had failed to surface hardly anything on this family after they reached the U.S. A search of U.S. census records in Massachusetts, New Hampshire, and Rhode Island, both as "Mcs" and "Macs," failed to find any of them, except for my grandfather. A look at vital records, particularly, death and marriage records in New Hampshire and Massachusetts, had proven equally fruitless.

Given the lack of records, my hypothesis ran along the following lines. Perhaps, not long after the family's arrival in 1891, Daniel obtained work in southern New Hampshire and the family moved from Boston or vicinity to that area. Prior to 1900, Hannah died, or possibly, Daniel and Hannah separated. At any rate, the family broke up and was not recorded, at least not as an identifiable unit, anywhere in the 1900 census or any later census. According to the old family story, James Alfred ran off to make it on his own. The girls were either off with their mother or, if she died, were living with their father. Perhaps Daniel was unable to cope with the young girls and found some accommodation for them and began to live on his own. There *are* census records of persons named Daniel McDonald living in boarding houses in New Hampshire and Massachusetts, in 1900 and 1910. Proving that any of them is *the* Daniel McDonald would be next to impossible.

Then, in March of 2014, I finally found a key piece of the puzzle. This is a record I should have found at the NEHGS library in one of my searches there, but had not. A search of a relatively new database prepared by Ancestry.com, based on the NEHGS material, produced a Record of Divorce for Hannah McDonald, residing at Nashua, New Hampshire, from Daniel McDonald, dated 1 December 1899. The grounds of the libelant, Hannah, were "extreme cruelty." There is no doubt about the identity of the couple involved in this divorce since the record contains the date and place of marriage which perfectly match the 1887 marriage record of Daniel McDonald and Hannah Carr on Prince Edward Island.

Thus, some elements of my hypothesis were confirmed by the divorce record. The family did break up, so there would be no record of them as a unit in the 1900 U.S census or subsequent censuses. The 1899 divorce also fits very well with the story of my grandfather having run off at the age of twelve. The girls though, given the grounds for the divorce, no doubt went with their mother. As the only male left in the family, albeit only twelve years old, perhaps the girls viewed James' running off as an abandonment which may account for the reportedly poor reception he received from at least one of his sisters when he tried to reconnect years later. As for the women involved, the question is how long did they carry the McDonald name? Since Hannah divorced Daniel, then she may have remarried, or perhaps reassumed the Carr name. It is highly likely that the two daughters would have eventually married, as well, taking new surnames in the process, and making these two women yet harder to trace.

And there the story rests—for now. In my record, James Alfred's mother, Hannah Amelia Carr, now has a known family dating back to the 1700's on PEI and in England. Happily, my own family has met some of her living relatives. But of Hannah's later life after her arrival in the U.S. in 1891, there is, as yet, no trace, other than the record of her divorce from Daniel. As for Daniel, it is neither clear who his progenitors on PEI were, nor what happened to him after the divorce. He too disappears. James Alfred's two sisters are no longer total phantoms, however. They now both have names, and I know where they were born and when. But, I have found no trace of them after their arrival at Boston with their mother in 1891.

In 1997, the Canadian government completed a bridge across the Northumberland Strait between PEI and New Brunswick. It reaches eight miles across the straight and enters PEI only minutes from Albany and Tryon. I haven't seen it or crossed it yet, but undoubtedly a bit of the mystique of an island and an island people, set apart from the rest of the landlubbers by miles of ocean, has been lost. This is the prevailing way of things, old ways change and much of what came before is forgotten—but, not everything. With the artifacts that are left behind, archeologists and historians can reconstruct much from the past. The same is true for those interested in family history. The artifacts turn up in the most interesting places sometimes. The art is imagining where they might be hidden. The science is determining how to seek them out. The scope of the effort is only as big as your imagination and the time available to pursue the possibilities. Somewhere, there are clues that lead in the direction of Daniel McDonald and those who came before him, as well as hints that lead to those who followed him to the States in 1891. I haven't imagined well enough where all those clues are, so have yet to find them. The search continues.

FIVE LIVES AND AN ENIGMA: SOURCES

INTRODUCTORY QUOTE (p. v)

Ghosh, Amitav. *The Glass Palace.* Hammersmith, London: Harper Collins Publishers, 2000, p 552, in recognition of the work of Walter A. Desai.

CHAPTER 1: THE WILL TO ENDURE

Barry, Helen (Covert) (Pennell) (Jepson). Unpublished personal diaries, 1933 and 1935. (maternal grandmother of the author)

Brockton Times (now the Enterprise). Articles from the Times or Enterprise obtained from microfilmed copies held by the Brockton (Massachusetts) Public Library.

Brown, Richard D., and Jack Tager. *Massachusetts: A Concise History.* Amherst, MA: University of Massachusetts Press, 2000.

Carroll, Walter F. *Brockton, From Rural Parish to Urban Center.* Northridge, CA: Windsor Publications, 1989.

Commonwealth of Massachusetts, Executive Office of Health and Human Services, Department of Mental Retardation, Monson Developmental Center, Palmer, MA. *The records of June Pennell, admitted August 21, 1934 and discharged November 16, 1950.* Photocopy received by the author, 2005.

Fisher, Carl W., William V. Covert, and Maurice Patterson, compilers. *The Covert Family.* Interlaken, NY: Interlaken Historical Society, 1989.

History of Monson State Hospital. 4 pages, possibly part of a larger history of the Town of Monson, Mass. Photocopy provided by The Director of Placement, Planning and Training, Monson Developmental Center, Palmer, MA, 2005.

MacDonald, June M. Unpublished account of June (Pennell) MacDonald's life, from childhood to the time of her marriage in 1948. Written in the 1980s and 1990s. (mother of the author)

Phinney, Clara Pennell. *The Pennell Family in Portland, Maine.* Unpublished manuscript, 1916, held by the LDS Family History Library, Salt Lake City, Utah.

Rosen, Ronald, Superintendent. *Monson State Hospital: A Short Past, But A Long History*. Six pages, originally published as a three part series in *The Aurora* (a publication of the hospital?), 1978. Photocopy provided by the Director of Placement, Planning and Training, Monson Developmental Center, Palmer, MA, 2005.

CHAPTER 2: THE DOUGHBOY

The principal source for this chapter is an unpublished series of letters written from Percy Covert, to his sister Grace. The letters were given by Grace to her niece June (Pennell) MacDonald, and passed from June to the author. Found in an envelope marked "My Letters from Percy from World War I while in action," the letters cover the period from 5 October 1917 through 14 March 1919 with one additional undated letter from Fort Heath in Winthrop, MA, written in the spring or summer of 1919. (Percy Covert was a great uncle of the author.)

Other sources:

Albertine, Connell. *The Yankee Doughboy*. Boston, MA: Branden Press, 1968.

Battery A of the 101st Field Artillery. Cambridge, MA: Brattle, 1919. (The introduction states that sixteen members of the Battery helped write the book; no overall editor is named.)

Benwell, Harry A., *History of the Yankee Division*. Boston, MA: The Cornhill Company, 1919.

Carter, Russell Gordon, *The 101st Field Artillery, A.E.F. 1917-1919*. Boston, MA: Houghton, Mifflin, 1940.

Gilbert, Martin. *The First World War, A Complete History*. New York, NY: Henry Holt and Co, 1994.

Hallas, James S., ed. *Doughboy War, The American Expeditionary Force in WW I*. Mechanicsburg, PA: Stackpole Books, 2009.

Marshall, S.L.A. *The American Heritage History of World War I*. New York: American Heritage/ Bonanza Books, 1964.

Sibley, Frank. *With the Yankee Division in France*. Boston, MA: Little Brown, 1919.

Stallings, Lawrence. *The Doughboys, The Story of the AEF, 1917-1918*. New York, NY: Harper and Row, 1963.

CHAPTER 3: THE SANGUINARY NEWSMAN

This chapter depends heavily on archival material related to Samuel Haynes Jenks, and other Jenks family members, maintained by:

America's Historical Newspapers (AHN), published by Readex, a division of Newsbank, Inc, in association with the American Antiquarian Society, including the following:

- *American Federalist/ Columbian Centinel* —Boston, MA.
- *Baltimore Patriot* —Baltimore, MD.
- *Boston Recorder* —Boston, MA.
- *New Bedford Mercury* —New Bedford, MA.

The Nantucket Atheneum (NA), Nantucket, MA: copies of the following Nantucket newspapers reviewed on microfilm (they are now also available in digital form):

- *The Inquirer*: 1821-1846.
- *The Islander*: 1840-1843.
- *The Mirror*: 1846-1847.
- *The Warder*: 1846.

Nantucket Historical Association (NHA) - Research Library, Nantucket, MA:

- *The Eliza Starbuck Barney Genealogical Record*, database at www.nha.org.
- MS 57: *Grace Brown Gardner Collection, 1900-1962* (including "Fifty Famous Nantucketers").
- MS 99: *Admiral Sir Isaac Coffin's Lancastrian School Papers, 1806-1837.*
- MS 129: *Worth Family Papers, 1743-1912.*
- MS 133: *Samuel Haynes Jenks Papers, 1834-1849.*
- MS 133-Folder 3: *The Atlantic Silk Company.*

- MS 335: *Edouard A. Stackpole Collection, 1750-1990*, including material on the Jenks Family in Folder 405.

New England Historic Genealogical Society (NEHGS), Boston, MA:

- Carlson, Stephen P., *Joseph Jenks, Colonial Toolmaker and Inventor*, 1975 (revised).

- Mss. 1017: *Genealogy of the Jenks Family.* NEHGS manuscript collection, handwritten record in a ledger-style book, author unknown.

Other sources:

Brown, Richard and Jack Tager. *Massachusetts, A Concise History.* Amherst, MA: University of Massachusetts, 2000.

Browne, William B. *Genealogy of the Jenks Family of America.* Concord, NH: Rumford Press, 1952.

Burns, Eric. *Infamous Scribblers: The Founding Fathers and the Rowdy Beginnings of American Journalism.* New York, NY: Public Affairs, 2007.

Byers, Edward. *The Nation of Nantucket, Society and Politics in an Early American Commercial Center, 1660-1820.* Boston, MA: Northeastern University Press, 1987.

Douglas-Lithgow, Robert Alexander. *Nantucket, A History.* New York, NY and London, England: G.P. Putnam's Sons, 1914.

Emery, Michael and Edwin Emery. *The Press and America, an Interpretive History of the Mass Media.* Boston, MA: Allyn and Bacon, 1996.

Godfrey, Edward K. *The Island of Nantucket, What it Was and What it Is.* Boston, MA: Leeand Sheppard, Publishers, 1882.

Holt, Michael F. *The Rise and Fall of the American Whig Party: Jacksonian Politics and the Onset of the Civil War.* New York, NY: Oxford University Press, 1999.

Howe, Daniel Walker. *What Hath God Wrought, The Transformation of America, 1815-1848.* New York, NY: Oxford University Press, 2007.

Kettle, Samuel, ed. *Specimens of American Poetry*, 1829, an anthology that contains several poems by Samuel H. Jenks.

Nantucket Argument Settlers, Island History at a Glance, 1602-1993. Nantucket, MA: *Inquirer and Mirror*, 1994.

Pasley, Jeffrey. *The Tyranny of Printers, Newspaper Politics In the Early American Republic.* Charlottesville, VA: University Press of Virginia, 2001.

Philbrick, Nathaniel. *Away Off Shore, Nantucket Island and Its People, 1602-1890.* Nantucket, MA: Mill Hill Press, 1994.

Starbuck, Alexander. *The History of Nantucket, County, Island and Town.* Rutland, VT and Tokyo, Japan: Charles E. Tuttle, 1969.

White, Barbara Ann. *A Line in the Sand, The Battle to Integrate Nantucket Public Schools, 1825-1847.* New Bedford, MA: Spinner Publications, 2009.

CHAPTER 4: THE LAND SPECULATOR

Historic Documents

This chapter owes much to the collections held by the Massachusetts State Archives, and others, as follows:

Massachusetts Archives, 222 Morrisey Blvd, Boston, MA:

- *Massachusetts Archives Collection, 1629-1799.* A 328 volume series which contains original records of the governor, Council, General Court and other officials of various governments of Massachusetts, including the Massachusetts Bay Colony. Agency code: SC1/series 45X. Microfilm. Records cited in this book as "MAC" by volume and page(s).

- *Suffolk Deeds, 1629-1687.* A series of volumes containing handwritten transcriptions of early deeds from throughout Suffolk County, Massachusetts. Agency code: CY 1.03/series 1205. Records cited in this book as "SD" by volume and case number.

Suffolk Files Collection, nos. 1885 and 2053. Massachusetts Supreme Judicial Court Records. These cases, involving the Thayers, are from volume 3 of a microfilm series reviewed at the Massachusetts Archives. Records are cited in this book as "SCR" by case number.

Braintree Indian Deed of 1665. Signed by the Massachusett Sachem Wampatuck and members of his council, witnessed by other Massachusett Indians and Town of Braintree residents. Original document held by the Office of the Town Clerk, Braintree, MA. A transcription is found in Pattee's *History of Braintree* (see below).

Other sources on the Thayers, Mass Bay Colony and Braintree:

Bates, Samuel A. *Records of the Town of Braintree, 1640-1793*. Randolph, MA: D. H. Huxford, printer, 1886.

--- *The Ancient Iron Works of Braintree, Mass. (The first in America)*. Probably Quincy, MA: Frank A. Bates, publisher, 1898. Reprinted in Muno's *Descendants of Richard Thayer* (see below).

Brown, Richard D. and Jack Tager. *Massachusetts, A Concise History*. Amherst, MA: University of Massachusetts Press, 2000.

Dunn, Richard S. and Laetitia Yeandle, eds. *The Journal of John Winthrop, 1630-1649*, abridged edition. Cambridge, MA and London, England: The Belknap Press of Harvard University, 1996.

Faxon, Walter, Edward H. Whorf and Henry E. Woods. "Tayer (Thayer) Family Entries in the Parish Register of Thornbury, Gloucestershire, England." *New England Historic Genealogical Register* 60 (1906): 281-289.

Holly, H. Hobart, ed. *Braintree Mass, Its History*. Braintree, MA: Braintree Historical Society, 1985.

Muno, Patricia Thayer. *A Comprehensive Genealogy of the Thayer Family of America — Vol III, Descendants of Richard Thayer Immigrant to America 1641, Through his Grandson, Richard Thayer*. Braintree, MA: Braintree Historical Society, 2003.

Ojeda, Luis Thayer. *Genealogy of the Descendants of William Turpin Thayer of Bellingham*. Valp[araiso, Chili]: around 1933. (Copy held by the New England Historic Genealogical Society, Boston, MA.)

Ojeda, Tomas Thayer. *The Thayer Family of Thornbury, A Study Trying Its Reconstitution*. possibly Santiago, Chili?: Imprenta Moderna, "2015-Modena-2015," 1907. (Copy held by the New England Historic Genealogical Society, Boston, MA.)

Osgood, Franklin Baker, et. al. *A Thayer Family History, Ancestors and Descendants of Walter Tisdale Thayer and Anne Elizabeth Levere*. 2005. (Copy found at the New England Historic Genealogical Society, Boston, MA. Its focus is Thomas Thayer, the immigrant.)

Park, Lawrence. *Major Thomas Savage of Boston and His Descendants*. Boston, MA: Press of David Clapp and Son, 1914.

Pattee, William S., M.D. *A History of Old Braintree and Quincy, with a Sketch of Randolph and Holbrook*. Quincy, MA: Green and Prescott, 1879.

Records of the Suffolk County Court, 1671-1680, Vol XXX. Boston, MA: Publications of the Colonial Society of Massachusetts, The University Press, 1933. (Volume of court case transcriptions reviewed at the New England Historic Genealogical Society, Boston, MA.)

Sanders, Joanne McRae. *Barbados Records, Wills and Administrations, Vol 1, 1639-1680*. Sanders Historical Publications, 1979.

Smith, Dean Crawford. *The Ancestry of Eva Belle Kempton, 1878-1908, Part III*. Ed. Melinde Lutz Sanborn. Boston, MA: New England Historic Genealogical Society, 2004.

Sprague, Waldo C. *Genealogies of the Families of Braintree, Mass*. Boston, MA: New England Historic Genealogical Society. Database created from original records donated to NEHGS by Mr. Sprague in 1962. (See www.americananancestors.org.)

--- *Genealogies of the Families of Braintree, Mass*. Boston, MA: New England Historic Genealogical Society, 2001.This microfilm version provides images of cards on which Sprague recorded findings on each family containing key information on land holdings and other details not available on the electronic database. Cited in this book as Sprague's Braintree, followed by the number of the card prepared by Sprague.

--- *The Braintree Iron Works: Erected in 1644 and 1645 by John Winthrop, Jr*. Quincy, Mass: Premier Press, Printers, 1955.

Strong, Sydney, ed. *Roger Clap's Memoirs with account of the voyage of the "Mary and John," 1630*. Toledo, OH: Mary and John Clearing House, undated.

Thayer, Bezaleel, *Memorial of the Thayer Name, From the Massachusetts Colony of Weymouth and Braintree, Embracing Genealogical Sketches of Richard and Thomas Thayer and Their Descendants, from 1636 to 1874*. Oswego, (New York?): R. J. Oliphant Steam Book and Job Printer, 1874. Reprinted by Rockwell Foundation, (1976?).

Wilson, James. *The Earth Shall Weep, A History of Native America*. New York, NY: Atlantic Monthly Press, 1998.

CHAPTER 5: MAN OF THE TEMPEST

Anderson, Robert Charles. *The Pilgrim Migration, Immigrants to Plymouth Colony, 1620-1633*. Boston, MA: New England Historic Genealogical Society, 2004.

Austin, John D. *Mayflower Families Through Five Generations: Stephen Hopkins*. Vol 6, 3rd Edition. Plymouth, MA: General Society of Mayflower Descendants, 2001.

Beals, Kathleen C. *Early Families of Bethlehem, New Hampshire*. Bradford, NH: self-published, 2009.

Bradford, William. *Of Plymouth Plantation*. Ed. Samuel Elliott Morrison. New York, NY: Alfred A. Knopf, 1999.

Bradford, William and Edward Winslow, et al. *Mourt's Relation: A Journal of the Pilgrims at Plymouth*. 1622. Original published in 1622. Ed. Dwight B. Heath. Bedford, MA: Applewood Books, 1963.

Doherty, Kieran. *Sea Venture: Shipwreck, Survival and the Salvation of the First English Colony in the New World*. New York, NY: St. Martin's Press, 2007.

Emerson, William A. *History of the Town of Douglas, Mass. through 1878*. Boston, MA: Frank W. Bird, 1879.

Hammond, Isaac W. *Documents in New Hampshire, Vol II*. Concord, NH: Parsons B. Cogswell - State Printer, 1882.

Horn, James. *A Land As God Made It: Jamestown and the Birth of America*. New York, NY: Basic Books, 2005.

Johnson, Caleb. *Here Shall I Die Ashore — Stephen Hopkins: Bermuda Castaway, Jamestown Survivor, and Mayflower Pilgrim*. United States: Xlibris Corporation, 2007.

Kilbourne, Frederick W. *Chronicles of the White Mountains*. 1916. Ed. by Heritage Books Inc.

Kingman, Bradford. *The History of North Bridgewater, Plymouth County, Mass. from its First Settlement to the Present Time*. Boston, MA: self-published, 1866.

Middleton, Richard. *Colonial America: a History, 1585-1776*. Cambridge, MA: Blackwell Publishers, 1996.

Philbrick, Nathaniel. *Mayflower, A Story of Courage, Community and War*. New York, NY: Viking - Penguin Group, 2006.

Records of the Town of Lyman, New Hampshire. Salt Lake City, UT: LDS Family History Library. Microfilm, no. 2,257,489.

Reich, Jerome. *Colonial America.* Upper Saddle River, NJ: Prentice Hall, 2001.

"Stephen Hopkins." *The Great Migration Begins: Immigrants to New England 1620-1633, Vols I-III.* Boston, MA: New England Historic Genealogical Society. Database at www.newenglandancestors.org.

Welch, Sarah N. *A History of Franconia, New Hampshire, 1772-1972.* Littleton, NH: Courier Printing Co, 1972.

Woodward, Hobson. *A Brave Vessel: The True Story of the Castaways Who Rescued Jamestown and Inspired Shakespeare's The Tempest.* New York, NY: Viking - the Penguin Group, 2009.

Wooley, Benjamin. *Savage Kingdom, The True Story of Jamestown, 1607, and the Settlement of America.* New York, NY: Harper Collins, 2007.

CHAPTER 6: THE IRONIC ENIGMA

Barrett, Beryl (Prince Edward Island genealogist). Unpublished personal correspondence on the search for the author's McDonald and Carr genealogical lines, 1980-1983.

Crapaud Women's Institute, compilers. *History of Crapaud, Prince Edward Island.* Apparently self-published about 1955. Obtained from the Prince Edward Island Heritage Society, Charlottetown, PEI, Canada.

Fernald, Charles A., M.D. *Fernald Genealogy.* Boston, MA: apparently self-published, 1910.

Hood, Arlene. Unpublished genealogy of the Joseph Carr family of Crapaud, Prince Edward Island, his descendants and prior generations. Obtained from the author.

Nashua History Committee. *The Nashua Experience: History in the Making, 1673-1978.* Canaan, NH: Phoenix Publishing, 1978.

Roberts, Elias, Elder. *Baptisms (children) 1869-1900.* Charlottetown, PEI, Canada: Prince Edward Island Provincial Archives. Church of Scotland Records, Vol 1, Record Book 1, p 130. Microfilm of a handwritten record.

Sorensen, Arlene. Unpublished genealogy of the Joseph Carr family, his descendants and prior generations. Obtained from the author.

Weale, David. *Them Times*. Charlottetown, PEI, Canada: Institute of Island Studies, 1992. (A series of sketches of life on PEI prior to World War I.

FIVE LIVES AND AN ENIGMA: GENEALOGY

Provided in this section are the genealogical data that demonstrate the linkages between the author and the principal individuals highlighted in this book. The sources and related abbreviations used in this section are listed below:

AHN (name of paper, date, volume, issue): *America's Historical Newspapers*, published by Readex, a division of Newsbank, Inc., in association with the American Antiquarian Society; available on-line at: www.readex.com/content/americas-historical-newspapers.

Americanancestors (database): Any of a series of databases maintained by the New England Historic Genealogical Society (hereafter NEHGS), Boston, MA.

Ancestry.com (database): Any of a series of databases maintained by Ancestry.com, Provo, UT.

Braintree VR (volume, page): A subset of the collection of Waldo C. Sprague (see the note on Sprague's Braintree below), containing Braintree, MA vital records for the period 1643-1793; maintained by NEHGS as a database at www.americanancestors.org.

Browne: Browne, William B. *Genealogy of the Jenks Family of America*. Concord, NH: Rumford Press, 1952.

Covert Family: Fisher, Carl W., William V. Covert and Maurice Patterson, compilers. *The Covert Family*. Interlaken, New York: Interlaken Historical Society, 1989.

Covert Bible: Bible of the Leroy and Edith Covert family, from which the original listings of births, deaths, and marriages are in possession of the author.

Kempton Genealogy: Smith, Dean Crawford. *The Ancestry of Eva Belle Kempton, 1878-1908, Part III*. Ed. Melinde Lutz Sanborn. Boston, MA: New England Historic Genealogical Society, 2004.

Kingman: Kingman, Bradford. *The History of North Bridgewater, Plymouth County, Massachusetts, from its First Settlement to the Present Time*. Boston, MA, 1866.

LDS IGI: International Genealogical Index of the Church of Jesus Christ of Latter Day Saints, material from which is now incorporated in the new LDS website: www.familysearch.org.

MA VR (town, type of record, year, vol, page - where available): Massachusetts vital records compiled by the NEHGS and now available in on-line databases, as follows: MA VR to 1850, MA VR 1841-1910, MA VR: 1911-1915, at www.american ancestors.org.

MA VR-Index (town, type of record, year, vol, page - where available): Volumes of indices of vital records compiled by the State of Massachusetts; consulted in hard copy at NEHGS for vital records which post-date the year 1915.

NEHGR (year, vol, page): New England Historic Genealogical Record, the journal of the NEHGS.

NEHGS-Mss 1017: A handwritten genealogical record of the Jenks family, including the Richard H. and Eliza H.W. Heaton family, maintained by NEHGS (manuscripts section). No author given. While unsourced, Mss 1017 is generally consistent with known sources of the Jenks genealogical record, and contains some details not found elsewhere.

NH VR (town, type of record): Vital Records from the towns of New Hampshire compiled by the State of New Hampshire's Office of Registrar of Vital Statistics. Collection maintained by the New Hampshire State Archives, Concord, New Hampshire.

NHA-Barney: Genealogical information for Nantucket collected by Eliza Starbuck Barney and maintained by the Nantucket Historical Association. On-line database at www.nha.org/library.

Nickerson Family: *The Nickerson Family, The Descendants of William Nickerson, 1604-1689, First Settler of Chatham, Mass., Part 1*, Nickerson Family Association, self-published, 1973.

PEI VR: Vital records maintained by the Public Archives and Records Office, Government of Prince Edward Island, Charlottetown, PEI, Canada, on microfilm, and now made available through an on-line database.

Savage: Savage, James, *Genealogical Dictionary of the First Settlers of New England Showing Three Generations of Those Who Came Before May, 1692*, Vol I-IV. Boston, MA, 1860-1862.

Sprague's Braintree: Sprague, Waldo C. *Genealogies of the Families of Braintree, Mass.*, NEHGS, Boston, MA, 2001. The original records, in notebooks and small cards, were donated to NEHGS by Mr. Sprague in 1962; available on microfilm, and now on CD, through NEHGS.

<u>Sprague's Randolph</u>: Sprague, Waldo C. Transcriptions of Randolph, MA vital records from town records and cemeteries, made available from NEHGS as an electronic database entitled *Randolph, MA—Vital Records to 1875*, at: www.americanancestors.org.

<u>Sorensen-Carr Genealogy</u>: Genealogy of the descendants of Joseph Carr by his grand-daughter, compiled by Arlene (Carr) Sorensen, generally without sources, unpublished. Copy in possession of the author.

<u>Thayer Memorial (1874)</u>: Thayer, Bezaleel. *Memorial of the Thayer Name, From the Massachusetts Colony of Weymouth and Braintree, Embracing Genealogical Sketches of Richard and Thomas Thayer and Their Descendants, from 1636 to 1974*. Oswego, (New York?): R. J. Oliphant Steam Book and Job Printer, 1874. Reprinted by Rockwell Foundation, (1976?)

<u>Tower Genealogy</u>: Tower, Charlemagne. *Tower Genealogy, An Account of the Descendants of John Tower of Hingham, Mass*. Cambridge, MA: John Wilson and Son, University Press, 1891.

ABBREVIATIONS USED IN THIS SECTION

ca. - about

aft. - after

b. - born

bap. - baptized

bef. - before

bet. - between

bpl. - birthplace

bur. - buried

d. - died

div. - divorced

d/o - daughter of

int. - intentions to marry

m. - married

m. (1), m. (2), m. (3) - first marriage, etc.

poss. - possibly

prob. - probably

rec. - recorded

s/o - son of

unm. - unmarried

In the sections for each chapter that follow, there is a brief introduction that lists the generations for which genealogical data is presented. Each of these lists is numbered, from the oldest generation to the most recent. When generations of a family line overlap from chapter to chapter, the reader is referred to the appropriate section of this genealogical record to avoid repetition. Following this introduction is a presentation of genealogical data organized by family group. Direct ancestors of the author are highlighted in bold print. The endnotes for each chapter contain the source material that supports the genealogical data.

The bulk of the family history recorded in this book is from the current state of Massachusetts or the colonial entities that preceded it. For brevity's sake, all towns or cities that are now part of Massachusetts are listed without a state designation. Only in a few cases where no town or city is known, or where there is specific need for clarification, is the abbreviation "MA" used.

GENEALOGY — CHAPTER 1: THE WILL TO ENDURE

1a: Leon Pennell and Helen C. Covert
1b: James A. MacDonald and Theresa F. Fernald
2:   Irving F. MacDonald and June M. Pennell
3:   Barry J. MacDonald

LEON and HELEN CORNELIA (COVERT) PENNELL

LEON PENNELL b. Wareham, 10 Feb 1897, s/o George Woodbury Pennell, bpl. unclear, and Harriet D. Beswick, b. Blackburn, Lancashire, England.[1] Leon d. Long Island Hospital, Boston, 05 Mar 1925.[2] He m. Rockingham, VT, 28 Nov 1916, **HELEN CORNELIA COVERT**,[3] b. Holbrook, 09 Apr 1898, d/o Leroy Leighton Covert, b. Farmer (later Interlaken), NY, and Edith Gertrude Wood, b. Randolph.[4] Helen d. Brockton, 26 Jul 1981.[5]

Children (PENNELL) of Leon and Helen (Covert) Pennell:

i.   LEON WILLARD b. Brockton, 06 May 1917; d. Brockton, 07 Jun 1920.[6]
ii. **JUNE MIRIAM** b. Brockton, 04 Jun 1919; d. Boston, 03 Apr 2009.[7]

Helen m. (2) West Bridgewater, 03 May 1925, HARROLD [HAROLD] DUSTIN JEPSON,[8] b. prob. West Bridgewater, 30 Jun 1900, s/o Axel Jepson, b. Sweden, and Angenora S. Dustin, b. CT.[9] Helen and Harold, div. 15 Mar 1937.[10] Harold d. San Bernardino, CA, 11 Jun 1960.[11]

Child (JEPSON) of Harrold and Helen (Covert) (Pennell) Jepson:

i.   LAWRENCE LEROY b. West Bridgewater, 18 Nov 1926; d. West Bridgewater, 15 Feb 1933.[12]

Helen m. (3) Syracuse, NY, 15 Aug 1944, HERBERT HENRY BARRY,[13] b. Brockton, 15 Apr 1885, s/o Edward (or Edwin) J. Barry, b. North Bridgewater (later Brockton), and Catherine A. Scrivens, b. Ireland. Herbert d. NH, 1962.[14] No children of this marriage.

JAMES ALFRED and THERESA FRANCES (FERNALD) MACDONALD

JAMES ALFRED MCDONALD b. prob. Albany, Lot 27, Prince Edward Island (hereafter PEI), Canada, 03 May 1887, s/o Daniel McDonald, b. Canada, and Hannah Amelia Carr, b. Tryon, Lot 28, PEI, Canada.[15] James A. bap. Albany, Lot 27, PEI, Canada, 23 Jun 1889.[16] He d. Brockton, 08 Mar 1964.[17] James A. m. Lee, NH, 10 Nov 1915, **THERESA FRANCES FERNALD,**[18] b. Haverhill, 24 Jan 1890, d/o Daniel Fernald, b. Lee, NH, and Maria (Minnie) Price Heaton, b. Baltimore, MD.[19] Theresa d. Boston, 01 Nov 1959.[20] James Alfred became a naturalized U.S. citizen on 03 Apr 1922.[21] At some point after this date, he changed the spelling of the family's surname to MacDonald.

Children (MACDONALD) of James Alfred and Theresa (Fernald) MacDonald:

i.   GEORGE ALFRED b. Nashua, NH, 15 Jul 1917; d. prob. Boca Raton, Palm Beach, FL, 23 Sep, 1971. His name was legally changed from McDonald to MacDonald in 1958. [22]

ii. **IRVING FRANCIS** b. Boston, 10 Oct 1922; d. Brockton, 05 Aug 1985.[23]

iii. ARTHUR WILLIAM b. Boston, 14 Jan 1928; d. San Diego, CA, 04 Jul 1991. [24]

IRVING FRANCIS and JUNE MIRIAM (PENNELL) MACDONALD

IRVING FRANCIS MACDONALD b. Boston, 10 Oct 1922; d. Brockton, 05 Aug 1985.[25] He m. Boston, 31 May 1948, **JUNE MIRIAM PENNELL,**[26] b. Brockton, 04 Jun 1919. June d. Boston, 03 Apr 2009.[27]

Child (MACDONALD) of Irving and June (Pennell) MacDonald:

i.   **BARRY JAMES** b. Boston, 11 May 1950.[28]

---

[1] MA VR, Wareham, births, 1897, vol 467, p 699. Original town records reviewed at Wareham Town Hall: *Town Records of Wareham, Births: 1893-1936.*

[2] MA VR-Index, Brockton, deaths, 1925, vol 7, p 172, and probably a duplicate: MA VR - Index, Boston, deaths, 1925, vol 1, p 182. Copy of original record issued by City Clerk of Brockton, in possession of the author.

³ Certified copies of marriage record, dated 21 March 1994, "Marriage - Bride" and "Marriage - Groom," Public Records Division, VT, in possession of the author.

⁴ MA VR, Holbrook, births, 1898, vol 476, p 541, no 6.

⁵ Certificate of Death, City Clerk of Brockton, 27 July 1981, in possession of the author.

⁶ Birth: MA VR, Brockton, births, 1917, vol 642, p 160. Death: MA VR, Brockton, deaths, 1920, vol 28, p 418. Name and date also recorded in Covert Bible.

⁷ Birth: Birth Certificate, Brockton, 1919, p 130, Reg. no 611, in possession of the author. Death: Death Certificate, Registry Division of the City of Boston, Certificate R No. 22956, dated 09 Apr 2009, in possession of the author.

⁸ Original marriage record signed by the pastor, Rev. F. Burton Long, in possession of the author.

⁹ Deposition by Angenora Jepson, Harold's mother, 09 August 1916, stating that Harold Jepson was born to Angenora and Axel Jepson on 30 June 1900 at West Bridgewater. This unusual record most likely formed the basis for MA VR - Index, West Bridgewater, births, 1900, vol 217, p 123, found in MA VR Index to Births, Corrections and Additions, Commonwealth of Massachusetts, 1929.

¹⁰ Copy of certificate, Massachusetts Probate Court at Plymouth, signed 03 August 1944, stating that a divorce from Helen C. Jepson was granted to Harold D. Jepson on 15 March 1937. This divorce decree became absolute on 15 September 1937. In possession of the author.

¹¹ Ancestry.com (*California Death Index, 1940-1997*); data from *California Death Index, 1940-1997*, California Dept of Heath Services, Center for Health Statistics.

¹² Birth: MA VR-Index, West Bridgewater, births, 1926, vol 94, p 438. Abstract issued 18 May 1931 by the Town Clerk of West Bridgewater, attesting to the birth of Lawrence Leroy Jepson in that town on 18 November 1926, in possession of the author. Death: MA VR-Index, West Bridgewater, deaths, 1933, vol 87, p 481.

¹³ Copy of Affidavit for License to Marry, State of New York, Onondaga County, City of Syracuse, NY, signed 14 August 1944 by the Commissioner of Deeds.

Copy of wedding certificate, dated 15 August 1944 at Syracuse, by the Minister of Onondaga Valley Presbyterian Church. Both in possession of the author.

[14] Birth: MA VR, Brockton, births, 1885, vol 359, p 362, no 121. Death: unsourced family information.

[15] Birth information from a Certificate of Baptism issued 18 July 1977 from the records of the Free Church of Scotland in Prince Edward Island, Canada (see Note 16); in possession of the author.

[16] *Record of Baptisms by Elias Roberts, Elder*; Public Archives of Prince Edward Island, microfilm, accession no. 3095, item 1, p 58, no 247.

[17] MA VR-Index, Brockton, deaths, 1964, vol 33, p 213.

[18] Copy of certificate of marriage from the Town Clerk, Lee, NH, dated 08 Sept 1979, in possession of the author.

[19] MA VR, Haverhill, births, 1890, vol 403, p 268, no 47.

[20] Death Certificate, Boston, MA, 1959, vol 27, p 278, no 10348, in possession of the author.

[21] Intention No. 1184, Superior Court, Hillsborough County, NH, 16 July 1917. Petition dated 18 August 1921, provides information about the marriage to T[h]eresa Fernald, her birthplace and date, and birth data for son George A.

[22] Birth: copy of Corrected Birth Certificate based on a filing of Sep 15 1958, issued by the New Hampshire State Registrar on 28 Nov 2001. Purpose of this correction was to change George Alfred's surname from McDonald to MacDonald. Death: Ancestry.com (*Florida Death Index, 1877-1980;* data from Florida Dept. of Health, Office of Vital Records, 1998.

[23] Birth: Birth Certificate, Boston, 1922, vol 2, p 110, reg. no 14381, in possession of the author. Death: Death Certificate, dated 06 August 1985, issued by City Clerk, Brockton, in possession of the author. The certificate also refers to marriage to June M. Pennell and lists parents as James A. MacDonald and Theresa Fernald.

[24] Birth: MA VR-Index, Boston, births, 1928, vol 1, p 13 for Arthur William McDonald. Why the last name was recorded without an "a" in "Mac" is unknown. The same birth date and place for Arthur William are recorded in the James A. and Theresa MacDonald family bible in possession of the author. Death: Ancestry.com (*California Death Index, 1940-1997)*, based on original data from California Dept of Heath Services, Center for Health Statistics.

[25] See note 23.

[26] Certificate of Marriage, Boston, 1948, p 402, reg. no 3276; in possession of the author.

[27] See note 7.

[28] Birth Certificate No. 20393/H citing Boston birth record no. 7032 for 1950, in possession of the author.

GENEALOGY — CHAPTER 2:   THE DOUGHBOY

Percy Leon Covert, the principal subject of this chapter, was the uncle of the author's mother, June (Pennell) MacDonald, the subject of Chapter 1. Percy's sister, Helen, was June's mother. This record documents the families of Percy's grandparents, his parents' family, and his own family.

    1a: Martin V. Covert and Affa Antoinette Davis
    1b: William Henry Wood and Nancy Ann Tower
    2:    Edith Gertrude Wood and Leroy Leighton Covert
    3:    Percy Leroy Covert and Gladys Morton Dean

MARTIN and AFFA ANTOINETTE (DAVIS) COVERT:

MARTIN V. COVERT b. Seneca County, NY, 17 Dec 1837, s/o John E. Covert, b. prob. NJ, and Catherine _____, b. Seneca County, NY.[1] Martin d. Bath, NY, 18 Feb 1915.[2] He m. (1) Lodi or Ovid, NY, Dec 1861, ELIZABETH G. SEARS, of Trumansburg, NY.[3]

Child (COVERT) of Martin and Elizabeth (Sears) Covert:

    ?i.   CHARLES[4]

Martin m. (2) Ovid, NY, 27 Oct 1867, **AFFA (EFFIE or AFFIE) ANTOINETTE DAVIS,**[5] b. New Baltimore, MI, 7 Aug 1851, d/o Charles A. Davis, b. Seneca County, NY, and Louisa Caywood, b. Seneca County, NY.[6] Affa Antoinette d. Taunton, 5 May 1927.[7]

Child (COVERT) of Martin and Affa Antoinette (Davis) Covert:

    i.   **LEROY LEIGHTON** b. Farmer (later Interlaken), NY, Apr 1871; d. Brockton, 4 Feb 1937.[8]

WILLIAM HENRY and NANCY ANN (TOWER) WOOD:

WILLIAM HENRY WOOD b. Braintree, 8 Mar 1835, s/o Joel Wood(s), b. Braintree, and Eliza A. Howard, b. prob. Canton.[9] William Henry d. Holbrook, 26 Aug 1903.[10] He m. (1) Abington, 3 Jul 1859, HANNAH MARIA FRENCH,[11] b. prob. Randolph, ca. Mar 1843, d/o John French, b. Randolph, and Ellen Maria Gorham, b. Sandwich.[12] Hannah d. Randolph, 5 Nov 1863.[13]

Child (WOOD) of William Henry and Hannah (French) Wood:

i.   ANNIE (or ANNA) ELIZABETH b. Randolph, 6 Nov 1859.[14]

William Henry m. (2), Stoughton, 31 Aug 1865, **NANCY ANN TOWER**,[15] b. Braintree, 2 Jul 1848, d/o Isaac Pratt Tower, b. Braintree, and Susan Snow, b. Lyman, NH. Nancy Ann d. West Bridgewater, 30 Mar 1930.[16]

Children (WOOD) of William Henry and Nancy Ann (Tower) Wood:

i.   **EDITH GERTRUDE** b. Randolph, 4 Apr 1871; d. West Bridgewater, 25 Dec 1927.[17]

ii.   MARION (or MARIAN) ETHEL WOOD b. Braintree, 14 Feb 1878; d. Braintree, 25 Feb 1879.[18]

LEROY and EDITH (WOOD) COVERT FAMILY

LEROY LEIGHTON COVERT b. Farmer (later Interlaken), NY, Apr 1871, s/o Martin V. Covert and Affa Antoinette Davis. Leroy d. Brockton, 4 Feb 1937.[19] He m. Detroit, MI, 5 May 1890, **EDITH GERTRUDE WOOD**,[20] b. Randolph, 4 Apr 1871.[21] Edith d. West Bridgewater, 25 Dec 1927.[22]

Children (COVERT) of Leroy and Edith (Wood) Covert:

i.   PERCY LEON b. Detroit, MI, 23 Feb 1892; d. Medfield, 19 or 20 Dec 1964.[23]

ii.   GRACE EVELYN b. Detroit, MI, 21 Feb 1894; d. Brockton, 15 Jan 1983.[24]

iii.   LILLIAN ETHEL MAY COVERT b. Detroit, MI, 18 Jan 1896; d. Charlton, 18 Jun 1986. [25]

iv.   **HELEN CORNELIA** b. Holbrook, 9 Apr 1898; d. Brockton, 26 Jul 1981. [26]

v.   RUTH ALMA b. Holbrook, 7 Nov 1906; d. San Jose, CA, 25 Jan 1986.[27]

vi.   HARRIET ALOIS b. Holbrook, 3 Jun 1910; d. Nokomis, FL, 17 Oct 1999.[28]

vii.   EDITH ALBERTA b. Brockton, 30 Aug (or 2_ Sep) 1913; d. Plymouth, 20 Sep 1998.[29]

PERCY and GLADYS (DEAN) COVERT FAMILY

PERCY LEON COVERT b. Detroit, MI, 23 Feb 1892, s/o Leroy Leighton Covert and Edith Gertrude Wood. Percy d. Medfield, 19 or 20 Dec 1964.[30] He m. Brockton, 28 Jun 1910, GLADYS MORTON DEAN,[31] b. Brockton, 9 Jan 1892, d/o Edgar Dean, b. OH, and Louisa J. Austin, b. Taunton.[32] Gladys d. Brockton, 27 Aug 1931.[33]

Children (COVERT) of Percy and Gladys (Dean) Covert:

    i.   ALTA LOUISA b. Brockton, 26 Jan 1911; d. 23 Mar 1998, Glendale, AZ.[34]

    ii.   ALLISTON DEAN b. Brockton, 25 May 1912; d. Duval County, FL, 3 Mar 1972.[35]

    iii.   [child] b. Brockton, 1 June 1914; d. Brockton, 1 Jun 1914.[36]

    iv.   [child] b. Brockton, 1 June 1914; d. Brockton, 14 Jun 1914.[37]

---

[1] National Archives, Civil War Pension Files: affidavit dated 1 Feb 1907, signed by John H. Stevens, Justice of the Peace, Seneca County, NY, provides birth date. Covert Family, pp 132 and 290, provides names of parents, and states Martin was born Seneca County, NY about 1838.

[2] National Archives, Civil War Pension File: Pensioner Dropped, Department of the Interior, Certificate No. 650391; date and place of death cited.

[3] Card files of Betty Auten, County Historian for Seneca County, NY; transcription of marriage details.

[4] No birth record found. Family information places Charles in Washington, DC at the time of the Taft Administration (1909-1913). A possibility is: Charles C. Covert, age 57, born NY, parents born US (1920 U.S. Census for the District of Columbia). Year of birth for this Charles coincides with time period when Martin Covert was married to Elizabeth Sears.

[5] Covert Family, p 290: marriage at the 1st Reformed Dutch Church of Ovid, NY, 27 Oct 1867. Card files of Betty Auten, County Historian for Seneca County, NY, shows marriage at "Lodi Presby," same date.

[6] Covert Family Bible shows Affie Antoinett Covert born 7 August 1851. Her death certificate (see note 7) shows that she was 75 years, 8 months, and 28 days old on 5 May 1927 when she died which converts to within a day of the

birth date given in the bible. Death certificate lists Affa's father as Alfred Davis (the Alfred is scratched through and Charles penciled in), and her mother as _____Caywood, and Affa's place of birth as New Baltimore, MI. The 1850 US census for nearby Chesterfield, Macomb, MI shows: Charles Davis, age 25, born New York; wife Louisa, age 24, born NY; children — Mary, age 7; and Alfred, age 2; both born Michigan. Later census records show Affa as a member of this family.

[7] MA VR, West Bridgewater, deaths, 1927, vol 79, p 225, no 17, in possession of the author. Record was filed in West Bridgewater, but the certificate states that death took place in Taunton at the State Hospital where Affa Antoinette was living with "senile psychosis."

[8] Birth: Covert Family Bible states that Leroy was born on 4 April 1871 in Farmer, NY. Covert Family lists the place of birth as Interlaken, NY. At the time of Leroy's birth, the village was called Farmer and was later renamed Interlaken. His death certificate lists Interlaken, NY as the birthplace and gives his age at death as 65 years and 10 months which would place Leroy's birth in April 1871. Death: MA VR, Brockton, deaths, 1937, vol 27, p 536, no 107, in possession of the author.

[9] Covert Family Bible: birth at Braintree, 8 March 1836. Sprague's Braintree: March 1836, per the "Randolph Rebellion Record." Massachusetts Certificate of Marriage, dated 17 September 1903, for William Henry Wood and Nancy A. Tower provides names of both of William Henry's parents, found in William Henry's Civil War pension file, no 791939, National Archives, transcribing the Record of Marriages of Stoughton. MA VR, Randolph, deaths, 1874, vol 266, p266, no 3 for Eliza (Howard) Wood, gives Canton as her birthplace. MA VR, Randolph, deaths, 1890, vol 410, p 378, for Joel Wood, states his birthplace as Braintree.

[10] MA VR, Holbrook, deaths, vol 1903/26, p 87.

[11] MA VR, Abington, marriages, 1859, vol 127, p 223.

[12] No vital record yet found. William Henry Wood's pension file (see note 9) provides the data shown for Hannah's birth and the names of her parents as John and Ellen French. MA VR, Randolph, 1862, deaths, vol 157, p 291, for John French, states that Hannah's mother was Ellen M. Gorham of Sandwich.

[13] MA VR, Randolph, 1863, deaths, vol 166, p 235 for Hannah Woods, daughter of John and Ellen French. Her gravestone in the Central Cemetery, Randolph,

MA, reads as follows: "Hannah M., wife of William H. Wood and daur. of John and Ellen French, died Nov. 5 1863, aged 20 yrs, 8 mos."

[14] MA VR, Randolph, 1859, births, vol 124, p 259.

[15] MA VR, Stoughton, 1865, marriages, vol 181, p 246. Original marriage certificate signed by Charles M. Smith, DD, East Stoughton, in possession of the author.

[16] Copy of Massachusetts Certificate of Death for West Bridgewater, 1930, "483," obtained from the Boston Department of Public Health on 2 March 1994, in possession of the author.

[17] Birth: MA VR, Randolph, births, 1871, vol 233, p407. Death: MA VR, West Bridgewater, deaths, 1927, vol 79, p 244, no 35.

[18] Birth: MA VR, Braintree, births, 1878, vol 296, p 235, which reads: "Marian Ethel Wood d. William H. and N. Annie (Tower)." Death: MA VR, Braintree, deaths, 1879, vol 311, p 205.

[19] See note 8.

[20] Covert Family Bible. Original certificate of marriage, signed by Charles Haass, Pastor, St. John's Germ[an] Ev[angelical] Church, in possession of the author, confirms date and place.

[21] MA VR, Randolph, births, 1871, vol 233, p 407 for an Edith C. Wood; parents are listed as William Henry, born Braintree, and Nancy Ann (Tower) Wood, born Randolph.

[22] MA VR, West Bridgewater, deaths, 1927, vol 79, p 244, no 35, in possession of the author.

[23] Birth: Familysearch.org (Michigan, Births, 1867-1902), based on "A Return of Births in the County of Wayne, Michigan for 1892." Also, Covert Family Bible. Death: date of 20 Dec 1964 is from Percy's tombstone found in the Central Cemetery, Wareham. MA VR-Index, Medfield, deaths, 1964, vol 71, p 215: Medfield, 19 December 1964.

[24] Birth: Covert Family Bible. Death: family information.

[25] Birth: Covert Family Bible. Death: family information.

[26] Birth: MA VR, Holbrook, births, 1898, vol 1, p 67, no 9. Death: copy of Massachusetts Certificate of Death witnessed by the City Clerk of Brockton, 27 July 1981, in possession of the author.

[27] Birth: MA VR, Holbrook, births, 1906, vol 560, p 47, no 44. Death: family information.

[28] Birth: MA VR, Holbrook, births, 1910, vol 592, p 43. Death: family information, corroborated by Ancestry.com (Social Security Death Index).

[29] Birth: MA VR, Brockton, births, 1913, vol 616, p 167 lists the name as Edith; however the page for this document reviewed on the NEHGS website was incomplete and appears to show a date of 2_ Sep 1913. Covert Family Bible lists first name as Edith and lists birth date as 30 August 1913. Death: Ancestry.com *(Massachusetts Death Index, 1970-2003)*, certificate 044617, for Edith Billings (married name).

[30] See note 23.

[31] MA VR, Brockton, marriages, 1910, vol 596, p 165, no 264.

[32] MA VR, Brockton, births, 1892, vol 422, p 545, no 40. This record is for _____ Dean, male, to Edgar Dean and Louisa (Austin) Dean. While no name is given, and the child is identified as male, this is certainly the birth record for Gladys Dean. Edgar Dean and Louisa J. Austin are noted as the parents of Gladys Dean on her marriage record shown in Note 31 above. Edgar Dean's birthplace of Ohio is from 1860 U.S. Census for Cuyahoga County, OH, in the family of his parents David and Harriet B. Dean.   Louisa J. Austin's birthplace is from MA VR, Taunton, births, 1858, vol 114, p 169.

[33] MA VR-Index, Brockton, deaths, 1931, vol 26, p 360. Specific death date as well as place are given in the Covert Family Bible; corroborated by an article in the Brockton Times of 27 August 1931: "Mrs. Gladys M. Covert, wife of Percy L Covert, 359 Pleasant street, died today in her 40th year, after being ill for a year."

[34] Birth: MA VR, Brockton, 1911, births, vol 600, p 148 which lists a Covert born on this date, no first name given, to Percy and Gladys (Dean) Covert. Covert Family Bible confirms the MA VR record and provides the first name. Death: Ancestry.com (Social Security Death Index) for an Alta Williams (surname of Alta's first husband).

[35] Birth: MA VR, Brockton, births, 1912, vol 608, p 147. Death: Ancestry. com (Florida Death Index, 1877-1998), based on data from the Florida Dept. of Health, Office of Vital Records, 1998.

[36] Birth: Covert Family Bible records the birth of twins to Percy and Gladys on 1 Jun 1914. This is corroborated by MA VR, Brockton, births, 1914, vol 624, p 162, nos. 694 and 695 - both female. No names are given. Death: Familysearch. org (Massachusetts Deaths, 1841-1915) based on images of the original death certificates. No names are given.

[37] Birth and death: see Note 36.

CHAPTER 3: THE SANGUINARY NEWSMAN

The descent from Samuel Haynes Jenks to the author runs through his paternal grandmother, Theresa (Fernald) MacDonald. The first three generations of descent are documented below. The next three generations are found in Genealogy - Chapter 1.

1:    Samuel H. Jenks and Eliza Williams *(third wife)*
2:    Eliza H. W. Jenks and Richard H. Heaton
3:    Maria (Minnie) P. Heaton and Daniel C. Fernald
4:    Theresa F. Fernald and James MacDonald *(See Genealogy - Chapter 1)*
5:    Irving F. MacDonald and June M. Pennell *(See Genealogy - Chapter 1)*
6:    Barry J. MacDonald *(See Genealogy - Chapter 1)*

SAMUEL HAYNES JENKS and WIVES

SAMUEL HAYNES JENKS b. Boston, 20 Sep 1789, s/o Samuel Jenks, b. MA, and Mary Way of Philadelphia, PA.[1] Samuel d. South Boston, 3 Sep 1863.[2] He m. (1) Boston, 14 Jun 1812, LYDIA GROSE WILLIAMS,[3] b. prob. Boston, 03 Sep 1796, d/o James and Lydia Williams of Boston.[4] Lydia d. Boston, 25 June 1814; bur. Boston.[5]

Child (JENKS) of Samuel and Lydia (Williams) Jenks:

i.   LYDIA MARIA b. prob. Boston, 05 May 1814;[6] d. Nantucket, or Providence, RI, 29 May 1838.[7]

Samuel m. (2) Boston, 28 Jan 1816, LYDIA A. STEVENS,[8] b. prob. Nantucket, 22 Jan 1799, d/o Dennis Stevens, bpl. unknown, and Phebe Arthur, b. Nantucket.[9] Lydia d. Boston, bet. 15 and 18 May 1817; bur. Prospect Hill Cemetery, Nantucket.[10]

Child (JENKS) of Samuel and Lydia (Stevens) Jenks:

i.   MARIA LOUISA JENKS b. prob. Boston, 16 Feb 1817; d. Nantucket or Boston, 3 Jul 1817; bur. Prospect Hill Cemetery, Nantucket.[11]

Samuel m. (3) Nantucket, 23 Sep 1818, **ELIZA WILLIAMS**,[12] b. prob. Boston, 25 May (or Mar) 1801, d/o James and Lydia Williams of Boston.[13] Eliza d. prob. Nantucket, 20 Aug 1822; bur. prob. Boston.[14]

Children (JENKS) of Samuel and Eliza (Williams) Jenks:

    i.   WILLIAM ALFRED b. Nantucket, 29 Aug 1819; d. Camden, NJ, 21 July 1887.[15]

    ii.   **ELIZA HAYNES WILLIAMS** b. Nantucket, ca. 16 August 1822; d. Boston, 12 Aug 1892.[16]

Samuel m. (4) Nantucket, 01 Jan 1823, MARTHA WASHINGTON COFFIN,[17] b. Nantucket, 21 or 28 Apr 1801, d/o William Coffin, Jr., b. Nantucket, and Deborah Pinkham, b. Nantucket.[18] Martha d. Boston, 20 Feb 1887.[19]

Children (JENKS) of Samuel and Martha (Coffin) Jenks:

    i.   MARTHA COFFIN b. Nantucket, 29 Jan 1824; d. Nantucket, 01 Aug 1825.[20]

    ii.   MARTHA COFFIN b. MA, 19 Sep 1825, or 1826; d. Boston, 27 Sep 1888.[21]

    iii.   SAMUEL HAYNES Jr. b. Boston, 09 May 1828; d. Boston, 19 Jan 1858. [22]

    iv.   LUCY CATHERINE b. Boston or Nantucket, 13 Jun 1830; d. Boston, 06 Feb 1891 [23]

    v.   MARY HARRIET b. prob. Nantucket, 18 Jul 1832; d. Boston, 09 Mar 1851.[24]

    vi.   FRANCIS HENRY b. prob. Nantucket, 07 Dec 1834; d. Nantucket, 30 May 1836.[25]

    vii.   FRANCIS HENRY b. Nantucket, 02 Jun 1838; d. Boston, 09 Dec 1894.[26]

    viii.   CHARLES EDWARD b. Nantucket, 10 Feb 1844; d. Nantucket, 19 Jun 1844.[27]

RICHARD H. and ELIZA H. W. (JENKS) HEATON

RICHARD H. HEATON b. prob. New York City, NY, poss. 15 Apr 1821, s/o Richard Heaton, b. NY, and Eliza b. NY. Richard d. Baltimore, MD, 7 Nov 1905.[28] He m. Boston, 21 Jan 1847, **ELIZA HAYNES WILLIAMS JENKS**,[29] b. Nantucket, ca. 16 Aug 1822. Eliza d. Boston, 12 Aug 1892.[30]

Children (HEATON) of Richard and Eliza (Jenks) Heaton:

i.   SAMUEL JENKS b. prob. Boston, or Baltimore, MD, 13 Mar 1848;
      d. Baltimore, MD, 16 Apr 1857.[31]

ii.   FRANK (or FRANCIS) JENKS b. prob. Baltimore, MD, 11 Jun 1851;
      d. Boston, 5 Aug 1927.[32]

iii. HOWARD GRIFFITH b. prob. Baltimore, MD, poss.
      16 Oct 1853; d. Baltimore, MD, 12 Aug 1873.[33]

iv.   MARIA PRICE b. Baltimore, MD, 28 Nov 1856; d. Boston,
      27 Oct 1919.[34]

v.   GEORGE BARTLETT b. prob. Baltimore, MD,
      6 Aug 1861; d. Boston, 26 Feb 1936.[35]

DANIEL and MARIA PRICE (HEATON) FERNALD

DANIEL C. FERNALD b. Lee, NH, Oct 1865, s/o Charles Fernald, b.
Barrington, NH, and Mary Elizabeth (Lizzie) Randall, b. Lee, NH.[36] Daniel
d. Claremont, NH, 20 May 1944.[37] He m. Nottingham, NH, 28 Apr 1888,
MARIA ("MINNIE") PRICE HEATON,[38] b. Baltimore, MD, 28 Nov 1856.
Minnie d. Boston, 27 Oct 1919.[39]

Children (FERNALD) of Daniel and Maria ("Minnie") (Heaton) Fernald:

i.   **THERESA FRANCES** b. Haverhill, 24 Jan 1890; d. Boston,
      01 Nov 1959.[40]

ii.   ELSIE HOWARD b. Haverhill, 19 Nov 1891; d. prob. Claremont,
      NH, Jan 1969.[41]

iii. CLARENCE GEORGE b. Nottingham, NH, 06 Oct 1895; d.
      Boston, 1960.[42]

---

[1] MA VR, Nantucket, births, vol 2, p 211: "20th, 9 mo, 1789 [dup _____,
1794] in Boston." The date in 1789 is corroborated by a baptismal record of the
New North Church, Boston, p 175 (Americanancestors.org): "Jenks, Samuel-
Haynes (2 yrs old), [son of] Samuel & Mary, bp. Sep. 25, 1791."

[2] MA VR, Boston, deaths, 1863, vol 167, p 132.

[3] Browne, p 153. Also, Ancestry.com (*Massachusetts, Town Vital Collections*),
1620-1988: handwritten record of "Marriages Registered in Boston," including

marriage of Samuel Jenks and Lydia G. Williams on 14 June 1812 by Rev. John Eliot.

[4] Browne, p 153. Americanancestors.org *(Records of the New North Church in Boston)*, p 175 shows a Lydia-Grose Williams, child of James and Lydia, baptized 10 September 1797.

[5] MA VR, Nantucket, deaths, vol 5, p 384, based on a gravestone record, Prospect Hill Cemetery, Nantucket. The memorial stone, in poor condition, notes that Lydia was buried in Boston. Americanancestors.org *(Records of the Hollis Street Church in Boston)*, p 149, states that, "Jenks, Lydia, W. Samuel H., buried June 27, 1814, a 18 y." Ancestry.com *(Record of the Deaths and Burials in the North District [of Boston] for the year 1814)*: death was due to typhus. Ancestry.com (Deaths in the City of Boston - 1801-1848): Lydia buried Copps Hill Cemetery, Boston.

[6] Since Lydia was from Boston and there is no indication that Samuel was living or working on Nantucket at the time of their marriage, their daughter Lydia Maria was probably born Boston. However, the only vital record found is MA VR, Nantucket, births, vol 2, p 210: date of birth "5th, 5 mo, 1814;" no place specified.

[7] Browne, p 153 provides only the date, May 1838. MA VR, Nantucket, deaths, vol 5, p 100 provides a death date of 29 May 1838; no place is specified. NEHGS-Mss 1017 concurs on the date but states that death occurred at Providence, RI. American ancestors.org *(Index of Deaths at Providence)* does not show a record for Lydia Maria. Providence remains a possibility since Lydia Maria married William Burroughs, printer of the Providence Journal *(AHN, Bedford Mercury, September 12, 1834, Vol XXVIII, Issue 10, p 2)*.

[8] Browne, p 153, corroborated by AHN, Boston Recorder of January 31, 1816, Vol 1, Issue 5, p 19: "In this town. - On Sunday evening, Mr. Samuel H. Jenks, to Miss Lydia A. Stevens, only daughter of Capt D Stevens, formerly of Nantucket." NEHGS-Mss 1017 provides the same date and place of marriage.

[9] Browne, p 153. NHA - Barney notes Lydia Stevens as the daughter of Dennis Stevens and Phebe Arthur, but a specific place and date of birth are not given. NEHGS-Mss 1017 concurs with Browne on the date, gives the place as Nantucket, and states that Lydia's middle name was Arthur.

[10] MA VR, Nantucket, deaths, vol 5, p 384: gravestone record shows date of death as 17 May 1817; church record states 15 May 1817. Ancestry.com *(Massachusetts, Town Vital Collections, 1620-1988:)* indicates that Lydia died Boston, 18 May 1817, bur. 20 May 1817, with the following note: "Her remains was carried to Nantucket & was there interred."

[11] Birth: MA VR, Nantucket, births, vol 2, p 384: full birth date, no place specified. Highly likely that Maria Louisa was born Boston, since her mother was brought from Boston to the island for burial three months after Maria Louisa's birth. Death: MA VR, Nantucket, deaths, vol 5, p 385 provides the date, no place specified. Since there is evidence that her father Samuel remained on the island for a year after the burial of his wife Lydia, Maria Louisa may have died on Nantucket. Per the stone at Prospect Hill Cemetery, Maria Luisa was buried in the same grave with her mother.

[12] MA VR, Nantucket, marriages, vol 4, p 97, no place specified. Ancestry.com *(Massachusetts, Town Vital Collections, 1602-1988)*: one of a series of marriages notified on 23 September 1818 to the Town Clerk of Nantucket by Seth F. Swift, Minister of the Gospel.

[13] Browne, p 153, provides date of 25 May 1801. However, the gravestone record discussed in both Notes 5 and 14, and NHA-Barney, both point to a birth date of March 1801. Boston as the location of birth is probable given the statement in the marriage record (Note 12) that her father, James Williams, was "of Boston." NHA-Barney and Nantucket VR both state that James Williams was the father of both Lydia-Grose and Eliza Williams. NEHGS-Mss 1017 states that James and Lydia Williams were the parents of both Lydia and Eliza Williams, wives of Samuel H. Jenks.

[14] MA VR, Nantucket, vol 5, p 384, based on a gravestone record (Note 5). This stone memorializes both Eliza and her sister Lydia, the first wife of Samuel H. Jenks. It states that Eliza died 20 August 1822, age of 21 years, 5 months, and appears to indicate that she was buried in Boston.

[15] Birth: MA VR, Nantucket, births, vol 2, p 211. Death: Browne, p 153 provides the date. NEHGS-Mss 1017 concurs in the date and provides the place of Camden, NJ.

[16] Birth: MA VR, Nantucket, births, vol 2, p 209 provides year only. Browne, p 153 shows Eliza's date of birth as 16 August 1822. This date may be based on

data in Eliza's death record. Death: MA VR, Boston, deaths, 1892, vol 429, p 310, no 23: at Boston, 12 August 1892, aged 69 years, 11 months, 26 days.

[17] MA VR, Nantucket, marriages, vol 4, p 97.

[18] MAVR, Nantucket, births, vol 1, p 302 lists both 21 and 28 April 1801 as birth dates.

[19] MA VR, Boston, deaths, 1887, vol 384, p 53.

[20] Birth: Browne, p 153, states all children of Samuel and Martha (Coffin) Jenks born at Boston. This is not likely since during many of their child-bearing years, the couple was living on Nantucket. NEHGS-Mss 1017 states that this birth occurred on Nantucket. Death: Prospect Hill Cemetery, Nantucket, gravestone death date, 1 August 1825. See also, NEHGR, 1946, vol 100, p 187.

[21] Birth: Browne, p 153: date only. MA VR, Nantucket, births, vol 2, p 210 provides the year, 1826. NEHGS-Mss 1017: birthplace, Nantucket and date, 19 September 1825. Death: MA VR, Boston, deaths, 1888, vol 393, p 334. No 7763.

[22] Birth: Browne, p 153: date only. Death record and NEHGS-Mss 1017 corroborate: Boston, 09 May 1828. Death: MA VR, Boston, deaths, 1858, vol 122, p 4, no 174: "age 29 yrs, 8 mos, 10 days."

[23] Birth: Browne, p 153: date only. MA VR, Nantucket, birth, vol 2, p 210: no place, 1830. The death record shows birthplace as Nantucket. NEHGS-Mss 1017: Boston, date per Browne. Either birthplace is possible. Death: MA VR, Boston, deaths, 1891, vol 420, p 44, no 1004 for Lucy C (Jenks) Bartlett; age 60 yrs, 7 mos, 24 days.

[24] Birth: Browne, p 153: date only. MA VR, Nantucket, births, vol 2, p 210: birth year, 1832. NEHGS Mss- 1017: Nantucket, birth date per Browne. Death: MA VR, Boston, deaths, 1851, vol 59, p 116.

[25] Birth: Browne p 153: date only. MA VR, Nantucket, births, vol 2, p 209: birth year, 1834. NEHGS-Mss 1017 concurs with Browne on the date; birthplace, Nantucket. Death: MA VR, Nantucket, deaths, vol 5, p 385; also, AHN, *New Bedford Mercury*, 03 June 1836, Vol XXIX, Issue 45, p 3, death notice: "On Monday morning, Francis Henry, son of S. Haynes Jenks, age 18 mos."

[26] Birth: MA VR, Nantucket, births, vol 2, p 209: year, 1838 only. Browne, p 153 and Universal Encyclopedia of Music by Louis Charles Elson, p 292: birth date, 02 June 1838. Elson and NEHGS-Mss1017: birthplace, Nantucket. Francis Henry was a professional music critic, an organist and an early member of Boston's Handel and Hayden Society. Death: MA VR, Boston, deaths, 1894, vol 447, p 494, no 10849.

[27] Birth: MA VR, Nantucket, births, vol 2, p 209. Death: MA VR, Nantucket, death, vol 5, p 385; died at the age of 4 mos, of "Consumption." No first name given, but the dates correlate with the MA VR birth record. NEHGS-Mss 1017 provides the same information.

[28] Maryland State Archives, Certificate of Death, City of Baltimore City, Accession No. MSA Sc 5458-103-10213: Richard Heaton, died Baltimore City, 7 Nov 1905. Certificate states that Richard born New York City, 15 April 1821, child of Richard and Eliza Heaton, both born New York; informant, Frank J. Heaton, son of Richard.

[29] MA VR, Nantucket, vol 4, p 96: Boston, January 1847. Ancestry.com *(Massachusetts Town Vital Collections, 1620-1988)*: Boston, 21 January 1847. Marriage recorded in the Nantucket Mirror of 30 January 1847: "In Boston, Mr. Richard H. Heaton of Baltimore, to Miss Eliza W., daughter of Hon. S.H. Jenks, formerly of this place."

[30] See Note 16.

[31] *Baltimore Sun*, 17 April 1857, death notice: "On Thursday morning, 16th instant, Samuel Jenks [Heaton], aged 9 years, 1 months and 3 days, eldest son of Richard H. and Eliza W. Heaton." This is the only record found of either the birth or death of this child. He clearly died in Baltimore, MD. Birth most likely to have occurred either in Boston, where his parents married, or in Baltimore, where they settled.

[32] Birth: Numerous U.S. Census records indicate that Frank and all remaining Heaton children were born in Maryland. No actual birth records yet found for any of these children. The 1870 U.S. Census for Baltimore gives Frank's age as 19, providing an approximate birth date of 1850 or 1851. NEHGS - Mss. 1017 provides an unsourced specific birth date: 11 June 1851. Ancestry.com *(Massachusetts, Mason Membership Cards, 1733-1990)*: same birth date, at Baltimore, for Frank Jenks Heaton. Death: MA VR - Index, Boston, deaths, vol 2, p 99, for Francis J. Heaton. It is likely that Francis J. and Frank J. are the same

individual. The Mason Membership Card noted above states he died 5 August 1927.

[33] Birth: 1860 and 1870 U.S. Census records for Baltimore indicate a birth date of about 1853 or 1854. However, the Baltimore Sun's death notice for Howard G. indicates that this birth may have occurred as early as 1852. If NHA - Barney is correct (see below), the birth may have occurred in 1853. NEHGS - Mss 1017 provides a specific, but unsourced, date of 16 October 1853. *Death: Index of Obits and Marriages in the Baltimore Sun* - 1871-1875, Vol 1 A-J, p 255: "Heaton, Howard G. (20 yrs, 10mos) d. on 73-Aug-12." NHA-Barney: same date and place of death but provides Howard G.'s age as "19, 10 mos."

[34] Massachusetts death certificate, Office of the Secretary, Division of Vital Statistics - certified copy, 02 March 1994: provides death date and place , and states, Minnie Heaton born Baltimore, MD, 28 November 1856.

[35] Birth: Based on U.S. Census, 1870, for Baltimore, Richard H. Heaton family, and Ancestry.com *(Massachusetts, Mason Member ship Cards, 1733-1990)* which states: George Bartlett Heaton born Baltimore, MD, 6 August 1861. Death: MA VR-Index, deaths, Boston, 1936, vol 9, p 492. The Masonic record, cited above notes the death on 29 February 1936.

[36] NH VR, birth record reported from Lee, NH: Daniel born Lee, October 1865; father, Charles Fernald; mother, Mary E. Fernald. Daniel's death record (Note 37) and marriage record (Note 38) lead to the conclusion that his mother's full maiden name was Mary Elizabeth (Lizzie) Randall.

[37] NH VR, death record reported from Claremont, NH.

[38] NH VR, marriage record reported from Nottingham, NH: Daniel's spouse, Minnie P. Heaton. NHfamilies.com *(Nottingham, New Hampshire Annual Report for 1888)* provides the same data. The 1860 and 1870 U.S. Census records for Baltimore show Daniel's wife as Maria P. in the family group with father Richard and mother Eliza. Minnie appears to be a commonly used nickname for this Maria; the name Minnie appears on some vital records.

[39] Birth and death: see note 34.

[40] Birth: MA VR Haverhill, births, 1890, vol 403, p 268, no 47. Death: MA VR, Boston, deaths, 1959, vol 27, p 278, no 10348.

[41] Birth: MA VR, Haverhill, births, 1891, vol 412, p 356, no 693. Death: Ancestry.com *(Social Security Death Index)* for Elsie Woodman, her married name. Specific date and place of death not otherwise confirmed; based on family knowledge, Claremont, NH is the probable place.

[42] Birth: NH VR, birth record from Nottingham, NH. Also, NH families.com *(Nottingham, New Hampshire Annual Report of 1895)*. Death: MA VR-Index, Boston, deaths, 1960, vol 16, p 136.

GENEALOGY — CHAPTER 4: THE LAND SPECULATOR

There are thirteen generations from the senior Richard Thayer to the author. The line runs as follows:

1:    Richard Thayer and Dorothy Mortimore
2:    Richard Thayer and Dorothy Pray *(principal subject of Chapter 4)*
3:    Richard Thayer and Rebecca Micall
4:    John Thayer and Rebecca French
5:    Micah Thayer and Mehitable French
6:    Mehitable Thayer and John Tower
7:    Alexander Tower and Selah (known as Celia) Pratt
8:    Isaac P. Tower and Susan Snow
9:    Nancy A. Tower and William H. Wood *(See Genealogy - Chapter 2)*
10:   Edith G. Wood and Leroy L. Covert *(See Genealogy - Chapter 2)*
11:   Helen C. Covert and Leon Pennell *(See Genealogy - Chapter 2)*
12:   June M. Pennell and Irving F. MacDonald *(See Genealogy - Chapter 1)*
13:   Barry J. MacDonald *(See Genealogy - Chapter 1)*

In those cases where there is no vital record or other evidence of a specific birth or death place for individuals in this chapter, those places are listed as unknown. For births, however, the birthplace is most probably Braintree, since the Thayers, in particular, lived there for a number of generations.

Richard Thayer (1, see above) and his children, including Richard Thayer (2, see above), immigrated to the Massachusetts Bay Colony from Thornbury, Gloucestershire, England, arriving at the town of Braintree by 1641.

RICHARD THAYER (TAYER) and WIVES:

RICHARD THAYER bap. Thornbury, Gloucestershire, England, 5 Apr 1601, s/o Richard Thayer, bap. Thornbury, Gloucestershire, England, and ANN GIBBS. Richard d. St. Michael's Parish, Barbados, bef. 10 Apr 1663.[1] He m. (1) Thornbury, Gloucestershire, England, 5 Apr 1624, **DOROTHY MORTIMORE,** d/o William Mortimore.[2] Dorothy bur. Thornbury, Gloucestershire, England, 17 Jan 1640/41.[3]

Children (THAYER) of Richard and Dorothy (Mortimore) Thayer, all baptized Thornbury, Gloucestershire, England:

i.   **RICHARD** bap. St. Mary's Church, Thornbury, 10 Feb 1624/25; d. Braintree, 27 Aug 1695.[4]

ii.   DEBORAH bap. Thornbury, 4 Feb 1629/30; bur. prob. Thornbury, 16 Mar 1630/31.[5]

iii. SARAH bap. Thornbury, 9 Feb 1631/32.[6]

iv.   JAEL bap. Thornbury, 2 Jun 1633; d. Braintree, 10 Mar 1701.[7]

v.   DEBORAH bap. Thornbury, 27 Mar 1633/34; d. 31 May 1662.[8]

vi.   ZACHARIAH bap. Thornbury, 6 Mar 1634/35; d. Braintree, 29 Jul 1693.[9]

vii. HESTER bap. Thornbury, 24 Nov 1636; d. Norton, 1724.[10]

viii. NATHANIEL bap. Thornbury, 11 Apr 1639; d. Boston, 1693.[11]

ix.   CORNELIUS, bap. Thornbury, 10 Dec 1640; d. Weymouth, ca. Jun 1663.[12]

RICHARD THAYER m. (2) Boston, 15 Jul 1646, JANE (HELLYER) PARKER, widow of John Parker. She was of Marlboro, England. Jane sold her own home in Boston and land in Brookline, and returned to England with children from her previous marriage. She d. prob. England bef. 1660.[13]

Children of Richard and Jane (Hellyer) (Parker) Thayer:

Some family histories record children of this marriage, including a Hannah and an Abigail. There is no definitive information on these children, however. The information on Abigail indicates she was born in 1661, at least a year after Sprague assumes that Jane (Hellyer) (Parker) Thayer died. By this time, Richard Thayer was definitely in Barbados and married to his third wife, Katherine.

RICHARD THAYER m. (3) prob. England, bef. Mar 1660, KATHERINE _____, who d. St. Michaels, Barbados, 1 Feb - 05 Apr 1687.[14] No children known.

RICHARD AND DOROTHY (PRAY) THAYER:

RICHARD THAYER bap. St. Mary's Church, Thornbury, Gloucestershire, England, 10 Feb 1624/25, s/o Richard Thayer and Dorothy Mortimore.[15] Richard

d. Braintree, 27 Aug 1695.[16] He m. Braintree, 24 Dec 1651, **DOROTHY PRAY**, b. prob. England, ca. 1634, d/o Quinton Pray, b. England, and Joan, b. England.[17] Dorothy d. Braintree, 11 Dec 1705.[18]

Children (THAYER) of Richard and Dorothy (Pray) Thayer:

i.   DOROTHY b. Braintree, 30 Aug 1653; d. "on board a ship," 5 Jul 1693.[19]

ii.   **RICHARD** b. Braintree, 30 Aug 1655; d. Braintree, 11 Sep 1729.[20]

iii.   NATHANIEL THAYER b. Braintree, 1 Jan 1657/58; d. Braintree, 28 Mar 1728/29.[21]

Thayer Memorial (1874), p 7 provides names and birth dates for three other children of Richard and Dorothy: Abigail, Joannah, and Sarah. There are, however, no Braintree vital records to support this. Sprague's Braintree (card 4621) states: "He [Richard Thayer, spouse of Dorothy Pray] was in Barbados in 1660 with his father, and probably stayed there some time as no children are of record [in Braintree] between 1658 and 1670." On this basis, Sprague excludes these children from his record of the Richard Thayer-Dorothy Pray family. A search of the records of St. Michael's Parish, Barbados, where Richard's father lived until 1664, with his wife, Katherine, who lived there until 1687, did not locate any children of Richard the younger. It seems unlikely that Richard would have spent twelve years in Barbados given the many disputes and issues concerning his real estate holdings in Braintree and the Blue Hills area. Perhaps, the three children noted above were simply not recorded on the Braintree records for unknown reasons. With the caveats noted above, they are included in this record, along with the last child Cornelius, for whom there is a Braintree record.

iv.   ABIGAIL b. 10 Feb 1661.

v.   JOANNAH b. 13 Dec 1665.

vi.   SARAH b. 13 Dec 1667.

vii.   CORNELIUS b. Braintree, prob. 18 Sep 1670.[22]

RICHARD and REBECCA (MICALL) THAYER:

RICHARD THAYER b. Braintree, 30 Aug 1655, s/o Richard Thayer and Dorothy Pray. Richard, the younger, d. Braintree, 11 Sep 1729.[23] He m. Braintree,

16 Jul 1679, **REBECCA MICALL**,[24] b. Braintree, 22 Nov 1658, d/o James Micall and Mary Farr.[25]

Children (THAYER) of Richard and Rebecca (Mycall) Thayer:

    i.   REBECCA b. Braintree, 16 Aug 1680.[26]
    ii.   BENJAMIN b. Braintree, 4 Oct 1683; d. Braintree, 4 May 1712.[27]
    iii.   RICHARD, aka Lt. Richard, b. Braintree, 26 Jun 1685.[28]
    iv.   **JOHN** b. 12 Jan 1687/88.[29]
    v.   MARY b. Braintree, 10 Feb 1689/90.[30]
    vi.   JAMES b. Braintree, 16 Nov 1691.[31]
    vii.   DEBORAH b. "11, 2m[onth], 1695."[32]
    viii. ANNA b. "14, 9m[onth], 1697."[33]
    ix.   GIDEON b. Braintree, 26 Jul 1700; d. Braintree, 7 Feb 1741/42.[34]
    x.   OBADIAH b. Braintree, 1 May 1703; d. Braintree, 5 Apr 1721.[35]

JOHN and REBECCA (FRENCH) THAYER:

JOHN THAYER b. Braintree, 12 Jan 1687/88, s/o Richard Thayer and Rebecca Micall.[36] He m. Braintree, 26 May 1715, **REBECCA (or REBEKAH) FRENCH**,[37] b. Braintree, 13 May 1694, d/o Dependence French, b. Braintree, and Rebecca.[38]

Children (THAYER) of John and Rebecca (French) Thayer:

    i.   JOHN b. Braintree, 18 Feb 1715/16; d. Braintree, 15 Apr 1716.[39]
    ii.   JOHN b. Braintree, 27 Jul 1717; d. Braintree, 10 Sep 1745.[40]
    iii.   BENJAMIN b. Braintree, 11 Jan 1719/20.[41]
    iv.   OBADIAH b. Braintree, 31 Dec 1721; bap. Braintree, 7 Jan 1721/22.[42]
    v.   **MICAH** b. Braintree, 31 Oct 1723; d. Randolph, 6 Jan 1802.[43]
    vi.   RICHARD, b. Braintree, 15 Dec 1725; d. Braintree, 30 Jan 1725/26.[44]
    vii.   RICHARD b. Braintree, 26 Jan 1726/27; bap. Braintree, 29 Jan 1726/27.[45]
    viii. ABIAH b. Braintree, 25 Jun 1729; bap. Braintree, 29 Jun 1729.[46]
    ix.   SIMON (or SIMEON) b. Braintree, 22 May 1732; bap. Braintree, 4 June 1732.[47]
    x.   ELIJAH b. Braintree, 16 Jul 1736.[48]

MICAH and MEHITABLE (FRENCH) THAYER:

MICAH THAYER b. Braintree, 31 Oct 1723, s/o John Thayer and Rebecca French. Micah d. Randolph, 6 Jun 1802.[49] He m. Braintree, 14 Jan 1748, **MEHITABLE (or MEHETABEL) FRENCH**,[50] bap. Braintree, 4 Mar 1727/28, d/o Alexander French, b. Braintree, and Mary White, b. Braintree.[51]

Children (THAYER) of Micah and Mehitable (French) Thayer:

i. MICAH b. MA, 9 Oct 1749.[52]
ii. **MEHITABLE** b. MA, 3 Jun 1751; d. Weymouth, 16 May 1825.[53]
iii. ZERIAH (or ZERVIAH) bap. Braintree, 10 Jun 1753.[54]
iv. REBECCA bap. Braintree, 7 Dec 1755.[55]
v. ALEXANDER bap. Braintree, 10 Jul 1757; d. prob. Brockton, 10 May 1833, age 76.[56]
vi. MARY bap. Braintree, 18 Mar 1759; d. Randolph, 19 Oct 1822.[57]
vii. LUCY bap. Braintree, 2 Nov 1760; d. Randolph, 4 Nov 1825.[58]
viii. EZRA b. MA, 21 Dec 1762; d. poss. Holbrook, 10 Nov 1806, in his 44th year. [59]
ix. THADEUS b. MA, 19 Oct 1765; bap. Braintree, 1765.[60]
x. ALPHEUS b. MA, 3 Apr 1768; bap. Braintree, 1769; d. prob. Boston, 30 Nov 1804, age 36. [61]

JOHN and MEHITABLE (THAYER) TOWER:

JOHN TOWER b. MA, ca. 1752, s/o John Tower, b. Braintree, and Rebecca Staples, b. Pembroke.[62] John d. Randolph or Braintree, 22 Feb 1823.[63] He m. Braintree, 23 Feb 1776, **MEHITABLE THAYER**,[64] b. 3 Jun 1751, d/o Micah Thayer and Mehitable French. Mehitable d. Weymouth, 16 Aug 1825.[65]

Children (TOWER) of John and Mehitable (Thayer) Tower:

There is little definitive data on the birth and death dates for these children. They are all recorded in the Tower Genealogy, p 138, where it states that all the children were born in Braintree. The Tower Genealogy provides a birth date for Mehitable; the other birth dates are approximations only.

i.   MEHITABLE b. Braintree, 29 Dec 1779; Mehitable (Tower) Orcutt d. Abington, 17 Jan 1873.[66]

ii.   LUCY b. Braintree, bet. 1780 and 1782; Lucy (Tower) Shaw d. Weymouth, either 28 Feb 1845 at age 63, or 3 Mar 1845 at age 65.[67]

iii.   NATHANIEL b. Braintree, ca. 1781.[68]

iv.   CHARLOTTE b. Braintree, ca.1783.[69]

v.   JOHN TOWER b. Braintree, ca. 1785.[70]

vi.   **ALEXANDER** b. MA, poss. 1788; d. Braintree, 1 Dec 1839.[71]

vii.   SAFIRA (or ZERVIAH), b. Braintree, ca. 1792.[72]

ALEXANDER and SELAH (PRATT) TOWER:

ALEXANDER TOWER b. MA, poss. 1788, s/o John Tower and Mehitable Thayer. Alexander d. Braintree, 1 Dec 1839.[73] He m. Weymouth, 11 May 1808, **SELAH (or CELIA) PRATT**,[74] b. Weymouth, 29 Jun 1787, d/o Joseph Pratt, Jr., b. Weymouth, and Mercy Shaw.[75]

Children (TOWER) of Alexander and Selah (also known as Celia) (Pratt) Tower:

i.   **ISAAC PRATT** b. Braintree, 25 Jan 1808; d. Braintree, 25 Jun 1854.[76]

ii.   MARY b. Braintree, 17 Jun 1811.[77]

iii.   EMELINE R. b. Braintree, 17 Feb 1813; Emeline (Tower) (Holbrook) Beales, d. Randolph, 20 Sep 1864, of typhoid.[78]

iv.   LUCY A., b. Braintree, 27 Mar 1816.[79]

v.   SELAH b. Braintree, 23 Mar 1819; Selah (Tower) Belcher, d. Braintree, 16 Mar 1888.[80]

vi.   ALEXANDER b. Braintree, 22 Oct 1822.[81]

ISAAC PRATT and SUSAN (SNOW) (LEACH) TOWER

ISAAC PRATT TOWER b. Braintree, 25 Jan 1808, s/o Alexander Tower and Celia (or Selah) Pratt. Isaac d. Braintree, 25 Jun 1854.[82] He m (1) (intentions) Braintree, 3 Apr 1826, RUTH POOL,[83] b. Braintree, 10 Jun 1810, d/o Thomas and Susannah Pool. Ruth d. prob. bef. Aug 1840, when Isaac remarried.[84]

Isaac m. (2) Braintree, 2 Aug 1840, **SUSAN (or SUSANNA) SNOW**,[85] b. Lyman, NH, 22 Dec 1822, d/o Ara Snow, b. Douglas, and Parmelia Briggs, b. prob. Norton.[86] Susan d. Rockland, 13 Oct 1912.[87]

Children (TOWER) of Isaac and Susan (Snow) Tower:

    ?i.   ALONZO TOWER b. MA, poss. 1841; d. bef. 1843, MA.[88]

    ii.   ALONZO E. TOWER b. MA, ca. 1843.[89]

    iii.   CHRISTOPHER P. b. MA, 1845; d. Weymouth, 1 Jun 1927.[90]

    iv.   MINOT A. b. Randolph, 7 Jul 1846.[91]

    v.   **NANCY ANN** b. Braintree, 2 Jul 1848; d. West Bridgewater, 30 Mar 1930.[92]

    vi.   ARA (or ORA, or IRA) SANFORD b. Braintree, 19 Jul 1853.[93]

    ?vii.   ANDREW TOWER b. bef. Mar 1855.[94]

Susan m. (2) Randolph, 27 Jan 1868, ELBRIDGE LYMAN LEACH, b. Hanson, s/o Elbridge Leach and Deborah H. Josselyn.[95] No children of this marriage.

---

[1] The family relationships, baptismal, and death data are all from Sprague's Braintree. Sprague may have relied on information from the Parish Register of St. Mary's, Thornbury, Gloucestershire, England, transcribed in *Tayer (Thayer) Family Entries in the Parish Register of Thornbury, Gloucestershire, England,* NEHGR, vol 60, pp 281-291. The data shown in Sprague and in the NEHGR article of 1906 are identical for all members of this family group. The baptism for Richard is given in NEHGR, vol 60, p 284. In some of these materials, Richard's mother is named as Dimery; in the Kempton Genealogy, Richard's mother is named as Ann Gibbs. Death: Kempton Genealogy, p 373. Sanders, p 350 provides a date of October 1664, which may be connected with the administration of Richard's will in which his wife, Catherine, is named as executrix.

[2] Sprague's Braintree; marriage, NEHGR, vol 60, p 287. Relationship to father based on will of William Mortimore dated 31 August 1626 per NEHGR, vol 60, p 291.

[3] Sprague's Braintree; NEHGR, vol 60, p 288.

[4] Sprague's Braintree; baptism: NEHGR, vol 60, p 285; Kempton Ancestry, p 373.

[5] Baptism and burial: Sprague's Braintree. Baptism: NEHGR, Vol 60, p 285; Kempton Ancestry, p 373. Burial: NEHGR, Vol 60, p 288. Parish register provides no mention of parents, so it only probable that this is the correct Deborah.

[6] Baptism: Sprague's Braintree; NEHGR, vol 60, p 286 (Sara); Kempton Ancestry, p 373.

[7] Baptism: Sprague's Braintree; NEHGR, vol 60, p 286 (Jaell); Kempton Ancestry, p 373. Death: Sprague's Braintree; Braintree VR, vol 1, p 133.

[8] Baptism: Sprague's Braintree; NEHGR, vol 60, p 286 (Deborah); Kempton Ancestry, p 373. Death: Sprague's Braintree.

[9] Baptism: Sprague's Braintree; NEHGR, vol 60, p 286 (Zacaria); Kempton Ancestry, p 373. Death: Sprague's Braintree.

[10] Baptism: Sprague's Braintree; NEHGR, vol 60, p 286 (Hester); Kempton Ancestry, p 374. Death: Sprague's Braintree.

[11] Baptism: Sprague's Braintree; NEHGR, vol 60, p 286 (Nathaniel); Kempton Ancestry, p 374. Death: Sprague's Braintree.

[12] Baptism: Sprague's Braintree; NEHGR, vol 60, p 286 (Cornelius); Kempton Ancestry, p 374. Death: Sprague's Braintree.

[13] See Sprague's Braintree (card 4617) for Richard Thayer. Greater detail regarding the source documents referred to in Sprague's sketch, and the family of John Parker, Jane's first husband, is given in "John Parker," *Great Migration: Immigrants to New England, 1634-5*, pp 364-7. While Sprague identifies Jane Parker's maiden name as Kember; the Kempton Genealogy identifies her maiden name as Hellyer.

[14] Sprague's Braintree (cards 4617 and 4618).

[15] See note 4.

[16] Sprague's Braintree, based on the gravestone in the Hancock Cemetery, Quincy, MA.

[17] Sprague's Braintree and Braintree VR, vol 1, p 125. Sprague notes that Dorothy and the other children of Quinton and Joan Pray were probably born in England; he estimates Dorothy's birth date as "about 1634." The English birthplace and date for Dorothy Pray correspond with other information which states that Quinton Pray first appeared in the Mass Bay Colony in 1643.

[18] Braintree VR, vol 1, p 103.

[19] Birth: Braintree VR, vol 1, p 19. Death: Sprague's Braintree, and Braintree VR, vol 1, p 38 where the statement "on board a ship" is found.

[20] Birth: Braintree VR, vol 1, p 19. Death: Braintree VR, vol 1, p 141.

[21] Birth: Sprague's Braintree. Death: Braintree VR, vol 1, p 140.

[22] Braintree VR, vol 1, p 29: "born 7th. mo 18 1670." Sprague gives the date as 18 Nov 1670. However, if the old-style date in the Braintree VR is brought into the modern dating system, it may be that the date is 18 September 1670.

[23] See note 20.

[24] Braintree VR, vol 1, p 126.

[25] Braintree VR, vol 1, p 257, twin of James; however there is no date given in this record; Savage provides a birth date of 22 November 1659.

[26] Braintree VR, vol 1, p 32.

[27] Birth: Braintree VR, vol 1, p 42. Death: Braintree VR, vol 1, p 134.

[28] Braintree VR, vol 1, p 42.

[29] Braintree VR, vol 1, p 46.

[30] Braintree VR, vol 1, p 51.

[31] Ibid.

[32] Thayer Memorial (1874), p 7: "11d, 2m, 1695;" source not known.

[33] Thayer Memorial (1874), p 7: "14d, 9m, 1697;" source not known.

[34] Birth: Braintree VR, vol 1, p 83. Death: Braintree VR, vol 1, p 149: "by falling through the ice," and Sprague's Braintree - PR 14 "bur. 10 Feb 1741/2, drowned," and CR1 (First Congregational Church Record of death): "in our river when coming to meeting on Sabbath day morning."

[35] Birth: Braintree VR, vol 1, p 187. Death: Braintree VR, vol 1, p 137.

[36] See note 29.

[37] Braintree VR, vol 1, p 164: married by Rev. Mr. Samuel Niel.

[38] Braintree VR, vol 1, p 58.

[39] Birth: Braintree VR, vol 1, p 106. Death: Braintree VR, vol 1, p 136.

[40] Birth: Braintree VR, vol 1, p 110. Death: Braintree VR, vol 1, p 150.

[41] Braintree VR, vol 1, p 114.

[42] Birth: Braintree VR, vol 1, p 118. Baptism: Sprague's Braintree, PR 14.

[43] Birth: Braintree VR, vol 1, p 122: "son of John Thayer and Rebekah his wife." Death: Sprague's Braintree, based on First Congregational Church Record: age 78, died of "lingering consumption and black jaundice."

[44] Birth: Braintree VR, vol 1, p 182. Death: Braintree VR, vol 1, p 139.

[45] Birth: Braintree VR, vol 1, p 184. Baptism: Sprague's Braintree, PR 14.

[46] Birth: Braintree VR, vol 1, p 190. Baptism: Sprague's Braintree, PR14.

[47] Birth: Braintree VR, vol 1, p 195. Baptism: Sprague's Braintree, PR14.

[48] Birth: Braintree VR, vol 1, p 204.

[49] See Note 43.

[50] Sprague's Braintree, based on First Congregational Church record.

[51] Baptism: Sprague's Braintree, PR14: her name is spelled Mehetabel and she is shown as the daughter of Alexander French.

[52] Thayer Memorial (1874), p 30. No vital records of birth or death found. However, there are as many as three marriage records that may involve this Micah Thayer, including one to an Abigail Wales on 27 February 1779 which is included in the Thayer Memorial (1874), p 31.

[53] Birth: Thayer Memorial (1874), p 30. Death: MA VR, Weymouth, deaths, vol 2, p 356; recorded as a widow, age 74 or 75.

[54] Sprague's Braintree, PR 14.

[55] Sprague's Braintree, PR 14.

[56] Baptism: Sprague's Braintree, PR 14. Death: MA VR, Brockton Deaths, vol 1, p 364. Alexander married Lucy Edson. Lucy Thayer died at Brockton in 1832 and is buried in the same cemetery as Alexander Thayer. Therefore, it is highly probable that this death record is for Alexander Thayer, son of Micah. Alexander's age of 76 at time of birth correlates with the year of his baptism in 1757.

[57] Baptism: Sprague's Braintree, PR 14. Death: Sprague's Randolph, Second or East Parish Church record: wife of Benjamin, age 64, "first death which has occurred in the church." Mary Thayer married Benjamin Paine in 1782 (Braintree VR, vol 2, p 267). Mary (Thayer) Paine's age at death yields a birth year that corresponds closely to the baptism date for Mary Thayer in Sprague's Randolph. Therefore, it is probable that this death record is for Mary, daughter of Micah Thayer.

[58] Baptism: Sprague's Braintree, PR 14. Death: Sprague's Randolph, Second or East Parish church record and a grave record for the East (now Union) Cemetery, East Randolph (now Holbrook). This record states that Lucy was wife of Joshua and died at age 65. Lucy Thayer married Joshua French in 1782 (Braintree VR, vol 2, p 234). Her age at death yields a birth year that corresponds closely with the date of baptism.

[59] Birth: Thayer Memorial (1874), p 30. Death: Cemetery Transcription, East Cemetery, now Union Cemetery, Holbrook (from Americanancesty.org).

[60] Birth: Thayer Memorial (1874), p 31. Baptism: Sprague's Braintree, First Congregational Church record.

[61] Birth: Thayer Memorial (1874), p 31. Baptism: Sprague's Braintree, First Congregational Church record. Deaths: Americanancestors.org (Boston, MA Deaths: 1799-1825). This is the most probable death record for Alpheus given the correspondence between age at death and Alpheus's birth and baptismal dates.

[62] Death records (Note 63) list his age as 71 when he died in 1823. No other VR found.

[63] Both Sprague's Braintree and Sprague's Randolph, from a First Congregational Church record.

[64] Braintree VR, vol 2, p 232: "both of this town"

[65] See Note 53

[66] Birth: Tower Genealogy. Death: MA VR, Abington Deaths, vol 257, p 349. Mehitable (Orcutt) Tower, age 93 yrs, 20 days. This record is probably the source of the birth date. Mehitable Tower married Benjamin Orcutt of Weymouth in 1806, recorded in both Braintree and Weymouth.

[67] All birth and death information based on MA VR, Weymouth, deaths, vol 2, p 337, for Lucy (Tower) Shaw. Lucy Tower, then of Abington, married Jabez Shaw at Weymouth in 1803. The death records (there is a duplicate) state that she died on either 28 February 1845 at age 63, or 3 March 1845, at age 65. The records state that Lucy was born at Braintree.

[68] Tower Genealogy. No other sources found.

[69] Tower Genealogy. Sprague's Braintree records a marriage intention in 1811 between a Charlotte Tower and an Ephraim Wills. No other vital records found.

[70] Tower Genealogy. MA VR, Bridgewater, marriages, vol 2, p 373, records a marriage between a John Tower and Mary Thompson at Bridgewater in 1816. Intentions for John Tower and Mrs. Mary Thompson were recorded at Weymouth. No other vital records found.

[71] Birth: Tower Genealogy; some LDS IGI records list his birth as at Braintree on 30 April 1788, however, no source document found. Death: Sprague's Braintree.

[72] Tower Genealogy. MA VR, Weymouth Marriages, vol 2, p 198, records intentions to marry in 1807 between a Zerviah Tower of Randolph and a Jonathan Agar, Jr. No other vital records found.

[73] See note 71.

[74] MA VR, marriages, Weymouth, V-2, p 197.

[75] Birth: MA VR, births, Weymouth, V-1. Duplicate records list the child's name as Sela or Selah, and the mother's name as Mercy or Marcy. Death: there is an LDS IGI entry which states that Selah died at Braintree, 10 June 1847, but no source found.

[76] Birth: Sprague's Braintree: Isaac Pratt Tower born Braintree, Massachusetts, 25 Jan 1808, child of Alexander and Selah. Death: MA VR, Braintree deaths, 1854, vol 85, p 148: Isaac Pratt Tower died Braintree, Massachusetts, 25 Jun 1854, of consumption, child of Alexander and Celia.

[77] Sprague's Braintree.

[78] Birth: Sprague's Braintree. Death: MA VR, Randolph, deaths, vol 175, p 257: age 51 yrs, 7 mos, 3 days, daughter of Alexander and Celia.

[79] Sprague's Braintree.

[80] Birth: Sprague's Braintree, first name written as "Seale." Death: MA VR, Randolph, deaths, vol 175, p 257.

[81] Sprague's Braintree.

[82] See note 76.

[83] Sprague's Braintree: intentions to marry, Isaac Tower and Ruthy H. Pool.

[84] Birth: Sprague's Braintree: Ruth H., child of Thomas and Susannah. Death: no vital record found.

[85] Sprague's Braintree: intentions to marry, Isaac P. Tower and Miss Susan Snow.

[86] Familysearch.org *(Massachusetts Deaths, 1845-1915)*: Certificate of Death from Rockland, Massachusetts for Susan Leach, nee Susan Snow: born at Lyman, NH, 22 December 22 1822; father, Ara Snow, born Douglas; mother, Pamelia Briggs, born Norton. Article from *The Brockton Times*, 20 December 1911, contains the same data.

[87] Death certificate discussed in Note 86. Susan buried at Union Cemetery, Brockton, 15 October 1912.

[88] This child appears in some histories of the family with a birth date of 1841. Since another child named Alonzo was born in 1843, the earlier Alonzo must have died by that date. No vital records found.

[89] Ancestry.com *(1850 U.S. Census for Braintree, Mass)*. This is the only record found for this child in the family of Isaac P. and Susan Tower which shows a son, Alonzo E., age 7, born MA.

[90] Birth: Census record (see Note 89) lists Christopher P. as a child of Isaac P. and Susan Tower, age 5, born MA. The birth year of 1845 is also given in Sprague's Randolph, based on a gravestone record from the Central Cemetery in Randolph. Death: Sprague's Randolph and Ancestry.com *(American Civil War Soldiers Database)*.

[91] Sprague's Randolph: son of Isaac P. and Susan

[92] Birth: Sprague's Braintree. This conforms to information in the 1850 U.S. Census record (Note 89 above). Death: Covert Family Bible.

[93] MA VR, Braintree, births, vol 73, p 194, no 32. It is possible that this Ara (or Era) Tower, married a Sarah F., per the 1900 and 1910 U.S. Census for Abington, Massachusetts (Ancestry.com).

[94] The existence of this child is based on family recollection. No vital or other record found.

[95] MA VR, Randolph, marriages, vol 209, p 314: Elbridge L. Leach married Susan Tower, 27 January 1868 at Randolph; second marriages for both.; Elbridge Leach born at Hanson to Elbridge Leach and Deborah H. Josselyn; Susan Snow, born at Lyman, New Hampshire to "Ira" and Pamelia.

GENEALOGY — CHAPTER 5: MAN OF THE TEMPEST

The descent from Stephen Hopkins to the author covers thirteen generations. For the first five generations, relevant material has been drawn from *Mayflower Families, Through Five Generations—Stephen Hopkins* (see Sources for Chapter 5), with the permission of the Director of the Five Generation series (The Silver Books Project), published by the General Society of Mayflower Descendants. These first five generations are presented here without source notes. The format of presentation is also slightly different for the first five generations than that found elsewhere in this book. A detailed record of sources is provided for the next two generations in the line: the Nathaniel and Azubah (Nickerson) Snow family, and the Ara and Parmelia (Briggs) Snow family. The descent through the remaining generations to the author is documented elsewhere in this book as shown below:

1:     Stephen Hopkins and Mary _____ *(From Mayflower Families)*
2:     Constance Hopkins and Nicholas Snow *(From Mayflower Families)*
3:     Mark Snow and Jane Prence *(From Mayflower Families)*
4:     Nicholas Snow and Lydia Shaw *(From Mayflower Families)*
5:     Nathaniel Snow and Elizabeth Eldredge *(From Mayflower Families)*
6:     Nathaniel Snow and Azubah Nickerson
7:     Ara Snow and Parmelia Briggs
8:     Susan Snow and Isaac P. Tower *(See Genealogy - Chapter 4)*
9:     Nancy A. Tower and William H. Wood *(See Genealogy - Chap 2)*
10:    Edith G. Wood and Leroy L. Covert *(See Genealogy - Chap 2)*
11:    Helen C. Covert and Leon Pennell *(See Genealogy - Chap 1)*
12:    June M. Pennell and Irving F. MacDonald *(See Genealogy, Chap 1)*
13:    Barry J. MacDonald *(See Genealogy - Chap 1)*

STEPHEN HOPKINS and WIVES

STEPHEN HOPKINS b. prob. Hampshire, England, ca. 1582, poss. s/o John Hopkins of Winchester. Stephen d. Plymouth, bet. 6 Jun and 17 Jul 1644. He m. (1) **MARY** ____, who was bur. Hursley, Hampshire, 9 May 1613. He m. (2) St. Mary Mallon, Whitechapel, London, England, 19 Feb 1617/18, ELIZABETH FISHER, who d. Plymouth bef. 6 Jun 1644.

Children, (HOPKINS) three oldest by first wife, all bap. Hursley, Hampshire, England; the remainder by second wife.

i.   ELIZABETH bap. 13 May 1604; alive 1613; no further record; note birth of dau. Elizabeth by second wife.

ii.   **CONSTANCE** bap. 11 May 1606; d. Eastham about the middle of Oct 1677.

iii. GILES (or GYLES) bap. 30 Jan 1607/08; d. Eastham bet. 5 Mar 1688/89 and 16 Apr 1690.

iv.   DAMARIS b. England ca. 1618; alive in 1627 but prob. the dau. reported by Bradford [of Plymouth] to have "dyed here"; note younger sister of same name.

v.   OCEANUS b. aboard the *Mayflower* on the Atlantic Ocean bet. 16 Sep and 11 Nov 1620; d. bef. 22 May 1627.

vi.   CALEB b. ca. 1623; a seaman, he d. aft. 6 Jun 1644 (date of Stephen Hopkins' will), and bef. 3 Apr 1651 (last date when he could have been mentioned by Governor Bradford as having "dyed at Barbadoes").

vii. DEBORAH b. Plymouth ca. 1626; d. prob. bef. 1674.

viii. DAMARIS b. Plymouth ca. 1628; d. bet. 20 Oct 1666 and 18 Nov 1669.

ix.   RUTH b. Plymouth ca. 1630; d. unm. after 30 Nov 1644, and prob. bef. 3 Apr 1651, when Governor Bradford indicated that she was dead; certainly bef. the settlement of the estate of her sister Elizabeth 5 Oct. 1659.

x.   ELIZABETH b. Plymouth ca. 1632; d. unm. after Oct 1657 and perhaps bef. 29 Sept 1659 [when her cattle were valued]. An agreement of 5 Oct 1659 by Andrew Ring, Jacob Cooke and Giles Hopkins as to Elizabeth's property was contingent "that in case Elizabeth Hopkins Doe Come Noe more," indicating that she had then disappeared and that her relatives thought she was prob. dead.

NICHOLAS and CONSTANCE (HOPKINS) SNOW

NICHOLAS SNOW may be the Nicholas bap. 25 Jan 1599/1600 at St. Leonard's, Shoreditch, London, England, son of Nicholas Snow of Hoxton, Co. Middlesex, England. Nicholas came on the Ann in 1623 and was made freeman at Plymouth in 1633. He d. Eastham, 15 Nov 1676.

Nicholas m. prob. Plymouth, by 22 May 1627, **CONSTANCE HOPKINS**, bap. Hursley, Hampshire, England, 11 May 1606, d/o Stephen Hopkins and his first wife, Mary. Constance d. Eastham, around the middle of October 1677. Her given name was sometimes rendered Constanta.

Governor Bradford wrote, bet. 6 March and 3 April 1651, that "Constanta is also maried, and hath 12 children all of them living, and one of them married."

Children (SNOW) all prob. b. Plymouth or Eastham.

i.   **MARK** b. 9 May 1628; d. Eastham bet. 23 Nov 1694 and 9 Jan 1694/95.
ii. MARY b. ca. 1630; d. Eastham 28 Apr 1704.
iii. SARAH b. ca. 1632; d. prob. Eastham aft. 8 Mar 1697.
iv. JOSEPH b. ca. 1634; d. Eastham 3 Jan 1722/23.
v.   STEPHEN b. ca. 1636; d. Eastham 17 Dec 1705.
vi. JOHN b. ca. 1638; d. Eastham bef. 4 Apr 1692.
vii. ELIZABETH b. ca. 1640; d. Eastham 16 Jun 1678.
viii. JABEZ b. ca. 1642; d. Eastham 27 Dec 1690.
ix. RUTH b. ca. 1644; d. Eastham 17 Jan 1716/17.
?x. CONSTANCE (The town clerk of Harwich wrote that Nicholas and Constance had a dau. named for her mother who was the first wife of Daniel Doane of Eastham.)
xi. [child]
xii. [child]

MARK SNOW and WIVES

MARK SNOW b. Plymouth, 9 May 1628; d. Eastham, bet. 23 Nov 1694 and 9 Jan 1694/95. He m. (1) Eastham, 18 Jan 1654 ANN COOKE, who d. Eastham, 24 or 25 July 1656; dau. of Josiah Cooke and Elizabeth (Ring) (Deane) Cooke. Mark m. (2) Eastham, 9 Jan 1660, **JANE PRENCE**, b. Duxbury, 1 Nov 1637; d. bet. late May and 28 Jun 1712; dau. of Governor Thomas and Mary (Collier) Prence.

Children (SNOW) b. Eastham, one by first wife and eight by second wife.

i. ANNAH b. 7 Jul 1656; d. prob. Eastham 7 Jul 1714.
ii. MARY b. 30 Nov 1661; d. prob. Harwich bet. 2 Apr 1718 and 27 Jan 1720/21.

iii.	**NICHOLAS** b. 6 Dec 1663; d. Rochester bet. 25 Jun 1751 and 29 May 1754.
iv.	ELIZABETH b. 9 May 1666; d. Eastham 18 Jan 1675.
v.	THOMAS b. 6 Aug 1668; d. prob. Eastham aft. 1 May 1737.
vi.	SARAH b. 10 May 1671.
vii.	PRENCE b. 22 May 1674; d. Harwich 7 Jul 1742.
viii.	ELIZABETH b. 22 Jun 1676; d. Eastham 22 Mar 1677/78.
ix.	HANNAH b. 16 Sep 1679.

NICHOLAS and LYDIA (SHAW) SNOW

NICHOLAS SNOW b. Eastham, 6 Dec. 1663, s/o Mark Snow and Jane Prence. Nicholas d. Rochester, bet. 25 June 1751 and 29 May 1754. Nicholas' intentions recorded at both Eastham and Harwich, 4 Apr. 1689, to marry **LYDIA SHAW**, b. prob. Plymouth about 1670, d/o Jonathan Shaw and Phoebe Watson. Lydia d., aft. 8 Dec 1714, but predeceased her husband.

Children (SNOW) first recorded both Eastham and Harwich; others all recorded Harwich:

i.	JONATHAN b. 30 Jan 1691/92; alive at Rochester 18 Apr 1764.
ii.	MARK b. 30 Apr 1695.
iii.	**NATHANIEL** b. 16 Oct 1697; alive at Rochester 16 Oct 1773.
iv.	JOSHUA b. 18 Aug 1700; d. prob. Rochester bet. 1731 and 26 May 1739.
v.	THANKFUL b. 7 Feb 1701/02; d. after 17 Feb 1755.
vi.	SARAH b. 20 Mar 1703/04; living 22 Mar 1758.
vii.	PHEBE b. 17 Nov 1705; d. prob. Rochester by 25 Jun 1751.
viii.	PRENCE b. 26 Dec 1707; d. bef. 22 Feb 1758.

NATHANIEL and ELIZABETH (ELDRIDGE) SNOW

NATHANIEL SNOW b. Eastham, 16 Oct 1697; son of Nicholas Snow and Lydia Shaw; alive at Rochester 16 Oct 1773. He m., int. rec. Eastham, 9 Jul 1720, **ELIZABETH ELDRIDGE**, b. prob. ca. 1702, poss. d/o Elisha Eldredge of Eastham. Nathaniel poss. m. (2) Rochester, 8 Sept. 1774, Abigail Dexter, b. Rochester, 6 Nov 1717; dau. of Jabez and Mary (Dexter) Dexter.

Children (SNOW), all rec. Rochester:

i.   NICHOLAS b. 9 Jul 1721; d. Rochester Feb 1744.
ii.   REBECCA b. 11 Aug 1723; m. John Arnol.
iii.   MARY b. 12 Apr 1726; m. Ebenezer Holmes.
iv.   WILLIAM b. 31 Jul 1728; m. (1) Priscilla Richmond; m. (2) Temperance (Nickerson) Rogers.
v.   JEAN b. 17 Sep 1730; d. Rochester in Jul 1738.
vi.   ELIZABETH b. 1 Feb 1732; m. Benajah Davis (Rev. service).
vii.   **NATHANAEL (or NATHANIEL)** b. 18 May 1735; m. Azubah Nickerson.
viii.   JAMES b. Aug 1737; bap. 18 Sep 1737; d. Rochester, in Aug 1738.
ix.   SETH b. 26 Dec 1739.
x.   SAMUEL b. 2 Jan 1742; m. Hannah Shaw.
xi.   NICOLAS b. 1 Jun 1745; m. Hannah Dexter (Rev. service).

NATHANIEL and AZUBAH (NICKERSON) SNOW

NATHANIEL SNOW b. Rochester, 18 May 1735, s/o Nathaniel Snow, b. Eastham, and Elizabeth Eldridge, b. poss. Eastham.[1] Nathaniel d. prob. Bethlehem, NH, bef. 1810.[2] He m. Rochester, 13 Oct 1761, **AZUBAH NICKERSON**, b. poss. Chatham, ca. 1740, d/o William Nickerson, b. prob. Chatham, and Hannah Baker, b. Yarmouth.[3] Azubah d. prob. Bethlehem, NH, aft 1822.[4]

Children (SNOW) of Nathaniel and Azubah (Nickerson) Snow:

There are only a few vital records that have been found which pinpoint the dates and places of birth and death for this family. As noted in the text for Chapter 5, there is documentary evidence of a Nathaniel Snow of Rochester buying land in Douglas, MA, and a Nathaniel Snow being involved in local government there in the period 1761 to 1776. If these two Nathaniel Snows are, in fact, the same individual, then his period of residence in Douglas covers the estimated birth dates of all his children. In only the case of his son, Ara, has a vital record been found, a death record that states that he was born at Douglas. An obituary record for Ono, and a prison record for Nathaniel, also point to Douglas as their birthplace. There are, however, no vital records at Douglas that cover the birth of any of Nathaniel and Azubah's six or seven children.

At some point after 1776, the family moved into the White Mountain area of New Hampshire. The presence of the family in and around Franconia and Bethlehem, NH, is attested to by a series of legal documents, deeds and other writings. *The Gazetteer of Grafton County, New Hampshire*, published at Syracuse, NY, in 1886, states that Nathaniel and "Ona" Snow were at Franconia, NH, in 1787. The Gazetteer also notes that in 1790, Nathaniel Snow, a land surveyor, was at Bethlehem, NH. Other documents show that he did the original survey of Bethlehem and was one of the founding settlers there. There are many land records involving Nathaniel and Azubah Snow and their children in this northern New Hampshire area. The Gazetteer notes that there were six children: Nathaniel, Jr.; Asa [or Ara]; Jerusha (Mrs. Deacon Hale); Mrs. Moses Eastman [Azubah]; Mahala [or Elizabeth] (Mrs. Major Amos Wheeler); and "one other" [Ono]. One other addition to this list is possible. Ezra Snow was also at Bethlehem in the earliest days of its existence. He was the only other Snow in the town. There was clearly a close family connection with Ezra; whether he was actually a child of Nathaniel and Azubah is unproven.

The death record of Ara Snow, and census records, collectively show that Ara moved his family out of the White Mountains to Massachusetts prior to 1830. Church, census and other records record the permanent relocation of Elizabeth (also known as Mahala) and her family to Ohio. Obituaries, gravestones, church and other records indicate that the others either certainly or most probably continued to live and die in New Hampshire, with the exception of Ezra of whom there is no word after he leaves Bethlehem, NH after 1808.

I am indebted to Kathleen C. Beals' *Early Families of Bethlehem, New Hampshire*, published in 2009, since this source provides the most complete data on the family as a whole. A birth record for Elizabeth (Mahala), however, was found in the Wheeler Family Bible documented in the NEHGS Register, vol 118, p 237. This record has required a change from the birth order shown in Beals' book to the one proposed below:

i.   ONO b. prob. Douglas, ca. 1762; d. Columbia, NH, 19 Feb 1839.[5]
?ii.   EZRA b. poss. Douglas, say ca. 1764.[6]
iii.   **ARA** b. Douglas, 7 May 1767; d. North Bridgewater, 20 Dec 1863.[7]
iv.   NATHANIEL b. prob. Douglas, ca. 1769; d. Bethlehem, NH ca. 1852.[8]

v.   ELIZABETH (or MAHALA) b. prob. Douglas, 16 Dec 1771; d. E. Liberty, Logan, OH, 18 Jun 1843.[9]

vi. AZUBAH b. prob. Douglas, say ca. 1773; d. prob. Bethlehem, NH, ca. 1802.[10]

vii. JERUSHA b. prob. Douglas, ca. 1775; d. Bethlehem, NH, 10 Apr 1853.[11]

ARA and PARMELIA (BRIGGS) SNOW

ARA SNOW b. Douglas, 7 May 1767, s/o Nathaniel Snow and Azubah Nickerson. Ara d. North Bridgewater (now Brockton), 20 Dec 1863.[12] He m. prob. NH, ca. 1810/11, **PARMELIA (or PAMELIA) BRIGGS**,[13] b. prob. Norton, 5 Mar, 1783, d/o Jacob Briggs and Sarah Cheney, both b. Norton. Parmelia d. North Bridgewater, 6 Nov 1869.[14]

Children (SNOW) of Ara and Parmelia (Briggs) Snow:

i.   PAMELIA b. Bethlehem, NH, 14 Jan 1812; d. poss. by 1838.[15]

ii. ARA b. Lyman, NH, 9 or 12 Feb 1814; d. Brockton, 11 Sep 1901.[16]

iii. THOMAS HALE b. Lyman, NH, 3 or 8 Feb 1816; d. Brockton, 10 Feb 1898.[17]

iv. JERUSHA b. Lyman, NH, 24 May 1819; d. Brockton, 5 Feb 1903.[18]

v.   JACOB CHENEY b. Lyman, NH, 14 Apr 1821; d. Kennebec, ME, 23 Jan 1900.[19]

vi. **SUSAN (or SUSANNA) SNOW** b. Lyman, NH, 22 Dec 1822; d. Rockland, 13 Oct 1912. [20]

---

[1] MA VR, Rochester, births, 1735, "s. Nathaniel and Elisabeth." Information on Nathaniel and Elizabeth Eldridge and family is from *Mayflower Families - Hopkins,* p 141.

[2] The U.S Census for 1810 shows a "Widow Zuba Snow" in Bethlehem, NH. Nathaniel and his family were founding members of the town of Bethlehem, NH and he appears on the tax rolls in the town until 1808. So, he is likely to have died at Bethlehem, NH sometime before 1810.

[3] MA VR, Rochester, marriages, 1761. There are two versions of this record, one which states that the date is of an intention to marry. Date of birth for Azubah

is an approximation. Place of birth and the name of her parents are given in Nickerson Family.

[4] Beals' Bethlehem: based on the Baptist Church membership record for Azubah Snow at Bethlehem, NH, 1822.

[5] Beals' Bethlehem: approximate date of birth, birthplace and date and place of death are based on an obituary in the *Democratic Republican of Littleton*, NH dated 6 March 1839: "in his 77th year . . . a native of Douglas, Mass."

[6] There is no certainty that Ezra is a child of this family. However, he is the only other Snow to appear in the early records of Bethlehem, NH and he is among those who engage in land sales with this family, so there is a possibility that he may be a child of this family. The position of his birth is based on a likely gap in the births of the other children.

[7] Birth: death record states that Ara was born at Douglas, Massachusetts. The specific age at time of death in this record yields a birth date of 7 May 1767. Kingman states that Ara was born 8 May 1767 and was "of Douglas." Death: MA VR, North Bridgewater, deaths, 1863, states that Ara Snow died on 20 December 1863, aged 96 years, 7 months, 13 days. This date corresponds with the date found on the gravestone at the Union Cemetery, Brockton.

[8] Beals Bethlehem: birth date derived from 1830 and 1840 census information; place of birth from an 1818 NH prison record. Death date based on a Bethlehem, NH town record for funds paid to Phineas Allen for digging the grave of "N. Snow."

[9] Date of birth from the NEHGS Register, vol 118, p 237, which contains records from a Wheeler family bible. Place of birth is not stated. Eliza [Elizabeth or Mahala] Snow married Amos Wheeler at Bath, Grafton, NH on 11 October 1788, according to this record. Death date and place from Beals' Bethlehem, based on Free Baptist Church death records in Ohio.

[10] Beals' Bethlehem places Azubah's birth at "say 1771." Given the birth record in 1771 for Elizabeth cited in Note 9, I have moved Azubah's birth date to "say ca. 1773." There is no vital record or other data that confirms this birth date. The approximate date of death and place is from Beal's Bethlehem, based on the remarriage of Moses Eastman sometime around 1802.

[11] Beals' Bethlehem: citing an obituary in the *Ammonusuc Reporter* of Littleton, NH of 16 April 1853 - "In Bethlehem, on the 10th inst., Jerusha, consort of

Dea. Thomas Hale, aged 78 years . . . daughter of Nathaniel Snow . . . ." Death: findagrave.com, memorial 82068178; Mt. Washington Cemetery, Bethlehem, NH.

[12] See Note 7.

[13] No vital record for this marriage has been found. However, the gravestones at Union Cemetery in Brockton, MA, U.S. census records and numerous mentions in the vital records of their children confirm that Ara and Parmelia were a couple. The place of Lyman, NH is probable given the presence of both the Snow and Briggs families in the area at the probable date of marriage. The most likely date for that marriage is the 1810/11 time period based on the date of birth of their first child in 1812. The Records of the Town of Lyman, NH, cited in Note 15 below, list two children of "Mrs. Snow," Sarah Barnes and Jane Barney. An NEHGS database, *New Hampshire Births to 1901*, vol Births B to 1901, provides a record for Sarah Barney, "daughter of Mrs. Snow by a former husband," born 9 December 1800 at Lyman, N.H. The father's name in this record, Asa Snow, has been crossed out. NEHGS database, *New Hampshire, Deaths and Marriages to 1937*, vol Brides B to 1901, provides a marriage record for Samuel J. Barron to Mrs. Parmelia Briggs at Lyman, NH on 9 August 1798. Clearly, Parmelia Briggs had another husband prior to her marriage to Ara Snow. Whether that husband's name was Barron, Barney or Barnes remains an open question.

[14] Birth: no vital record of this birth found. Parmelia's gravestone states that she died 6 November 1869, aged 86 years, 8 months, 1 day. The same information is found in her death record, which also confirms that Parmelia was a Briggs, daughter of Jacob and Sarah. From this is derived the birth date of 5 March 1783. Parmelia's death record, and the death records of three of her children, state that she was born at Norton, Massachusetts, therefore this location is most probable, despite the lack of a vital record. Death: MA VR, North Bridgewater, 1869, vol 221, p 330.

[15] Birth: *Records of the Town of Lyman, New Hampshire* - Ara Snow's Family, p 136, Microfilm 2,257,489, LDS Family History Library, Salt Lake City, Utah, state that Pamelia was both at Bethlehem, NH. The State of New Hampshire later made transcriptions of these records that can be found at Americanancestors *(New Hampshire: Births to 1901)*. Death: No vital record found. Kingman states that Pamelia married Cyrus Willis of Randolph. MA VR, Brockton, 1833, vol 1, p 305 confirms intentions for a marriage of Cyrus A. Willis, of Randolph, to "Permelia" Snow on 14 April 1833. There is an 1838 Brockton marriage record of

a Cyrus A. Willis to a Betsy Foss. If this is the same Cyrus A. Willis who married "Permelia" Snow, then possibly she was dead by 1838.

[16] Birth: *Records of the Town of Lyman, New Hampshire* (Note 15) provides a date of 12 February 1814 in Lyman, NH. NH VR, birth record from the town of Lyman, also carries the 12 February 1814 date. Kingman shows the date of birth as 9 February 1814, which matches the gravestone at Union Cemetery, Brockton, and the death record from the City Clerk's Office, Brockton, MA, in possession of the author. Ara's death record states his place of birth as Lyman, NH and the names and birthplaces of his parents as Ara Snow, born Douglas, and Pamila Briggs, born Norton. Death: death record, City Clerk's Office, Brockton. Gravestone provides the same date of death. For whatever reason, this record does not appear in MA VR, 1841-1910.

[17] Birth: *Records of the Town of Lyman, New Hampshire* (Note 15). Kingman notes the same date of 3 Feb 1816. NH VR: birth recorded at Lyman, NH, shows a date of 8 Feb 1816. Death: MA VR, Brockton, deaths, 1898, vol 482, p621.

[18] Birth: *Records of the Town of Lyman, New Hampshire* (Note 15). This record, Kingman and the gravestone record are all in agreement. Death: MA VR, Brockton, deaths, 1903: aged 83 years, 8 months, 12 days.

[19] Birth: National Archives *(Civil Ward Pension Records)*, application 767.279; certificate 539.409 provides the birth date and place. Kingman and the gravestone at Union, Cemetery, Brockton, are in agreement on the date. Death: at the time of his death, Jacob Cheney was living in Kennebec, ME in an institution for disabled soldiers. The date of his death, and the notation, "body sent to Brockton, Mass." are found in: Ancestry.com *(U.S National Homes for Disabled Volunteer Soldiers, 1866-1938)*, complied by the U.S. National Archives. The gravestone agrees with the death date in this record.

[20] See Notes 86 and 87, Genealogy - Chapter 4.

GENEALOGY — CHAPTER 6: THE IRONIC ENIGMA

This section documents what is known of the parents of Daniel McDonald and his wife, Hannah A. Carr, and their families. Daniel and Hannah were the parents of James Alfred M(a)cDonald whose family is documented in the Genealogy section for Chapter 1.

   1a: The parents of Daniel McDonald
   1b: Joseph Carr and Mary E. (or Elizabeth F.) MacNeil or MacNeill
   2:    Daniel McDonald and Hannah A. Carr
   3:    James A MacDonald and Theresa F. Fernald *(See Genealogy - Chapter 1)*
   4:    Irving F. MacDonald and June M. Pennell *(See Genealogy - Chapter 1)*
   5:    Barry J. MacDonald *(See Genealogy - Chapter 1)*

A note on Canadian sources. Public vital records for Prince Edward Island were not collected systematically prior to 1906, although some records do exist for earlier dates. Prior to that year, the primary sources of births and deaths are church records. On PEI, some such records are available and have been transcribed for public use; others are not available. Some church information conflicts with other source data such as census records. Therefore, I have had to rely on a variety of sources including, in some cases, unsourced information. While I am not in doubt about the existence of any of the individuals recorded here, the particulars on dates and places are not as firm in all instances as I would wish.

PARENTS OF DANIEL MCDONALD

Data on the father or mother of Daniel McDonald have not yet been found. Family tradition has it that Daniel's mother was a Mi'kmaq Indian. To date, there is no evidence to substantiate that claim.

JOSEPH and MARY ELIZABETH (MacNEIL or MacNEILL) CARR

JOSEPH CARR b. prob. Skirpenbeck or Harswell, Yorkshire, England, 28 May 1829 or 1830.[1] A Joseph Carr s/o John Carr and Elizabeth, christened at Harswell, Yorkshire, England, 08 Jun 1829.[2] Joseph d. Augustine Cove, PEI, Canada, 12 Jan 1916.[3] He m. **MARY ELIZABETH (or poss. ELIZABETH F.) MacNeill** [poss. MacNeil or McNeil], b. Nova Scotia, Canada, 02 Aug 1830.[4] She d. 17 (or 25) Dec 1911; bur. Crapaud, PEI, Canada.[5]

Children (CARR) of Joseph and Mary Elizabeth (MacNeill) Carr:

   i.   SARAH ELIZABETH b. Lot 29, PEI, Canada, 06 May _____;
         bap. 14 Jun 1861 Crapaud, PEI, Canada.[6]
   ii.   ROBERT MacNEILL b. Tryon, PEI, Canada, 28 Jun 1862;
         d. 29 Oct 1923.[7]
   iii. **HANNAH AMELIA** b. Tryon, Lot 28, PEI, Canada, 28 Oct 1867;
         bap. 02 Aug 1869, Bedeque, PEI, Canada.[8]
   iv.   S. EVELINE b. Tryon, PEI, Canada, 28 Oct 1867; bap. 02 Aug 1869
         Bedeque, PEI, Canada.[9]
   v.   THOMAS JAMES DIENSTADT b. Tryon, PEI, Canada,
         17 Jan 1869; bap. 19 May 1870, Bedeque, PEI, Canada.[10]
   vi.   CAROLINE b. PEI, CANADA, 02 Feb 1873.[11]
   vii. CHRISTIANN b. PEI, CANADA, 24 Mar 1875.[12]
   viii. GEORGE ARTEMUS b. PEI, CANADA, 25 Nov 1881.[13]

DANIEL and HANNAH AMELIA (CARR) MCDONALD FAMILY

DANIEL MCDONALD b. Canada, date unknown. Some records list his first name as either Donald or David. No record of death yet found.[14] Daniel m. prob. Tryon, PEI, Canada, 24 Apr 1886, **HANNAH AMELIA CARR**; marriage performed by I.J. Skinner, Baptist minister, Tryon, PEI, Canada.[15] Hannah b. Tryon, Lot 28, PEI, Canada, 28 Oct 1867; d/o Joseph Carr and Mary Elizabeth (or Elizabeth F.) MacNeill or McNeil.[16] Daniel and Hannah McDonald, residents of Nashua, NH, div. 01 Dec 1899.[17]

Children (MCDONALD) of Daniel and Hannah (Carr) McDonald:

   i.   **JAMES ALFRED** b. prob. Albany or Tryon, PEI, Canada, 03 May
         1887; bap. Albany, Lot 27, PEI, CANADA, 23 Jun 1889; d. Brockton,
         08 Mar 1964.[18] Emigrated from PEI to Boston with family members,
         Aug 1891.[19]
   ii.   RACHEL FLORANCE (or Florence) b. prob. Albany or Tryon, PEI,
         Canada, 08 Dec 1888; bap. Albany, Lot 27, PEI, Canada,
         23 Jun 1889.[20]
   iii. MARY b. prob. Tryon, PEI, Canada, ca. Jan or Feb 1891.[21]

---

[1] Birth date of 28 May 1830 from Canada Census, 1901, PEI, District No 133, Prince East, Township No. 28,   p 3, reviewed on microfilm at Provincial Archives, Charlottetown, PEI, Canada. This record states that Joseph was born in England and emigrated to PEI in 1831 [possibly 1834 — record is faint]. The 1829 birth date and place are from the Sorensen-Carr Genealogy. Since family records place this Carr family at Skirpenbeck, Yorkshire, England, before their emigration to PEI, Canada, it is probable that Joseph Carr's birth occurred at Skirpenbeck, or at Harswell where he was baptized.

[2] LDS IGI: Baptism record extracted from Harswell, Yorkshire, England records; reviewed on microfilm at LDS Family History Library: batch C106731, 1813-1852, 919427.

[3] Sorenson-Carr Genealogy.

[4] Canada Census, 1901, PEI District No 133, Prince East, Township No 28; shows Elizabeth F. Carr as wife of Joseph Carr and states that she was born in Nova Scotia, Canada on 2 August 1830. Her maiden name of McNeil is from the Sorenson-Carr Genealogy.

[5] Sorenson-Carr Genealogy lists date as 17 December 1911. Another genealogy by Arlene Hood of Charlottetown, PEI, Canada, another descendant of the Carr family, lists date as 25 December 1911, and place of burial as St. John's Anglican Church, Crapaud, PEI, Canada based on records of the church.

[6] PEI VR reviewed at Provincial Archives, Charlottetown, PEI, Canada, citing St. John's Anglican Church, Crapaud, Record Book No.1, p 21.

[7] Sorenson-Carr Genealogy.

[8] PEI VR citing Rec. Book No. 1, p. 130, Bedeque United Church. Reviewed at Provincial Archives, Charlottetown, PEI, Canada. Bedeque United is a Methodist church located in Bedeque, PEI, Canada. Thomas Dienstadt was the first minister of the church.

[9] Ibid.

[10] PEI VR citing: Rec. Book 1, p. 136, Bedeque United Church. Reviewed at Provincial Archives, Charlottetown, PEI, Canada.

[11] Sorenson-Carr Genealogy.

[12] Ibid.

[13] Ibid.

[14] Family knowledge and marriage records (Note 15) list his name as Daniel. The baptismal records of two of his children list his name as Donald. The marriage record of his son, James Alfred, lists his name as David. Daniel was born in Canada and his native tongue was English, according to a census record for son, James Alfred MacDonald: U.S. Census for Massachusetts, 1920, vol. 120, ED 494, Sheet 8, line 75.

[15] Prince Edward Island, Canada Marriage Register No. 13 (1870-1887), p 457, provides date of marriage and name and location of the minister. Also, Prince Edward Island Marriage License issued 17 April 1886 by the Deputy Prothonotary of Prince County, PEI, Canada. This record states that the bride and groom were both residents of Tryon, Prince County, PEI, Canada. The bondsman was John A. Carr, likely the brother of Joseph Carr, the bride's father.

[16] See Note 8.

[17] Ancestry.com *(New Hampshire Marriage and Divorce Records, 1659-1974)*; data from an NEHGS database of the same name citing New Hampshire Bureau of Vital Records, Concord, New Hampshire. This record is from the Superior Court of Hillsborough County, NH, certified as correct by the Clerk of the Court, 06 March 1903. The divorce case was brought by Hannah; cause: extreme cruelty.

[18] *Baptisms (children)* 1869-1900 performed by Elias Roberts, Elder, Church of Scotland Records, vol. 1, Accession No. 3095, Item No. 1. Microfilm of this record reviewed at PEI Archives, Charlottetown, PEI, Canada. This record does not specifically list the birth place. The baptism took place in Albany, PEI, Canada, a town just west of Tryon. Death: MA VR-Index, Brockton, deaths, 1964, vol 33, p 213.

[19] See Note 21.

[20] See Note 18; the baptism of Rachel Florance appears in the same record as that of her brother. Also, the Canada Census for 1891 for Lot 28, PEI, pp 51-52, family number 249, shows Hannah (Carr) McDonald and children James A. and Rachel F. living with the family of Hannah's father, Joseph. Death: no record found.

[21] The name Mary is from the list of passengers of the *S.S. State of Indiana* from the Port of Charlottetown [PEI] and Halifax [Nova Scotia] as sworn 24 August 1891 at Boston, MA. This list is from *Passenger Lists of Vessels Arriving at Boston, Massachusetts, 1891 - 1943*, Micropublication T843; RG085, Rolls #1-454 and *Passenger Lists of Vessels Arriving at Boston, Massachusetts, 1820-1891*, Micropublication M277; RG036, Rolls #1-155, both published by the National Archives, combined by Ancestry.com as an on-line database in 2006 as: *Boston Passenger Lists, 1820-1943*. This on-line record shows the arrival of: Hannah McDonald, age 27; James F. (should be A.), age 3; Rachael, age 2 and Mary, age 1/2. The Canada Census for 1891 for Lot 28, PEI, Canada shows an unnamed grandson living with the family of Hannah's father, Joseph. This child is listed as age 4/12 in an enumeration that took place in May, 1891. Although this child is listed as male in the census record, the evidence strongly suggests that the unnamed child in the 1891 census is Mary, Hannah's third child, although no PEI VR or church record has been found to date. Death: no record found.

INDEX

www.ingramcontent.com/pod-product-compliance
Lightning Source LLC
Chambersburg PA
CBHW030427290526
45786CB00001B/170